The Irish Art of Controversy

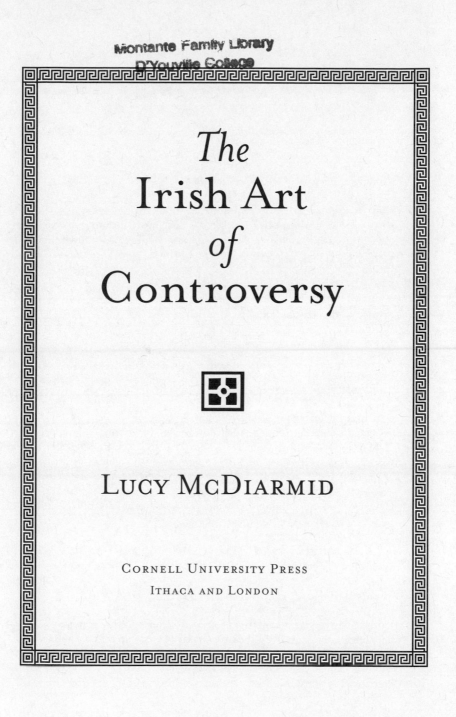

The
Irish Art
of
Controversy

Lucy McDiarmid

Cornell University Press
Ithaca and London

First published 2005 by Cornell University Press

Printed in the United States of America

Library of Congress Cataloging-in-Publication Data

McDiarmid, Lucy.
    The Irish art of controversy / Lucy McDiarmid.
        v. cm.
    Includes bibliographical references and index.
    Contents: Introduction : the Irish controversy—Hugh Lane and the decoration of Dublin, 1904—The man who died for the language : Rev. Dr. O'Hickey and the Irish language controversy, 1908—The shewing-up of Dublin Castle : Lady Gregory, Shaw, and Blanco Posnet, August 1909—Hunger and hysteria : the "save the Dublin kiddies" campaign, October–November 1913—The afterlife of Roger Casement : memory, folklore, ghosts, 1916—Epilogue : controversy as "heritage"—Chronologies of the controversies.
    ISBN 0-8014-4353-9 (cloth: alk. paper)
    1. Ireland—History—1901–1910. 2. Ireland—History—1910–1921. 3. Ireland—Civilization—20th century. 4. Ireland—Intellectual life—20th century. I. Title.
    DA960.M423   2005
    941.5082'1—dc22   2004030942

Cornell University Press strives to use environmentally responsible suppliers and materials to the fullest extent possible in the publishing of its books. Such materials include vegetable-based, low-VOC inks and acid-free papers that are recycled, totally chlorine-free, or partly composed of nonwood fibers. For further information, visit our website at www.cornellpress.cornell.edu.

Cloth printing   10 9 8 7 6 5 4 3 2 1

For Emily and Katie

aoibhneas máthar grá dá hiníonacha
a mother's joy: love for her daughters

✦ Contents

⊞ Illustrations

▦ Acknowledgments

To the scholars whose generous letters led to my receipt of a fellowship from the John Simon Guggenheim Memorial Foundation I owe warm thanks: David Bromwich, Daniel Hoffman, Sam Hynes, and Edward Mendelson. And to the Guggenheim Foundation I am grateful for the funds that enabled me to begin work on this project. I believe I innocently wrote in my application that I thought the writing would take me one year, 1993–94.

Five devoted friends—Maria DiBattista, Adrian Frazier, Nicholas Grene, Deirdre McMahon, and Mary Helen Thuente—have seen me through the many years of writing and revising this book. I can never thank them enough. At last, they can delete from their files all the messages whose attachments held varying versions of the manuscript.

For friendship, moral support, hospitality, research help, and controversy-related conversations over many years, thanks to Angela Bourke, Terence Brown, Carol Coulter, Theo Dorgan, Mary Hickman, Beth Kiberd, Declan Kiberd, Siobhán Kilfeather, Seth Koven, Bill Labov, Edna Longley, Michael Longley, Margaret MacCurtain, Sinéad Mc-Coole, Paula Meehan, Nuala Ní Dhomhnaill, Margaret O'Callaghan, Nancy Pepper, James Pethica, Yopie Prins, Paula Robison, Gillian Sankoff, Bruce Shapiro, Pat Sheeran, Philomena Sheeran, Margaret Spillane, Harry Vince, and Maureen Waters. I am especially grateful to Patricia Lysaght for creating the proverbial-sounding Irish in the dedication.

An essay including brief analysis of the Lane, O'Hickey, and "Dublin kiddies" controversies was published as "Revivalist Belligerence: Three Controversies," in *The Irish Revival Reappraised,* edited by J. H. Murphy and E. Taylor-Fitzsimon (Dublin: Four Courts Press, 2003), 132–44. Talks on the same three controversies were delivered as a lecture series at the National University of Ireland, Galway, in March 1999; I thank Kevin Barry for his generosity in planning the visit and Riana O'Dwyer and Adrian Frazier for their hospitality. On a few occasions, several controversies were packed into one lecture, and I am happy to thank the hosts who organized those visits: James H. Murphy, Betsey Taylor-Fitzsimon, and Margaret Kelleher of the Society for the Study of Nineteenth-Century Ireland (2002); Adrian Frazier of the Synge Summer School (2002); Eileen Reilly and Joe Lee of Glucksman Ireland House, New York University (2002); and Michael Kenneally and Rhona Richman Kenneally, Concordia University, Montreal (2003).

Because each controversy generated its own distinct social life and research network, I am thanking people in terms of the chapters to which they contributed.

For chapter 1, grateful thanks to Barbara Dawson, director of the Hugh Lane Municipal Gallery of Modern Art, for taking the time to talk with me on several occasions; to Liz Forster, who gave generous help whenever I needed it during many visits to the gallery; and to Christine Kennedy, who opened up the archives for me. Thanks also to Bruce Arnold for a copy of his Orpen biography. I am grateful also to my hosts on the occasions when I delivered talks about this controversy: Colbert Kearney of National University of Ireland, Cork (1995); Nicholas Grene at the Synge Summer School (1998); Rhoda Nathan of the Shaw Society of New York (1999); Marilynn Richtarik of Georgia State University (1999); Andy McGowan of the New York Yeats Society (2000); Maura McTighe and Perry Share of the Yeats Society, Sligo (2000); Paul Muldoon of the Fund for Irish Studies at Princeton (2002); and Marc Conner of Washington and Lee University (2003).

An earlier version of chapter 2 was published as "The Man Who Died for the Language: The Rev. Dr. O'Hickey and the Essential Irish Controversy of 1909," *Éire-Ireland* 35, 1–2 (Spring–Summer 2000): 188–218 (© 2000: Irish American Cultural Institute, 1 Lackawanna Place, Morristown, NJ 07960. Reproduced by permission of the publisher). This chapter originated in Margaret MacCurtain's suggestion that I write on something to do with the university and the language requirement; it was Séamus Blake who first pointed me toward O'Hickey and who for nine years lent me his copy of Msgr. Mac Fhinn's biography of O'Hickey and helped with many linguistic matters. Michael Coady gave me brochures, newspaper clippings, stories, a vivid understanding of precisely what O'Hickey meant to the community of Carrick-on-Suir, and, in the summer of 2001, a wonderful tour of all the O'Hickey-related sites in Carrick. Without his extraordinary generosity, I couldn't have written this chapter. O'Hickey's descendants have been similarly generous: Nora Briody, O'Hickey's niece, told me family stories in a telephone interview, and her son Mícheál Briody, who has also written about his great-uncle, has been unfailingly helpful with information, manuscripts, photographs, and ideas. O'Hickey's great-niece Maura Cronin has helped me with her great-uncle's allusions to Young Ireland ballads and much else. In 2000 she set up an interview with her mother, Mary Murphy, née Hickey, enabling me to speak with one of the few people then alive who had met and remembered Father O'Hickey. For other help with my research on O'Hickey, thanks to Gearóid Denvir, the late Michael Durkan, the Very Reverend Robert Forde of Charleville, County Cork, Patrick Maume, Deirdre McMahon, Thomas J. Morrissey, S.J., Philip O'Leary, Gary Owens, Bruce Stewart, and Seán Tobin.

An earlier version of chapter 3 was published as "Augusta Gregory, Bernard Shaw, and the Shewing-up of Dublin Castle," *PMLA* (special topic: Literature and Censorship) 109, 1 (January 1994): 26–44. My essay "The Abbey and the Theatrics of Controversy, 1909–1915," in *A Century of Irish Drama: Widening the Stage*, edited by Stephen Watt, Eileen Morgan, and Shakir Mustafa, 57–71 (Bloomington: Indiana University Press, 2000), also includes a few paragraphs used in this chapter. I am especially grateful to Dan H. Laurence for letting me know about the photograph from "The Sketch"; and to Tony Bradley, Rand Brandes, James Cahalan, Nicholas Grene, Patricia Haberstroh, the late Janet Oppenheim, Ann Saddlemyer, and Domna Stanton. Thanks also to my hosts on the occasions when I delivered talks about this controversy: Deborah Thomas of Villanova University (1992); Rhoda Nathan of the Shaw Society of New York (1995); Sheila O'Donnellan and Lois Tobin of the Lady Gregory Autumn Gathering (1998); Tina Mahony, Robert Mahony, and Timothy Meagher of the Centre for Irish Studies, Catholic University of America (1999); and Steve Watt of Indiana University (1999).

Chapter 4 has been enriched by the help of Karen Hunt, biographer of Dora Montefiore, who sent me clippings from the Liverpool newspapers of October 1913 and corresponded with me about many aspects of the "kiddies" campaign. Seth Koven discussed with me all the issues involved in bathing (and helping) the poor, and his conversation was wonderfully enlightening. Special thanks to Angela Bourke, whose brilliant book *The Burning of Bridget Cleary* has helped my thinking in this chapter, as well as to Colin Ireland, Paula Meehan, Mick Moloney, and Harry Vince. Thanks also to my hosts on occasions when I delivered talks about this controversy: Edna Longley of Queen's University, Belfast (1997); Vera Kreilkamp and Robert Savage of Boston College (1999); and Richard Bizot of the ACIS, Southern Region (2001).

A shorter version of chapter 5 was published as "The Posthumous Life of Roger Casement," in *Gender and Sexuality in Modern Ireland*, edited by Anthony Bradley and M. Valiulis, 127–58 (Amherst: University of Massachusetts Press, 1997), and a related short essay on Casement was published as "Martyr for Many Causes" in the *New York Times Book Review*, February 8, 1998, 31. After only one year of working on Roger Casement (1991–92), I began to suspect that Casement was the secret of the universe. After a few more years, I knew for certain that was the case. Casement left the world's biggest paper trail, a trail too exhausting for even a few hundred people to follow. I've followed it long enough, as have many later Casementistas. I intend to leave my collection of Casementana, all ten files and two trunks of it, to the National Library of Ireland. In the meantime, thanks to the many people who have augmented my collection: Nigel Acheson, Rosita Barone, Kevin Barry, Philip Brady, Robert Caserio, Marion Casey, Anne Colman, Mary Daly, Jeff Dudgeon, the late Michael Durkan, Antony Farrell, Liam Fay, Roy Foster, Thomas Hachey, Kieran Kennedy, Michael Keohane, Patricia King, Derek Mahon, Róisín McAuley, Sinéad McCoole, Mary McGrath, Medbh McGuckian, Sarah McKibben, Deirdre McMahon, Angus Mitchell, Patrick Mullen, Maureen Murphy, Ben Novick, Brian Ó Conchubhair, Séan Seosamh Ó Conchubhair, Bernard O'Donoghue, Eunan O'Halpin, Séamas Ó Síocháin, Eilis Pearce, Tom Rapp, Elizabeth Brewer Redwine, Robert Rhodes, Emily Savin, Harris Savin, Roger Sawyer, Lucy Selligman Schneider, and Sandra Siegel. Thanks also to Helen O'Carroll for a memorable tour of the area around Banna Strand. On my behalf, Philip O'Leary sat through a four-hour play about Casement, and this seems the appropriate place to acknowledge his sacrifice. Thanks to Beatrice Bartlett and Caroline Bynum for reading early drafts of this chapter. Apologies to anyone I've neglected who ought to be thanked in this category. Thanks also to my hosts on occasions when I gave talks about this controversy: the Yeats International Summer School, Sligo (1993); Tony Judt and the late Jocelyn Baltzell of the New York Institute for the Humanities, New York University (1994); John Hildebidle of the MIT Center for Cultural Studies (1994); Andy McGowan of the Yeats Society of New York (1994); Thomas Heffernan of the Columbia Irish Seminar (1994); Lee Mitchell of Princeton University (1995); Seamus Deane and Spurgeon Thompson of the Keough Center for Irish Studies, Notre Dame (1997); Yopie Prins of the University of Michigan (1997); William McCormack of Goldsmiths College, University of London (1998); and Margot Backus of the ACIS (2002).

For help of various kinds not related to any one chapter, I am grateful to Brendan Barrington, John Devitt, Bonnie Bryant Hiller, Liam Irwin, William Kennedy, Joep Leerssen, Sophie McCoy, William Murphy, Eiléan Ní Chuilleanáin, Andra Oakes, and Nuala O'Faolain. My students in Irish Studies at Villanova, Princeton, the Yeats International Summer School, and the Synge Summer School have given me great joy with their intelligence, enthusiasm, and warmth. I especially thank Sally Bachner, Abby Bender, Lee Blyer, Mary Burke, Crystal Cline, Sharon Cournoyer, Carly Daniels, Scott Dill, Beth Gilmartin, Rachel Glenn, Jonathan Greenberg, Thomas Jackson, Joe Johnson, Wei-Hung Kao, Howard J. Keeley, Jim Kennedy, Laura Kirton, Maureen Lees, Amanda Mandia, Caroline McCarthy, Frank McCormick, Kathryn Mullan, Kirri O'Brien, Eileen Rafferty, Jennifer Sherman Roberts, Mary Ann Ryan, and Elizabeth Sawyer. Joe Johnson provided excellent research help, and Deirdre McFeely performed wonders in finding obscure permissions. Katy Chiles of Northwestern University made proofreading a pleasure, and Kathryn Rutigliano of Villanova gave timely help with the final notes.

I am grateful to the patient, helpful, and wonderful librarians of Falvey Library, Villanova University: Luisa Cywinski, Domenick Liberato, Bente Polites, and Meryl Stein; and Therese Dougherty and Phylis Wright of Falvey's Interlibrary Loan. David Sheehy of Dublin Diocesan Archives was always cheerful, welcoming, and generous in his help with Archbishop Walsh's papers, which I read and reread over several years. Other librarians and archivists were also helpful: Penelope Woods at Russell Library, National University of Ireland, Maynooth; Mary Clark at the Dublin City Archives; Father John Gates at the Diocesan Archives at Armagh; Gerard Lyne and the staff at the National Library of Ireland; Robert Cannin, RTÉ Radio Archives; John Killen at the Linen Hall Library; Teresa Kane of the Abbey Theatre Archives; Isacc Gewirtz, Philip Milito, and Declan Kiely at the Albert A. and Henry W. Berg Collection, New York Public Library; and the staffs of the Abbey Theatre; the Bodkin Papers, Trinity College Dublin; the Department of Early Printed Books, Trinity College Dublin; the Gilbert Library, Dublin; the Maloney Collection of Irish Historical Papers, New York Public Library; and the National Archives of Ireland.

My agent, Jonathan Williams, has been excellent beyond words. I would also like to thank Bernhard Kendler of Cornell University Press for taking such good care of this manuscript at all stages of production. Grateful thanks also to Antony Farrell of Lilliput Press. When, in the final years of this book's composition, even my mother, Lucy Selligman Schneider, started sending me Casement references, I knew it was time to end. As a sophisticated, literate, but nonacademic humanist, she remains the audience I try to write for. I always ask myself how she would respond to a particular word or sentence, and for that reason I have tried to limit the use of the word *ludic* in this book. And finally, the young lives of my children, Emily Clare Savin and Katharine Eliza Savin, have been blighted by this book. Sometime in the mid-1990s my older daughter embroidered a tricolor with the words, "In this room Roger Casement, Lady Gregory, & Father O'Hickey live on." My daughters were small enough to be carried when I began writing this book, and now they are driving. With the hope that it will offer some kind of pleasure, I dedicate it to them.

✦

For permission to quote from unpublished or copyright materials, grateful acknowledgment is made to the Abbey Theatre Archives, Dublin; The Marquess of Aberdeen; the Henry W. and Albert A. Berg Collection, Astor, Lenox and Tilden Foundations, New York Public Library; Berlin Associates for the Estate of Max Beerbohm; Bernard F. Burgunder Collection, Cornell University Library; Bodkin Papers, Trinity College Dublin, by permission of the Board of Trinity College; the Council of Trustees of the National Library of Ireland; Dan H. Laurence Collection, Archival & Special Collections, University of Guelph Library; the Department of Early Printed Books, Trinity College Dublin, by permission of the Board of Trinity College; the Dublin Diocesan Archives; the Hugh Lane Municipal Gallery of Modern Art; Irish American Cultural Institute; the *Irish Times*; Frank Kelly for the Estate of Charles E. Kelly; the Maloney Collection of Irish Historical Papers, New York Public Library; Iseult McGuinness for the Estate of Grace Gifford; Mitchell Library, State Library of New South Wales; Monsignor Corish on behalf of College Archives, Russell Library, St. Patrick's College, Maynooth; Radio Archives, Radio Telefís Éireann; to Colin Smythe and the heirs of Lady Gregory; Rafi Mohamed for R. M. Associates; Wake Forest University Press and Gallery Press for permission to print "Casement's Funeral" by Richard Murphy from *Collected Poems* (2001) and "Ceist na Teangan" / "The Language Issue" by Nuala Ní Dhomhnaill, translated by Paul Muldoon, from *Pharaoh's Daughter* (1990, 1993); A. P. Watt Ltd. on behalf of Michael B. Yeats.

◨ Abbreviations

The following abbreviations have been adopted for frequently occurring citations.

ALS   autograph letter sent
DDA   Dublin Diocesan Archives
HLG   Hugh Lane Gallery Archives
NLI   National Library of Ireland
NYPL   New York Public Library
RTÉ   Radio Telefís Éireann
TLS   typed letter sent

The Irish Art of Controversy

⊞ Introduction

The Irish Controversy

Is fearr an t-imreasc ná an t-uaigneas.
Argument is better than loneliness.
—Irish proverb

Yeats told me how popular noise was in Ireland, and controversy,
too, when accompanied with the breaking of chairs.
—George Moore, *Ave*

Out of Ireland have we come.
Great hatred, little room,
Maimed us at the start.
—W. B. Yeats, "Remorse for Intemperate Speech"

"Throw them into the Liffey!"
"Kill him!"
"I regret nothing . . . ; I withdraw nothing; I apologize for nothing."
"Are you content to abandon your children to strangers?"
"Tell them that they can depend on me to burn with a brighter blaze
and louder yells than all Fox's martyrs."
"The history of Irish land and language is a constant record of clerical
hate of Ireland."
"If we are defeated in the first battle, the fight must still go on."
"Are you going to cut off our heads?"

These are the voices of controversy, expressing all the insolence, rage,
and defiance Yeats heard echoing in his mind when he fashioned the

phrase "Great hatred, little room." Whatever "remorse" Yeats may
have felt, he certainly recognized an excellent subject for poetry. Belligerence always inspired him. Years earlier he had written to explain
the opening poems of *Responsibilities*, "Three public controversies
have stirred my imagination."[1] These were the debates over Charles
Stewart Parnell, *Playboy of the Western World*, and the Hugh Lane
Gallery: how could they not stir his imagination? All around Yeats,
people were speaking, in their real lives, lines as colorful and passionate as any recited on the Abbey stage.

This book studies five Irish cultural controversies that began in the
years just before the 1916 Rising. These five merit study not because
Irish people are genetically more "combative" or more "eloquent"
than other peoples but because high cultural nationalism lent a particular urgency to every cultural contest.[2] In the dozens of new organizations founded in the period bordered by the failure of the Second
Home Rule Bill (1892) at one end and by the Easter Rising at the
other, Irish people were creating institutions that anticipated the establishment of a new Irish state: the National Literary Society (1892),
the Gaelic League (1893), the Irish Literary Theatre (1899; succeeded
by the National Theatre Society, also known as the Abbey Theatre).
In 1908 Parliament passed the Irish Universities Act, establishing the
National University of Ireland and Queen's University, Belfast. In
that same year Hugh Lane founded the Dublin Municipal Gallery of
Modern Art, and Patrick Pearse founded the Irish-language school St.
Enda's. In 1909 Constance Gore-Booth Markievicz founded the Fianna Éireann (Irish Boy Scouts).

To its members, each of these associations was a miniature Ireland.
It stood as if by synecdoche for the entire nation, existing in a realm
of symbolic significance somewhat apart from the institutions of government. Each represented, in Seamus Deane's phrase, "the idea of a
culture that has not yet come to be in political terms."[3] If the five
controversies simply pitted the colonized, oppressed Irish against the
English colonial oppressors, there would be no story to tell. The high
moral ground would be obvious, the participants' roles predictable, and
the controversies unambiguous, reflecting the large-scale antagonisms of the great national narrative. What they reveal is instead more
complex, more subtle, and more dramatic: they show the way different people and subcultures within Ireland fought to control the sites
whose symbolic power they understood intuitively. The question ar-

ticulated through these controversies was not Irish Ireland or English Ireland, but whose Irish Ireland? Whose version of Ireland would dominate when independence was finally achieved?

The chief characteristic of the institutions and cultural forms that inspired these battles was their blankness: they could be stamped with any kind of Irishness. Would the National University have an Irish language requirement and thereby be made "truly Irish," or admit monoglot English-speakers and be merely "West Briton"? Would the permanent location of the Dublin Municipal Gallery be determined by its wealthy, knighted Protestant patron or by the business interests of the city? One of the fiercest battles took place over that notoriously blank slate, the child: would the children of the striking workers in 1913 be fed by Socialists in England or by Catholic priests and nuns in Dublin? Would their Irishness be identified with labor or religion, international charity or city parish, Jim Larkin or Archbishop Walsh? Yeats referred to the Ireland of the early 1920s, the new Free State, as "plastic," ready to be formed and molded. But Ireland was already being shaped and defined through controversies before an Irish government existed.

In the years of high cultural nationalism, between 1908 and 1913 approximately, an Ireland embodied in a theater or a museum or a language had enormous potency. The nation's future seemed to lie in the hands of whoever could control the discourse of nationality. Lady Gregory and Yeats issued press releases in 1909 claiming that "the liberty of the Irish theatre of the future" hung on the Abbey Theatre's production of Shaw's *The Shewing-up of Blanco Posnet*, a play banned by the lord chamberlain in England but not explicitly disallowed in Dublin. But the Abbey staged its great resistance to colonial authority not for the pathetic viceroy of Ireland, who had no power to stop the performance anyway, but for the radical nationalists of Sinn Féin, to demonstrate the theater's right to the word *national*. Surviving many such controversies, the Abbey became officially, in 1925, *the* national theater.

The colonial condition of Ireland provided the paradigm for these controversies: each side—any side—could claim to be the "Irish" side, thereby constructing the other as English. During the "Save the Dublin Kiddies" controversy, each side, at one time or another, belted out "God Save Ireland" belligerently at the other. All power struggles replicated the master struggle, even when empire and native people were not directly opposed. The colonial paradigm determined the way the argument would be understood, and the idea of "Ireland" functioned as an automatic guarantee of high-mindedness for anyone who invoked it. Father Michael O'Hickey articulated the principle perfectly. Chastised by the bishops (in 1909) because he had attacked them in his writings on the Irish language, O'Hickey explained why his speech was licensed:

> Restraint and moderation of language are relative things.
> Language which in one case and set of circumstances might be
> quite unjustifiable, in different circumstances might well be
> not only warranted, but actually called for. That the language I
> have used was in no way too strong for the occasion that called it
> forth, I am convinced. . . . By the part I have taken in this controversy,
> it is my profound conviction that I have done the College and the
> Catholic Faith as well as the cause of Irish nationality a service.[4]

O'Hickey's belligerence was righteous, his language "called for" by the situation. He stood up to the "West Briton" bishops, and he kept talking, certain in the faith that he had done Irishness, Catholicism, and St. Patrick's College "a service." For those high causes, as he saw it, he could use any tone.

In the light of O'Hickey's defense of a language that is "in no way too strong for the occasion that called it forth," it is worth considering what Yeats may have meant by the phrase "intemperate speech." His poem traces a life lived in all the vocal registers of controversy:

> I ranted to the knave and fool,
> But outgrew that school,
> Would transform the part,
> Fit audience found, but cannot rule
> My fanatic heart.
>
> I sought my betters: though in each
> Fine manners, liberal speech,
> Turn hatred into sport,
> Nothing said or done can reach
> My fanatic heart.
>
> Out of Ireland have we come.
> Great hatred, little room,

Maimed us at the start.
I carry from my mother's womb
A fanatic heart.

"Remorse for Intemperate Speech," 506[5]

Ranting to the knave and fool sounds like the way a post-controversialist might describe his past: this is Yeats haranguing the Abbey Theatre audience or the Dublin Corporation. But not all controversialists rant: Yeats's "betters"—Lady Gregory, perhaps—turn "hatred into sport," making agonistic language playful and even polite. Writing the poem in 1931, Yeats no longer believes that lofty purposes can dignify or "fine manners" disguise great hatred: the feeling has to be confronted directly as an unavoidable inheritance from "mother" Ireland. O'Hickey, writing in the heat of controversy, would never use an unpleasant word like *hatred* because his words are uttered *pro bono publico*. The great fiction of a controversy, accepted by O'Hickey and rejected (in this poem, at least) by Yeats, is that its participants feel no personal animosity but are required by their awareness of what is at stake—nothing less, in these cases, than the defense of Irishness—to speak with a righteous, public-spirited anger. In fact the rhetoric of controversy is heard simultaneously as the raw hatred Yeats describes and the principled passion O'Hickey argues for. One's own side is high-minded; one's enemies speak merely from anger.

Whether the speech of controversy is ludic, like Gregory's, or intensely serious, like O'Hickey's, it assumes performance. Every utterance implies an audience, ready to applaud the witty rejoinders or to choose sides in the debate. After Lady Gregory's private conversations with the viceroy about Shaw's banned play, in the summer of 1909, she went back to her hotel and wrote down every word both had said, confident that she would use this material in a book some day—as she did, four years later, in *Our Irish Theatre*. Her fearless answers to the king's representative in Ireland were not spoken for him alone. The knowledge that words reach some large "imagined community" makes a controversy different from a family fight. It is a fight that's noticed, and the feeling of being overheard governs its style (eloquent or snappy) and its invocation of high causes. The audience out there—listening to the speech, scanning the newspapers, reading the book—is composed of the controversy's potential beneficiaries, the Irish people for whom everything is at stake in a single argument, whatever it may be.

The controversies of Irish cultural nationalism developed in a public sphere constructed by many modes of quickly circulating communication—conversations, meetings, newspapers, pamphlets, books. In
the late eighteenth century the papers, songs, and songbooks of the
United Irishmen had begun the creation of a nationalist public culture, and those of Young Ireland in the mid-nineteenth century had
continued the project.[6] It was this culture that the young Augusta
Persse (later Lady Gregory) came into contact with as a young girl,
when she bought "the paper covered collections of national ballads,
The Harp of Tara, The Irish Song Book, and the like." The "old bookseller" in Loughrea, Gregory writes, noted her taste, saying, "I look to
Miss Augusta to buy all my Fenian books."[7] And while Miss Augusta
was reading her ballads in Galway, the young Michael O'Hickey was
reading Thomas Davis "by the banks of the silvery Suir" in Waterford.[8] In O'Hickey's and Gregory's work especially, words and phrases
from nationalist ballads resonate often, allying the position argued
with the unarguably Irish patriotism of Davis or John O'Hagan or
John Keegan Casey. Through such allusions, participants made controversies appear as culture militant, an Irishness challenged by "the
Sasanach" but some day to be victorious (to use the Irish word for
Saxon demonized the English enemy at the same time as it helped
the linguistic credentials of the speaker).

In so far as controversies made headlines and offered tabloid thrills,
they provided the same opportunities for vicarious involvement as
any public drama—a trial, a scandal, an election. But they were
messier and more sprawling than those dramas, on subjects of such
general interest and so loosely defined that any member of the audience could become a participant simply by speaking out at a meeting,
or giving money to a cause, or writing a letter to any of the hundreds
of newspapers printed in pre-1916 Ireland. Those who opposed the socialists' plan to "save the Dublin kiddies" and feed the 1913 strikers'
children in England could join one of the huge processions, six-
people wide, that made its way along the quays every night, singing
"Hail, Glorious Saint Patrick" and "Faith of Our Fathers." In the
frenzy of the 1913 debate over the Lane gallery location, or (years
later) the 1937 *Irish Press* letter controversy over Roger Casement's
sexuality, very little familiarity with the issues was needed to join
the fray: one need only write in attacking any previous letter writer.
However a controversy was sparked, fueled, or provoked, whether it
raged or brewed or exploded, as a ruckus, commotion, *cause célèbre,*

whirlwind, tempest in a teapot, or much ado about nothing, it was generally easy to join. The idle, the angry, or the passionate person who could always be heard sounding off was indeed "no stranger to controversy."

Such debates would not exist *as controversies* if they did not resonate in some way with a large public. In them large forces explode in a small site. They do not usually cause transformations, but they make visible social change as it is in the process of occurring. And because controversies tend to happen in border areas, unlegislated zones not definitively controlled by any single authority, their conflicts are often decided, if they are decided at all, by bluff and bravado, by performative skills and improvisational flair, rather than by any clear and consistent scoring system. Precisely because it is often irresolvable, a controversy registers with great clarity the tensions of a society at a particular moment. Cultural controversies did not in any sense cause the large political events that led to the independence of twenty-six of Ireland's thirty-two counties in 1922. They revealed social change in miniature, the kinds of changes that continued to occur in post-Treaty Ireland.

Three of the five controversies—those relating to Hugh Lane, Father O'Hickey, and Roger Casement—continued long past the heyday of cultural nationalism and well into the middle decades of the twentieth century. The issue of "whose Irish Ireland" took on a different form in the later period, as controversies, especially the old, familiar ones, offered a licensed opportunity for speech about topics otherwise unapproachable in public discourse.[9] To talk about Casement was almost always to talk about sexuality, or around sexuality. To broach the issue of homosexuality was not quite the same as to confront it, but circumlocutions were still a mode of expression. The remarkable number of letters to editors about Casement, indeed the astonishing number of outbreaks of the controversy, demonstrate a collective need to understand sexuality in a national field. Officially there was no birth control, no abortion, no divorce, no dirty books or movies; unmarried mothers were locked up in Magdalen laundries, and their babies shipped off to America. Unauthorized sexuality was punished: but there were always Casement controversies, during which anyone could write in to any number of papers and express outraged opinions on all sides of the conflict. If the Casement diaries had been forged, then it was a patriotic duty to talk about them as much as possible. Judging not only by the number of letters but by the number of

poems, plays, and uncompleted film scripts, Ireland was aching to
talk about Casement.

Recent Irish controversies have not generated the kind of broad
populist excitement of the pre-Rising days: each controversy appeals
to a particular constituency. It could be argued that *The Field Day
Anthology of Irish Writing* (1991, 2002), like the Lane Gallery or the
Abbey Theatre, stands for an idea of the nation, but those passionately engaged in fighting about the anthology's contents on feminist
or other political grounds have been primarily academics and writers.
The debate inspired by Dublin archbishop Desmond Connell's
thoughts on "planned children" (1999) did indeed inspire general
public debate. A storm of protest greeted Dr. Connell's claim that the
child conceived through family planning, in vitro fertilization, or sur-
rogate motherhood is not "welcomed as a gift" and is not "happy."[10]
The participants were not fighting over nationalist discourse, however, but over the definition of the family, a debate occurring at the
same time elsewhere in similar terms.

To study controversies that began in the years just before the Rising
is to enjoy an *embarras de richesses*. The available evidence is
enough for an entire book on any single controversy. Ireland was a
small society with a highly developed communications infrastruc-
ture, and even those people not directly involved in controversies
were the cousins or in-laws or neighbors of someone who was. Even
now, long after many of the controversies began, it is possible to talk
with people who met Father O'Hickey or whose parents saw Casement when he landed in Kerry in 1916. The century just past seems
very short, and memories cluster around famously contested people
and events. Three of these controversies are Dublin-centered (Lane,
Blanco Posnet, and "Dublin kiddies"), and their sources show all the
chance encounters that came to constitute small parts of the larger
story: the meetings in libraries or newspaper offices or hotels, the
missed appointment, the nocturnal visit, the argument on the bridge.
The same sense of a society whose members are in constant communication with one another exists even in the controversies that spread
in space over the country or in time over the century. Hundreds of
newspapers record the primary, secondary, and even tertiary events of
controversies, and dozens of archives preserve the letters of the participants. A diagram of the entire sequence of causes and effects,
major and minor, in the five controversies discussed in this book
would reveal a strange type of plenitude. Such a diagram would in-

evitably extend beyond mortal sight, because controversies run deep, wide, and long.

The material of controversy exists in the large overlap of history, folklore, and the arts. To limit its sources to printed materials and manuscripts would be to restrict its meaning, to misconstrue it as a debate between clearly distinguishable parties over clearly defined issues, like an election, a trial, a tribunal, or some other official public conflict. However, to limit its sources to gossip, interviews, anecdotes, and conversations would be to restrict its significance in another way, to misunderstand it as a cluster of trivial animosities about ephemeral issues too marginal to matter in the larger society. And to emphasize the poems, plays, paintings, and other artistic evidence of controversy would be to treat it as a charming but merely decorative transformation of events made to entertain an audience. All these forms of evidence belong to controversy. Attracting social thought at its most unstable, giving form to the articulation of antagonisms, controversy provides the theater in which a society may view itself in the unfinished process of change.

⊡ 1 ⊡

Hugh Lane and the Decoration of Dublin, 1908–

Maireann an crann ar an bhfál, ach ní mhaireann an lámh a chuir.
The tree on the ditch survives, but not the hand that planted it.

How heavy and bulky most serious paintings are, and how very difficult to carry. Would Hugh Lane's notorious thirty-nine contested pictures—promised to Dublin, taken from Dublin, given back—ever have achieved the status of national treasures if they had been smaller or less numerous? The photographs in the archives of the Hugh Lane Municipal Gallery make it impossible to ignore the weight and the simple materiality of the paintings. Much of their life, the records show, has been spent being moved about: here they are in one photograph being loaded onto a horse-drawn cart in August 1913, stacked in two piles with thick fabric between the frames, being moved from the Harcourt Street gallery to the Mansion House. And here they are only seven weeks later, being removed from the Mansion House: "The 'Priceless Pictures' Again on the Move," noted the disrespectful headline of the *Irish Independent,* over a photo of workmen loading a huge painting onto a large cart. Years later, when two young men, acting on behalf of the "Irish national interest," stole another Lane painting, Berthe Morisot's *Jour d'été,* from the Tate Gallery in London, they thoughtfully summoned a photographer beforehand to record the theft: there is the young art student Paul Hogan, in 1956, walking down the steps of the Tate quite openly with his arms around a huge painting. But only five years later, here are some of the paintings "HOME AT LAST And without a hitch," according to the *Daily Mail.* Dangling in midair at Dublin's North Wall is a large rectangular object, ambiguously described as "the huge crate containing St. John the Baptist." An adjacent photograph shows three men in white aprons carefully unwrapping a painting, under the gaze of police and gallery officials. As valuable as Viking gold but the size of furniture, the paintings have always required special attention of one sort or another.[1]

In spite of all the brilliant color on their canvasses, color painted by Manet, Monet, Renoir, Courbet, Morisot, Pissarro, Degas, and others, the thirty-nine mostly Impressionist paintings are blank spaces onto which meanings could be projected. Although the paintings became talismanic national objects for the people of Ireland, they did not begin that way. They were culturally redefined and only gradually accrued Irishness and talismanic power.[2] Anyone wanting to understand their magic must study the series of meanings attributed to them by Irish people in the years following 1904, when some of them made up part of the Loan Exhibition at the Royal Hibernian Academy; meanings that had changed somewhat by January 1908, when for the first time they were defined as a collection and exhibited by Lane at the first Municipal Gallery of Modern Art in Dublin, a gallery Lane himself established; and meanings further revised in the course of numerous transfers. The paintings were given provisionally by Lane to the gallery in 1912; taken away from the gallery in 1913, after the Dublin Corporation refused support for the new building Lane wanted; bequeathed, in a will, to the National Gallery in London (1914); bequeathed once more, in a codicil to that will, to the Municipal Gallery in Dublin (1915); contested between the Dublin and London galleries after Lane's death in the sinking of the *Lusitania*, when the codicil proved to be unwitnessed; and divided between the two galleries in a series of agreements beginning in 1959.[3]

An art dealer and public benefactor, Lane was Lady Gregory's nephew, as well as her colleague and Yeats's in many cultural projects and public commotions. Both writers were active in the "long and dreary campaign" to get the paintings back from London, and to those seeking merely to understand the allusions in Yeats's poems or Gregory's journals, Lane's fortunes and misfortunes make excruciating footnotes.[4] But there is much in Lane's story to marvel at, not least the intense emotions generated by the objects themselves. Like Desdemona's handkerchief and the Stone of Scone, the paintings need to be considered as slightly magic and oddly vulnerable. No doubt because of their supernatural powers, they are susceptible to mischievous thefts, required to stay put but always in transit. "To lose't or give't away were such perdition / As nothing else could match," Othello threatens his wife, but the handkerchief moves swiftly from Desdemona to Emilia to Iago, and then to Cassio, to Bianca, and back to Cassio. It cuts a destructive swath through all the couples in the play, leaving in its passage anger, mistrust, and hysteria. The Stone of Scone is charged with a similar symbolic weight, sanctifying the national sphere as the handkerchief does the domestic. Beginning with Aidan in AD 575, the Stone was used in the coronation ritual of the kings of Scotland, validating the union between monarch and nation. But its history, also, has been one of thefts and displacements. For one reason or another, over the centuries, it has been moved from Iona to Dunstaffnage to Scone to Westminster to Edinburgh Castle, where, since 1996, it has been "on loan" to the people to whom it purportedly belongs.

Like the handkerchief, the thirty-nine paintings grew troublesome when they became gifts. Every time they were given, taken back, or moved about, some kind of public conflict emerged around the point of transference. This part of their history began after Lane bought the paintings. As his friend Alexander Martin of Christie's points out in a taped memoir, Lane earned his wealth dealing in Renaissance paintings, especially Old Masters, but he did not deal in modern paintings.[5] With the money earned by his dealing, he bought modern works only for the purpose of giving them away. He removed all the modern paintings he bought—many more than the contested thirty-nine—from the capitalistic world of investments, risks, bargains, fortunes made and lost, and put them into a gift economy that was quite different. Giving was the great central fact of Lane's life: it took him away from luxury goods and gained him entrance into a public realm of philanthropy. When Lane bought paintings, few people knew of it except dealers and his friends: buying was relatively private. The scale on which Lane gave paintings made his giving not only visible but theatrical. He wasn't just giving: he was bestowing paintings, donating them, presenting them to galleries, cities, and populations. The history of the Lane paintings is driven by the inevitable visibility and public drama entailed in transferring them. To give one is a serious presentation. To give hundreds, as Lane did over a lifetime, is major benefaction. To give thirty-nine, and then take them back, and then give them again, is theater.

A Visionary Sense of Objects

Hugh Lane was probably the only cultural nationalist who believed that Ireland could be changed by beautiful objects. He told his aunt Lady Gregory that he "had been converted to nationalism by discovering that the viceregal windows, which badly needed cleaning, could not be cleaned without long-pondered leave from London."[6] Lane had a visionary sense of objects and passionate convictions about the way things ought to look. Philanthropy for him was not generosity pure and simple; his civic-mindedness evolved from the militancy of his taste. The taste preceded the benefaction: it was a power he considered himself born with, like second sight for a psychic. Arriving home once to find guests already in the drawing room but the flowers unchanged, Lane said in shock, "I have nothing but my taste," and "he felt this outrage to it like an insult, a blow in his face."[7] In Grant Richards's novel *Caviare*, the Lane figure, Sir Peter Bain ("Collector of Pictures"), explains to the protagonist, "I can't write about painting. I express myself by acquiring pictures. That's my way of criticism, my method of expression."[8]

This aesthete got mixed up in controversy with Dublin's business leaders not because he was seeking an outlet for his nationalism, but because he transferred to exterior space his passion for interior decoration. The division of the material world into public and private "spheres," or into the "domestic" and the "political," was unknown to him. All surfaces—the body, the room, the city—were there to be made beautiful. They were distinct in degree but not in kind. Clothing, for instance, was a serious aesthetic project for Lane: as a child he dressed dolls in "brilliant coloured silken scraps," and as an adult he dressed other adults. When his friend Delia Tyrrell determined to wear a hat rather than a wreath and veil to her wedding, Lane "vehemently protested against this," told her he would not go to the wedding if she wore a hat, and then went out and bought a veil for her.[9] According to William Orpen, when his "lady friends" were "going out to Court or balls," Lane "would deck their tresses with jewels and their ears with rings."[10] Once, seeing a young woman of his acquaintance being painted in a "diaphanous dress, he had water-lilies brought in to deck her in the likeness of a Naiad."[11] Not everyone enjoyed the tyranny of Lane's attentions: Lily Yeats said that her father "had not liked being interrupted in the heat of argument by having his clothes brushed from neck to ankle by Hugh."[12] He seems to have irritated the whole family: W.B. did not like the small rose Lane wore in the buttonhole of his evening coat when he came down to dinner at Coole. But that rose, for Lane, was a rose on stage. His own clothes were no less theatrical: according to Thomas Bodkin, when Lane learned that as director of the National Gallery he was entitled to wear an "official Court uniform," he designed one himself. The nine large metal buttons, the hat with enormous plume, the white gloves, and the heavily embroidered collar and cuffs of this remarkable costume were no less "ceremonial" than the sword with its large tassel. As Bodkin observes, "I fancy it was the first and last of its kind."[13]

Not only was every piece of clothing a costume; every object was an *objet*, every drawing room a gallery or a theater. The visible was always becoming spectacle, as Lane reimagined its possibilities. To Lady Fingall he insisted "that the lovely walls of Killeen should never have paint or paper on them. Castle walls should be left as much like stone as possible."[14] Once he pulled down the curtains from a friend's drawing room window, saying, "You really must not have these in your house."[15] Visiting a hypnotist to calm his nerves, Lane took the occasion to redecorate the man's house. The hypnotist "told him to lie upon a couch in a room by himself and count slowly up to a thousand." Bodkin asked him if he did that, and Lane replied, "Not likely. When he went out I just popped up and arranged his beastly mantelpiece for him, and when I heard him coming back I lay on the couch and pretended to be asleep."[16] Even when he gave gifts to friends, Lane made theater out of his presentations. In his memoirs the painter William Orpen tells the story of their parting in Madrid during their trip in 1904. Orpen had admired some statuettes of Adam and Eve that he could not afford. Lane secretly bought them for him and left them in Orpen's bed for him to discover after Lane had left. "When I got to bed that night," writes Orpen, ". . . there were Adam and Eve on the white sheet, with a little card 'H.P.L.' I can't tell you how it brought me up with a shock!" Orpen says Lane loved buying "just the thing" that some friends might need for a room, "and he would find out when they were away from home, and go there and 'place it,' so that the friends would get a surprise of joy when they returned."[17]

Such a man was an odd duck among cultural nationalists. Native Irish matters were never the center of his interest: he preferred Cunarders to currachs, spoke French but not Irish, and never step-danced. In Lady Gregory's diaries of the early 1890s he makes cameo

1.1 Hugh Lane in court uniform (designed by himself) as director of the National Gallery of Ireland, an office he was appointed to in 1914. Photo by permission of the Hugh Lane Municipal Gallery of Modern Art, Dublin.

appearances, gossiping about London art dealers and bargains and forgeries and other "fashionable talk."[18] When he visited Lady Gregory at Coole in 1901, he was at first, writes his aunt, "a little bored." Legend has it that he said to the wife of one guest that his aunt had "lost her position in the county by entertaining people like your husband."[19] But Lane was the only one of Adelaide Persse's eight children to have been born in Ireland, and as he wrote Lady Gregory, his "early romantic notion of Ireland was got in my childhood in Galway."[20] As the public-spirited message of Coole sank in, Lane began to exercise his talents in the larger symbolic space of the nation. Still only twenty-six, Lane commissioned a series of portraits of Irish men and women by Irish artists. In 1904 he organized a London exhibition of the work of Irish painters. And in January 1908 the first Municipal Gallery of Modern Art, organized by Lane and supported by the Dublin Corporation, opened in Clonmell House on Harcourt Street. Its contents were primarily paintings donated by Lane.

The Ireland that Lane imagined offered the supreme opportunity for decoration. With the same élan, the same extravagance, the same pleasure indulged in buying wedding veils or rearranging mantelpieces, Lane bestowed his taste on his native country. To the Irish cultural revival Lane did not bring anything Irish: he brought the exotic aura of European high culture that Joyce was just then leaving Ireland to find. The fresh air, the disturbing air that came in with many of the paintings evoked Manet's world of boulevards, flâneurs, sidewalk cafés, wives, mistresses, and female students, all with paintable bodies and beautifully paintable clothes. The first Irish meaning projected onto some of the paintings was the work of George Moore, who presented them to Dublin with typical provocation. In December 1904, at Lane's request, Moore lectured on behalf of the Loan Exhibition of Modern Art at the Royal Hibernian Academy, an exhibition arranged by Lane. It contained over three hundred works, among them Manet's *Eva Gonzales* and *Le concert aux Tuileries* and Renoir's *Les parapluies*, paintings Lane had bought in Paris, with Orpen's guidance, the previous summer. Moore's lecture did not cause a controversy, but it caused discomfort. According to the *Irish Times*, "the doctrine upon which he insisted with almost painful reiteration last night was, 'Be not ashamed of anything but being ashamed.'"[21] Moore focused much of his sermon on the portrait of Eva Gonzales: to Joseph Holloway, in the audience, it seemed that Moore "almost raved over the unshaded arm of a lady . . . and pro-

pounded many strange things such as 'an artist should be almost unaware of any moral codes to succeed.' "[22]

Unlike Moore, Lane with his innocent idealism did not deliberately seek to provoke controversy. In his donations, the personal and
the national met and blended; cultural patronage was satisfying to
him. Paintings (so it seemed to Lane) could be both gifts and private
possessions, the gallery that he began to plan for housing his paintings a municipal space and at the same time a kind of home. It was
Lane's own space—chosen, approved, and decorated, if not owned,
by Lane—its contents given as benefaction to the city of Dublin. As
he put it, "I never sell a picture till I am driven to it. And if I sell it
to some millionaire it is lost, I don't see it again, it may not give any
very great pleasure to him and it is lost to everyone else. But if I give
a picture to a gallery, that is really good business. It is as much mine
as ever, I still possess it, I can see it when I like and everyone else
can see it too."[23] When, in 1914, Lane was being considered for the
directorship of the National Gallery of Ireland, he sent a message to
J. P. Mahaffy, then chair of the board, promising that "if I am appointed to the National Gallery I will make it my adopted child."[24]
And so he did: as director, Lane forsook the £500 director's salary to
use the funds for acquisitions, and he left bequests to the National
Gallery in his will. He treated the building as his own, painting
some of the smaller rooms and rehanging the paintings at his own
expense. Both galleries, municipal and national, offered stability to
Lane, who had spent a peripatetic childhood staying in rented rooms
in England, Ireland, and Europe with his mother after she left his father. Through these institutions the bachelor Lane constructed a
kinship with Dublin and with Ireland. The public—the putative audience for the paintings—constituted his symbolic heirs. The Municipal Gallery was a Big House that was national property from the
beginning.

As Orpen had developed Lane's taste during their European travels,
so Lane would develop Dubliners' taste. The Municipal Gallery as it
emerged in Lane's thought was characterized by its accessibility. In
the Prefatory Notice to the first catalogue, written for the 1908 opening, Lane wrote, "The Gallery is open free from 10 a.m. to 10 p.m., on
every week-day, and from 3 to 6 p.m. on Sundays."[25] The long hours
show the centrality of display to Lane's aesthetic: this was the civic
fulfillment of his interior decoration. The paintings collected specifically for the Municipal Gallery had not belonged to any one person

but came from a number of collections or from Lane's methodical acquisitions of representative modern European and Irish paintings.
They had never been under one roof before, and when Lane opened
the gallery to the public in its temporary home, Clonmell House on
Harcourt Street, on January 20, 1908, the construction of that "one
roof" was in his mind: "I have . . . deposited here my collection of pictures by Continental artists, and intend to present the most of them,
provided that the promised permanent building is erected on a suitable site within the next few years."[26]

Lane's interiors gestured to the nation outside the walls by the
choice and the hang of the paintings. When the Municipal Gallery
opened, its first room consisted entirely of works by Irish painters—
Nathaniel Hone, John Lavery, John Butler Yeats, Walter Osborne,
William Orpen, Dermod O'Brien, and others. The title read "Irish
Painters (by Birth or Descent)," indicating Lane's wish to claim as
many painters as possible for Ireland; not precisely Patrick Pearse's
brand of cultural nationalism, perhaps, but not incompatible with it.
The next room was "British Schools," including works by Constable,
Whistler, Gerald Kelly, Augustus John, William Rothenstein, and
others (paintings by Charles Shannon were shown in both Irish and
British rooms: Lane made allowance for hybridity). Over the staircase
hung portraits of contemporary Irish men and women. They were
mostly male and mostly Protestant, but not altogether: Douglas
Hyde, Standish O'Grady, Horace Plunkett, and Synge were joined on
the walls by Lady Gregory, Katharine Tynan, Jane Barlow, Willie Fay,
and Michael Davitt. The third room, "French Impressionists and
Others," included many of what would later become the famous
thirty-nine "Continental" paintings, works by Manet, Renoir, Pissarro, Vuillard, and Degas. Other rooms included paintings of the
French Barbizon school (Corot, Courbet, Puvis de Chavannes, and
others), as well as drawings, watercolors, etchings, lithographs, and
sculpture.[27]

It was a remarkable collection to find anywhere in 1908, but it was
in Dublin, where the hang of the pictures constructed its visitors as
Irish Europeans, taking their place among the nations of the earth.
"Perhaps no one but Dublin men who have lived abroad," wrote
Synge, "can quite realise the strange thrill it gave me to turn in from
Harcourt-street—where I passed by to school long ago—and to find
myself among Monets, and Manets and Renoirs, things I connect so
directly with the life of Paris."[28] The invitation to the opening was

bilingual, in Irish and English. In the original catalogue Lane wrote, "Till to-day Ireland was the only country in Europe that had no Gallery of Modern Art. There is not even a single accessible private collection of Modern Pictures in this country. That reproach is now removed."[29] Lane's vision was of a cosmopolitan Ireland, as worthy of visiting as Paris, Madrid, and Rome. And of course the gallery would not just draw foreign visitors: it would create sophisticated Irish audiences and Irish painters. "Nearly every country has had a great epoch in art," Lane had announced to a London committee in 1905; adding, in the idiom of cultural nationalism learned from his aunt, "It is now our turn."[30]

By displaying paintings he had given to the city of Dublin in a municipally supported gallery that had never been his home, Lane seemed to be avoiding the arrogant material statements of American millionaires such as Henry Frick, Isabella Stewart Gardner, and J. Paul Getty, whose cultural patronage created memorials to their own importance. Lane did not enshrine any private office space in perpetuity, with elegant desk, pens in marble holders, gold clocks, and other expensive business paraphernalia situated in museum space as if they were equal in importance to the surrounding artifacts of high culture. Nor did he want the gallery to bear his name. Only long after his death was the gallery he had established named after him.[31]

The "Bridge Site" and the Politics of Space, 1913

Lane's enthusiastic, almost evangelical notion of the Municipal Gallery's mission does not quite come across in the Beerbohm drawing "Sir Hugh Lane Producing Masterpieces for Dublin. 1909." Lane the magician—tall, tuxedoed, debonair, standing on a stage—pulls a painting of a landscape out of his top hat, while a Dubliner of distinctly unaristocratic mien stands nearby, staggering under a pile of paintings. Of those, the painting most visible shows a woman of leisure in a fancy hat, looking quite different from the shawled colleens in the audience. The man in the audience drawn in most detail holds his hat (with clay pipe attached) on his lap. Four years before the public commotion over Lane's "conditional gift" of paintings, Beerbohm's genius intuited the difficulties inherent in the distance between Lane and his intended beneficiaries. By drawing Lane on a stage high above the audience, Beerbohm literalized the public drama entailed in giving away the paintings. Lane acts as a magician because of the inevitable theatricality of patronage on such a scale—and because he appears magical to the people of Dublin, who have not been privy to his acquisition of wealth painting by painting, deal by deal, year by year. To them he bursts onto the scene already rich with a treasure hoard of art at his fingertips.[32]

But then, there was already a gulf between Lane and most other human beings, because, as *Le Figaro* pointed out, he had created a whole museum out of nothing: "créer, sans fortune, sans appui d'aucune sort . . . un musée complet . . . un musée envié des États les plus prospères et des cités les plus orgueilleuses, puis donner á une ville qu'on aime de trésor . . . voilà qui est agir mieux encore qu'un habile homme." ["To create without a fortune, without support of any kind . . . an entire museum . . . a museum envied by the wealthiest countries and the proudest cities, then to give it to a city one loves like a treasure, . . . that's what it is to do things even better than a skillful man."] To the hibernophile French, this feat was a patriotic act worthy of applause: "Quelle victoire pour l'Irlande!"[33] In Dublin, the scale and size of the thing was overwhelming. As Henry James might have said, Lane was "immense." So were his needs: there were too many paintings and too much space required for them. Where would *un musée complet* be put in a crowded city? By the spring of 1912, Lane must have assumed that the "promised permanent building," one that suited the paintings, the donor, and the Dublin Corporation, would soon be found, because he had already set up a competition for the design of panels to place in it.

Lane had long held strong feelings about the issue of location, location, location even before the opening of the Harcourt Street gallery. In the calm atmosphere created by the committee of inquiry of the Lords Commissioners of the King's Treasury in 1905, questioning witnesses about the Royal Hibernian Academy, Lane testified with a high seriousness and idealism. His answers tended to stray to the subject that really interested him, the gallery he had in mind to establish, and the issues that mattered the most, its location and architecture. Speaking of the RHA, but thinking of his own project, he characterized the habits of the audience for high culture:

> The general public are not energetic enough to go much out of their way for an Art Exhibition; they are much affected by the extent to which a place is easy to get to. They may go once, if out of the beaten

1.2. Max Beerbohm cartoon of Hugh Lane. "Sir Hugh Lane producing master-pieces for Dublin. 1909." Beerbohm's drawing emphasizes the class difference between Lane and his beneficiaries, though the people in the drawing resemble a Londoner's notion of Irish country people rather than actual Dubliners. Permission of the Hugh Lane Municipal Gallery of Modern Art, Dublin. Copyright the Estate of Max Beerbohm, reprinted by permission of Berlin Associates.

track, or ten times, if they are within easy reach of it. The building should be in a prominent place, and also be an imposing one—not merely a place for the housing of pictures.[34]

Although the committee chair kept redirecting·Lane's attention to "the general question," Lane interpolated his aims for what he was then calling the "Modern Gallery" at every possible moment. "That Gallery would be free of charges for admission," he noted, "and would be intended for the education of the taste of the man in the street as well as the art student." Asked if the RHA and the gallery should be situated near one another in Dublin, Lane thought not: "The more desirable thing for the Modern Gallery is to get a building where there is most traffic." Lane wanted his gallery to create, summon, and greet its public. The public art museum "addresse[s] its visitor as a bourgeois citizen who enters the museum in search of enlightenment and rationally understood pleasures," notes Carol Duncan. "It stands revealed as keeper of the nation's spiritual life and guardian of the most evolved and civilized culture of which the human spirit is capable."[35] Location, for Lane, was inextricable from this lofty educational mission. The gallery had to be where the people were, seducing them by its beauty.

For a while St. Stephen's Green seemed a likely spot, and in spite of the objections of Lord Ardilaun, whose approval was required, Lane asked the English architect Sir Edwin Lutyens to design a gallery for it. The design did not convince Lord Ardilaun, who felt it would ruin the green's "proportions and beauty."[36] Temperamentally impatient already, Lane now expressed his frustration in a letter to the Dublin city clerk on November 5, 1912, turning over to the Dublin Corporation one set of paintings "on the condition that they are always on view free to the public," but threatening that another group of thirty-nine Continental paintings would be removed at the end of January 1913 if no decision about the gallery's permanent site were made.[37] A Citizens' Provisional Committee (later called the Mansion House Committee) composed of people from artistic, political, and social circles in Dublin—Walter Armstrong of the National Gallery, W. F. Bailey of the Estates Commission, Thomas Bodkin, Oliver Gogarty, Mary Guinness, Count Markievicz, Dermod O'Brien, and Sarah Purser—was established under the leadership of the lord mayor. These citizens would raise all funds necessary for the acquisition of a site beyond the amount voted by the council. Approached by Lady

Gregory for his help, Bernard Shaw offered a hundred guineas, sending along a letter of rhetorical flourishes about the responsibility of "Irishmen . . . to keep and extend their share in forming the mind of the world."[38] This was the group doing the leg work while Yeats was writing his poem "To a friend who promises a bigger subscription than his first to the Dublin Municipal Gallery if the amount collected proves that there is a considerable 'popular demand' for the pictures," with its idealized image of a single wealthy duke who would foot the bill.[39]

In their own way, Yeats's poems on the subject of Lane's benefactions, like Beerbohm's drawing, focused on distinctions of class, wealth, and cosmopolitanism. Beerbohm had shawled women and men with clay pipes; Yeats had "Paudeen" and "Biddy":

> You gave, but will not give again
> Until enough of Paudeen's pence
> By Biddy's halfpennies have lain.
>
> (287)

The "wealthy man" (Lord Ardilaun, not Lane) is encouraged to model himself on the Duke of Urbino or the Medici, while "Paudeens play at pitch and toss." The poem's original title insults the Ardilauns as much as its ethnic diminutives insult the "people." The correspondence between Lady Gregory and Lane on the issue of the gallery's site shows that neither of them ever quite gave up the idea that the Ardilauns would relent and allow space in the green for a building. After the entire site controversy was over, Gregory wrote Lane, "I hope someone will attack the Ardilauns—they are worse than the Corporation." (Lane attacked them privately in a letter to Gregory, noting that Lord Ardilaun's "gift of the Green was only the purchasing price of his Peerage.")[40]

The middle classes, too, were at fault, as they generally are in Yeats's poetry, and like Lord Ardilaun, they were scolded and told to model their behavior on that of the illustrious dead. In "September 1913," the middle-class Dubliners who opposed the site and the architect Lane ultimately wanted for the permanent gallery are said to "fumble in a greasy till / And add the halfpence to the pence / And prayer to shivering prayer." To this unattractive group is opposed the elegance and self-sacrifice of martyrs—Edward Fitzgerald, Emmet, Wolfe Tone, O'Leary—whose idealism left them no money to save

and no time to pray. It was on behalf of Hugh Lane's Municipal
Gallery that Yeats wrote his most famous lines: "Romantic Ireland's
dead and gone, / It's with O'Leary in the grave." When the *Irish Times*
printed "September 1913" on the day of the Dublin Corporation's important meeting about the gallery, it appeared to accept Yeats's invid-
ious distinctions. An editorial urging a vote for the gallery announced, "We want a prosperous Ireland, but we must not sacrifice to
it the sweeter qualities which have formed the character of our
people. . . . if the day is lost, the city will deserve the reproach which
Mr Yeats makes against those who have grudged the money."[41]

Like Yeats's poems and most notes on Yeats's poems, narratives of
the so-called battles of the sites imply a highly polarized Dublin,
fierce hostility to Lane and all purveyors of high culture from the very
beginning, and a desire to do Lane in altogether. Opinions actually
developed more gradually and were more ambivalent. Initially Lane
had much support in Dublin, where he had been given the Freedom of
the City in February 1908, just after the opening of the gallery in
Clonmell House. Alderman Tom Kelly had long been his champion,
and on January 20, 1913, the Corporation determined by a vote of 29
to 2 to devote £22,000 to the gallery. Lord Mayor Lorcan Sherlock pol-
iticked actively on Lane's behalf, and even the nationalist paper *Sinn
Féin* originally urged the city not to lose the "unique collection of
modern pictures."[42]

Where was a good permanent site to hang the paintings? Where
was there "most traffic" but also an available space? The search
was on in the winter of 1913, and no stone was left unturned. Was
the best site perhaps in Lord Edward Street, near City Hall? What
about Kildare Street or at the Turkish Baths in Lincoln Place? Too
expensive. A "disused skating rink in Earlsfort Terrace"? Not central enough. Merrion Square? Too close to the National Gallery.
The Mansion House? Too small. Upper Ormond Quay? Essex
Quay?[43] A cartoon by Grace Gifford captured the burdensome quality of Lane's generosity: Lane is leading an elephant up to the lord
mayor, Lorcan Sherlock, who is saying, "Of course it's very kind of
you, sir—but where now will I house him?"[44] Another cartoon
shows the desperation of the search for a site: the gallery is balanced on top of Nelson's pillar.[45] In fact the problem was the opposite of a recent debate: in 1998 and 1999 there was an empty place,
the spot where Nelson's pillar used to be, but controversy over
what to put in it.

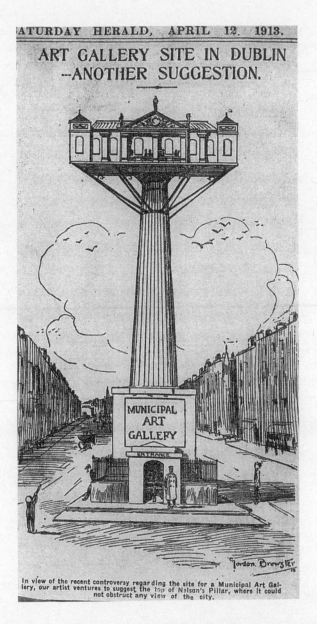

SATURDAY HERALD, APRIL 12. 1913.

ART GALLERY SITE IN DUBLIN
---ANOTHER SUGGESTION.

MUNICIPAL
ART
GALLERY

ENTRANCE

Gordon Brewster

In view of the recent controversy regarding the site for a Municipal Art Gallery, our artist ventures to suggest the top of Nelson's Pillar, where it could not obstruct any view of the city.

1.3. Art gallery site in Dublin—another suggestion. The original caption reads, "In view of the recent controversy regarding the site for a Municipal Art Gallery, our artist ventures to suggest the top of Nelson's Pillar, where it could not obstruct any view of the city." Courtesy of the National Library of Ireland and the Hugh Lane Municipal Gallery of Modern Art, Dublin.

THE LORD MAYOR OF DUBLIN EXPRESSES BEWILDERMENT ON SIR HUGH LANE OFFERING
HIS PICTURES TO DUBLIN.

1.4. Cartoon of Hugh Lane and Lorcan Sherlock, Lord Mayor of Dublin, by Grace Gifford, drawn during the bridge-site controversy. From *Irish Life*, August 1, 1913. The original caption reads, "The Lord Mayor of Dublin expresses bewilderment on Sir Hugh Lane offering his pictures to Dublin." At a special meeting of the Dublin Chamber of Commerce, one speaker referred to the collection as a "white elephant." Permission of the Hugh Lane Municipal Gallery of Modern Art, Dublin, and courtesy of Iseult McGuinness.

During the winter, the internationally acclaimed architect Sir Edwin Lutyens, who had already made a design for the possible Stephen's Green site, took up Frank Craig's suggestion of a bridge gallery spanning the Liffey.[46] The building he designed to replace the metal Ha'penny Bridge would have made a strong visual statement: two separate galleries, each with its own pavilion facing the water, were to be connected by a colonnaded pergola, the whole supported by a three-arched bridge. The roof of each gallery was topped with statuary. By the time of Lane's January deadline, no other acceptable location had been discovered. He had made known his preference for a bridge site, and by April it had become a stipulation. Without that design by that architect in that place, he would take back the conditional gift of the thirty-nine paintings (leaving, of course, the other group given only on the condition that they be permanently displayed free of charge). His conditions, wrote *Sinn Féin*, had increased "until he has deprived the gift of all grace, and rendered it impossible for the city, while it regards its own dignity, to accept them."[47] Even Lane's devoted aunt tried in the most affectionately tactful way to point out the problem created by an additional condition: "In my mind I see two great dangers, one that Ireland may lose the pictures—the other and more personal one that you, after your Great patience and Great Generosity—may put yourself in the wrong by getting away from your original promise."[48]

The palpable monumentality of what was required, and the nature of the site Lane demanded, made the alleged "gift" seem an imposition. The scale had changed: Lane was no longer simply giving paintings; he was demanding a monument. Or so said those who spoke and voted against it. The issue was a matter of great public debate in all the Dublin newspapers during the summer of 1913. *Sinn Féin* gradually withdrew its support, objecting both to the visibility and the centrality of the proposed building: "No visitor to Dublin could miss seeing that Gallery . . . a forty thousand pound monument to Sir Hugh Lane far more conspicuous than the memorials . . . to Daniel O'Connell and Charles Stuart Parnell. . . . if Sir Hugh Lane persists in demanding that this memorial to his generosity should be placed where he designs it, there is trouble ahead."[49] The scale of his gift, earlier the index of his munificence, became the measure of his grandiosity and condescension. Dublin was not Lane's demesne, and there seemed to be a seigneurial quality in someone who insisted on tearing down a bridge and inflicting a building on the city. The way Lady

1.5. Design by Sir Edwin Lutyens for the Municipal Gallery on bridge replacing the Ha'penny Bridge. Such a gallery, if built, would have made an easy target for the gunboat *Helga* during the Rising three years after the bridge-site controversy. Picture courtesy of the Hugh Lane Municipal Gallery of Modern Art, Dublin.

Gregory wrote of Dublin sites to Lane makes the whole city sound like a huge game board: "Would you take Mansion House if you approved of a plan? Or Merrion Square, tho' most uninteresting of all?"[50]

Like the movement of the handkerchief from person to person in *Othello*, the attempted transference of the paintings released anxieties that perhaps had been there all along. Suddenly, it seemed, Dublin businessmen were threatened by the paintings. They despised them. Quite possibly some residue of George Moore lingered about them too, an aura of shamelessness, of immoral continental ways, the painting of bare-armed and bare-breasted women by non-Irish painters—and all these pictures to be placed in an expensive and ostentatious building designed by an "English" architect (Lutyens's father was Dutch and his mother was Irish).[51] Why hadn't this general hostility to high culture, to sexy pictures, to rich people with English titles, been heard earlier, when the Corporation had voted money in support of the gallery? Lane's insistence on the one site and the one design excited feelings of territoriality. The gallery began to seem invasive, and all those who had ever felt the slightest bit of dislike for Lane, or high culture, or Yeats, or titled people, defended their space.

Moreover, the first hint of complaint opened the door to other complaints. All the antagonism had been there, but no one knew that other people felt the same way. Someone had to take the first step, and someone else the second: then it was open war on Lane. By summer, the vocal minority was clamorous.

The class conflict expressed itself in terms of the control of space in Dublin. "Earth being denied us, we took water and air for our site," Lady Gregory wrote breezily to the *Irish Times*, but water and air were denied also.[52] Public debate focused on ownership of the bridge, the river, the air, and the streets, as well as the taxes that would be required for maintaining the whole enterprise in perpetuity. The control of space was the particular concern of two deputations attending the August 11 meeting of the Dublin Corporation, the Central Highways Committee, and the River Liffey Protection Association. The Highways Committee urged "that nothing . . . be done . . . with the site . . . which would prevent the future improvement, development, and progress of the heart of the city." Mr. J. Hamilton Hunter (of the Highways Committee) said that "if this folly bridge—this picture bridge was going to be put up . . . , it would be swept away in a few years, because it would not be fair to the progress of a great city to allow it to stand in the course of the flow of traffic and prosperity."[53] It was he who introduced the notion of "effluvia" from the river that might damage the paintings, and he suggested they be kept in the Mansion House on Dawson Street. Richard Jones of the River Liffey Protection Association objected on aesthetic grounds to the architectural design and said that

> it would be an outrage on art and on common sense to adopt such a plan. It would obstruct a view painted by God Almighty, which no artist could imitate. It would be one of the most unsightly bridges ever erected in a large city, and [would] obstruct the diurnal passage of the sea air, which daily prevented the outbreak of disease in many filthy alleys.[54]

Mr. Jones added his personal aesthetic response to the paintings, that although "some of them were incomparable, there were others he would not hang in his back kitchen (Laughter)." In an editorial the next day, the *Irish Times* refused to take seriously the claim that a bridge gallery would "obstruct the traditional Liffey sunset."[55]

The bridge site was discussed at a specially summoned meeting of the Dublin Chamber of Commerce, whose president, William Martin

Murphy, had become Lane's chief antagonist. A former Dublin MP and notorious anti-Parnellite, wealthy from railroad construction in England, Ireland, Africa, and South America, Murphy was the most important businessman in Dublin: he controlled the Dublin United Tramways Company, the *Irish Independent* newspaper, Clery's department store, and the Imperial Hotel. The Chamber of Commerce was not by definition hostile to painting: the very next year it commissioned Lane's good friend Orpen to do a portrait of Murphy. (Although a copy, also done by Orpen, was made to "hang in the Chamber of Commerce," no copy was commissioned to join those of other famous Irish people in the Municipal Gallery.)[56] At the August 12 meeting, the chamber adopted a resolution protesting the proposed bridge site, and Mr. E. H. Andrews echoed the concern about health: "If they were going to erect such a block in the middle of their city the quays of Dublin would not maintain their reputation for promoting the health of the city as they had done in the past." Mr. Andrews said that his "own personal opinion was to let Sir Hugh Lane take himself and his pictures away from the city altogether, and not cause any more turmoil and trouble."[57]

Now that Lane and the Dublin civic leaders were at war, distinctions of status were frequently invoked. To James Walker of the River Liffey Protection Association, the bridge gallery seemed like a Big House that would be built in the center of Dublin. He said that

> they had lost sight of the fact that there were 20,000 families living in one room each, and living under conditions which were a disgrace to the City of Dublin. Like any other 'white elephant', the collection in question might be described as being worth £10,000, and they were asked to provide for them a magnificent palace and a great retinue of servants to take care of them. He could not help but regard such a proposition as a scandalous waste of money.[58]

William Martin Murphy's figures of speech (in a long letter to the *Irish Times* in August) implied that Lane insisted on the bridge site in order to assert his own dominance over the city:

> He is to choose the only site in the city against which he knows there is an intense public feeling . . . he figuratively wipes his boots in the architectural profession of Ireland, and a committee of Irish gentlemen are so obsessed by Sir Hugh Lane and his handful of pictures that

they meekly swallow all his conditions, and are prepared if they can succeed in doing so to place the citizens under his feet. It is a case of "no Irish need apply" for any job besides digging the foundations in the Liffey mud.[59]

The battle lines replicated to some extent those of several Abbey Theatre controversies; the colonial paradigm was made to fit in such a way that Lane, who had sent invitations to the 1908 opening in Irish and English, who wanted Dublin to take its place among European cities as an equal, was now understood to be neocolonial and anti-Irish. Clearly the Lane–Lutyens gallery was the camel's nose or the tip of the iceberg: Dublin was to be recolonized, and the gallery would be a "riparian advertisement" to the power of "an Irish gentleman" over the mud diggers. The imperious stubbornness of Lane's "taste" had turned him into a landlord.

Murphy's attitude was an affront to Lane's idealism, but Lane's attitude was an affront to Murphy's dignity. Not that Murphy believed in Lane's idealism: rejecting the assertion that Lane acted from "philanthropy, public spirit, and beneficence," he insisted, "I look upon it all as business, and very good business." After all, Lane's work "procured a knighthood for a very young man of 33 years of age, previously unknown to fame."[60] No doubt many readers of the *Irish Times* remembered the peculiar drama of 1907, when Murphy refused to accept a knighthood from Edward VII, even as the king was getting his ceremonial sword ready. Who was Lane to impose conditions on Murphy's Dublin?[61]

The heat and intensity of passions about the design of the gallery attracted to itself all the other antagonisms in the air that year. As the struggle over the gallery's site was coming to a close, in late August and early September, the great strike of the Irish Transport and General Workers' Union against Murphy and other Dublin capitalists was beginning. *Sinn Féin* astutely pointed out that all the participants in the gallery controversy tried to gain the high moral ground by linking their own point of view with that of the city's poor:

For long we have tried to awaken public opinion on behalf of the poor. We promulgated plans to remedy the awful conditions under which they exist. Our efforts proved abortive. Then the unlooked-for happens. We help to create a fuss about Lane's pictures. Mr. Yeats writes poems, piercing the public conscience, and lo, the pictures accom-

plished what our most strenuous efforts failed to achieve. Champions
arose on behalf of the poor. . . . Public spirited citizens come forward.
Tenements are to be swept away—the sick are to be cleansed. The des-
titute and forsaken are to be cared for. . . . The poor are indebted to
the pictures for the discovery of their deplorable condition. . . . Now
Lane's pictures may go—the Liffey flow on its course undisturbed and
undisfigured by wanton waste. . . . The poor will no longer be forgotten and ignored. Clearly, then, pictures are wonderful and thought
provoking. They are an influence to be reckoned with.[62]

Murphy may have been the first to associate his position with sympathy for the poor. Reading Yeats's poem "To a Friend Who Promises a
Bigger Subscription" in the *Irish Times* of January 11, Murphy had
(wrongly) assumed that he himself was the wealthy man and had responded six days later in his own paper, the *Irish Independent*, with a
resounding defense of practicality against culture: "Speaking for myself I admire good pictures and I think I can appreciate them but as a
choice between the two, I would rather see in the city of Dublin one
block of sanitary houses at low rents replacing a reeking slum than
all the pictures Corot and Degas ever painted."[63] Murphy, as is well
known, was not building those houses, but he introduced the notion
that paintings used up money better spent on rebuilding the slums.
But the other side could also claim to be helping the poor. Writing to
the *Irish Times* in March, Yeats invoked "an old man who was painting a friend's bathroom" and quoted the man's praise of Mancini,
adding that "the pictures once set up upon their bridge will be near to
many men and women of his sort."[64]
    Allied against their common enemy Murphy, James Larkin and
Lane, labor and culture, recognized in one another a common progressive mentality. They were alike transgressive and disruptive, attempting to exert power in Murphy's city. Socialist, trade unionist,
founder of the Irish Transport and General Workers' Union, Larkin
was beginning his battle with Murphy as Lane's was coming to temporary resolution. Like Lane, Larkin would be defeated by Murphy in
the short term but would have a powerful and more enduring hold in
Irish memory. The 1913 strike and lockout had begun in August, before the corporation's final vote on the gallery was taken. On July 28
Larkin "had moved a motion at Dublin Trades Council supporting
the building of the gallery." He was also quoted as recommending
that Murphy "should be condemned to keep an art gallery in Hell."[65]

After the infamous police charge against the Dublin strikers on August 31, in which two men were killed by baton blows, Lane wrote to Thomas Bodkin, "I hope that Murphy will get a crack on the head by one of the Police soon!" and in November, when Larkin was imprisoned, "I think that Larkin will beat Murphy yet—I hope so!"[66] The *Irish Citizen* pointed out the alliance between the two causes:

> The opponents of the Art Gallery employed many claptrap arguments, based on a fallacious opposition between the project and the slum-clearing work, which were calculated to appeal to the working classes, who cannot usually be expected to have time or training to appreciate questions of art. But the Labour Party, disregarding these arguments, voted steadily for the Art Gallery at every stage.[67]

To some extent the two constituencies overlapped. Lane's strongest support on the Dublin Corporation was the painter and suffragist Sarah Cecilia Harrison, the first woman elected to membership on the Corporation. Larkin had attended the party that celebrated her election in 1912, and the *Irish Citizen* called her a "sincere friend of Labour."[68] William Orpen, Lane's close friend, worked in the soup kitchens of Liberty Hall during the strike. And Casimir Markievicz, a painter and a member of the Mansion House Committee, supplied the frock coat and top hat that Larkin wore to disguise himself as a cleric so he could gain entrance to Murphy's Imperial Hotel on August 31 and address the workers from the balcony.[69]

In August and September, as the strike was beginning, the controversy over the site was coming to an end. Sentiment against Lane came from every possible direction: Councilor William Cosgrave (later the first president of the Executive Council of the Irish Free State and Yeats's ally) moved to offer the amendment that "no proposal for the erection of a Municipal Art Gallery can be contemplated by this Council which excludes Irish Architects from competing for the design."[70] Councilor David Quaid (long an opponent of anything to do with the gallery) said he "was opposed to the Gallery scheme at present because of the other needs of the city, the greatest of which was the housing of the poor."[71] When told that Lady Gregory had urged the value of appreciating Impressionist pictures, he came back with, "She's his aunt—a family affair, a family affair."[72] William McCarthy claimed that he was "neither against the architect nor the pictures" but only against the bridge site.[73] When, just

before the September 8 vote, Lorcan Sherlock warned that "the result would be, if Sir Hugh Lane were in earnest in his statement to
the Committee, that the pictures were gone," Quaid called out, "Let
them go."[74] As the aldermen and councilors were making amend-
ments and yelling at one another, and Yeats was writing poems, and
Lady Gregory was wondering what to do with all the money raised in
America for the gallery if the cause failed, Lane was expressing himself in the only way he knew, through objects. With great, dramatic
public flourishes, photographed eagerly by Murphy's *Irish Independent*, he removed the thirty-nine paintings. Retrieving them was, he
wrote Gregory, "my last trump card. . . . if they give me the river site
I will return the lot."[75] On July 31 he moved the pictures from the
Harcourt Street gallery to the Mansion House, and in the early autumn they were sent to the National Gallery in London, the location
that would send the strongest possible message to the ungrateful
Dubliners.

And shouldn't Dublin be grateful to those thirty-two negative
votes, to Councilors Quaid and McCarthy, Aldermen Coffey and Bew-
ley, and all the rest? They saved the Ha'penny Bridge for posterity,
they saved the Liffey from the gallery, and they saved the Manets,
Courbets, and Renoir from the Liffey, where they would surely have
ended up during Easter week 1916.

The Empty Room

When Yeats "revisited" the Municipal Gallery in 1937, five years
after Lady Gregory's death, he saw it as a monument to the culture of
the Big House, locating there the "deep-rooted" things he could no
longer visit at her house. In "The Municipal Gallery Revisited"
Coole is museumized. The poem is written in the ottava rima Yeats
uses for high subjects in his later poetry, and in the last four stanzas
Yeats wraps Coole into the Municipal Gallery, as he moves from grief
at the desolation of Coole to a reaffirmation of its values:

> John Synge, I and Augusta Gregory, thought
> All that we did, all that we said or sang
> Must come from contact with the soil, from that
> Contact everything Antaeus-like grew strong,

1.6. The removal of the Lane pictures to the Mansion House. Photo courtesy of the National Library of Ireland and the Hugh Lane Municipal Gallery of Modern Art, Dublin.

> We three alone in modern times had brought
> Everything down to that sole test again,
> Dream of the noble and the beggar-man.
>   *(603)*

Synge's socialism and Lady Gregory's Irish republicanism would hardly be compatible with the feudal "dream" Yeats claims as their common project. Its presence in a poem about revisiting the Dublin Municipal Gallery shows that Yeats's imagination moved quickly away from the portraits of his friends to what he saw as the sacred center of Irish culture, the west of Ireland, and its custodians, the denizens of the Big Houses. Nothing could be farther from Lane's vision of municipalized European paintings in a city-owned gallery, open long hours so working people could view them. But others before Yeats had understood its politics in the same way.

Whatever about the Big House, the strongest political statement made by the gallery in the late 1930s was something entirely different, embodied not in the presence of portraits of Yeats's friends but in the absence of paintings that should have been there. Lane's "trump card," the thirty-nine paintings, remained in London, and the magic or curse that decreed they would always cause trouble was now manifest. After Lane's death on the *Lusitania* in May 1915, the paintings entered a new phase, one in which their absence from Dublin made them far more conspicuous and more interesting than their presence ever would have.

Lane's will of October 11, 1913, written after the gallery site debacle, had left the paintings to the National Gallery in London, to "found a collection of Modern Continental Art" there. But there they lay unviewed in the basement; the board did not consider all thirty-nine worthy of display, and Lane, insulted, withdrew his gift but never repossessed the paintings.[76] Irritated now by a more sophisticated corporate body, and somewhat reconciled to Ireland after his appointment as director of the National Gallery of Ireland in April 1914, Lane had further thoughts about the collection. It had come to constitute a means of articulating his feelings about Ireland. Even when bequeathed to England, it was used to send a message to Ireland, the legacy indicating Dublin's "want of public spirit in the year 1913." Before leaving for the fatal visit to America in early 1915, Lane wrote a "codicil of forgiveness," as Lady Gregory called it in her biography of Lane. The codicil not only gave the paintings back to Dublin but explicitly required that if they did not go to the Municipal Gallery, they would not go to any gallery:

> Hugh Lane. 3rd February, 1915. This is a codicil to my last will to the effect that the group of pictures now at the London National Gallery, which I had bequeathed to that Institution, I now bequeath to the City of Dublin, providing that a suitable building is provided for them within five years of my death. The Group of pictures I have lent to Belfast I give to the Municipal Gallery in Harcourt Street. If a building is provided within five years, the whole collection will be housed together. . . . If within five years a Gallery is not forthcoming, then the group of pictures (at the London National Gallery) are to be sold, and the proceeds to fulfil the purpose of my will.[77]

Lane had told many people that "they will all be in Dublin yet," and he had initialed the codicil at the top of every page.[78] He simply had not got a witness for the initials, although, as the codicil's supporters were quick to point out, had he been a soldier at the Front writing a will under pressure of imminent death, or had he been in Scotland, the unwitnessed codicil would have been legal.[79] Death at sea from enemy attack was not covered by these exceptions.

"Never before, and probably never again, in the history of Ireland," wrote Thomas Bodkin of the 1918 Mansion House meeting called to claim the Lane paintings,

> will our people be found in such absolute unanimity on any question. At one time or another Arthur Griffith, General Michael Collins, President Cosgrave, Mr. De Valera, Mr. John Redmond, Lord Carson, Lord Craigavon, Protestant and Catholic Bishops, the Moderator of the General Assembly of the Presbyterian Church, Unionists, Nationalists, Sinn Feiners, judges and generals, peers and proletarians, artists, scholars, and professional and business men, rich and poor have found themselves working together towards the same end.[80]

The Continental paintings, their cosmopolitan shamelessness forgiven or forgotten, had become Irish national treasures, as Irish as the Book of Kells or the Blasket Islands, or as Irish as Roger Casement's remains and the six northern counties, those other properties that England kept but Ireland claimed. The ultimate hibernicization of the collection was accomplished in 1926 when the British government officially refused to return it. The National Gallery in London had said it could do nothing without an act of Parliament, and the Parliamentary Committee of Inquiry found that although Lane himself believed he was making a legal document when he wrote the codicil, there were many reasons why the paintings should be kept in London. One reason, the committee said, was that if Lane had "been spared to witness" the Tate Gallery, "he would have destroyed the codicil."[81] As John Reynolds, curator of the Municipal Gallery in 1932, put it, such reasoning "could be applied with equal force to all Testamentary Bequests since the world began."[82] However, with this definitive refusal, Lane and his thirty-nine paintings became definitively Irish, and the gap Beerbohm had represented in his 1909 drawing, the great distance between Lane and the people of Dublin, was overcome. The gift was given. What the Germans began with the torpedoing of the *Lusitania*, the British committee completed.

Thus the aura, if not the actual fact, of martyrdom surrounded Lane, and the British retention of the paintings gave the matter a

1.7. A page from the famous codicil to Lane's will. This is the document that bequeathed the thirty-nine paintings to the gallery in Dublin, "providing that a suitable building is furnished for them within 5 years of my death." Notice the signature in the upper right-hand corner, over the date; if only Lane had thought to have the signature witnessed. Permission of the Hugh Lane Municipal Gallery of Modern Art, Dublin.

strong postcolonial bitterness. The gift was given, but it wasn't received. Dublin Corporation unanimously supported it and appointed
a Lane bequest committee to work for the return of the collection. In
this effort the Corporation was aided by many others: the Friends of
the National Collections of Ireland was founded by Sarah Purser in
1924 and soon directed its efforts to the return of the Lane paintings.[83] Lady Gregory devoted hours to taking tea with the wives of
powerful men, begging them to convince their husbands of Ireland's
right to the paintings. She wore out the pavement to politicians' offices—Edward Carson, Eamon de Valera, anyone sympathetic—in her
continuing efforts on behalf of the collection, gathered personal testi-
monies to Lane's wishes and legal opinion supporting them, and
wrote the earliest pamphlet stating in its entirety the case for the return of the paintings to Ireland, as well as the first biography of Lane.
The Executive Council of the Irish Free State commissioned Bodkin's
1932 biography of Lane, for which both Cosgrave and de Valera wrote
introductory remarks. De Valera offered the martyr's crown, calling
Lane "an Irishman who strove nobly to serve the cause of culture in
his country," saying that the book was "a gift from the Government . . . to those who love justice."[84] In 1932, in response to Sarah
Purser's request, the Irish government gave Charlemont House to the
city of Dublin for use as the Municipal Gallery, and John Reynolds
wrote the *Statement of the Claim for the Return to Dublin of the 39
Lane Bequest Pictures Now at the Tate Gallery, London*, with the
seal of the city of Dublin on the title page. Their absence was made
conspicuous by the large room at the end of the gallery kept empty
for their return. All this for the man who had attempted to block the
Liffey sunset and keep the healthy air from the city's tenements! As a
final expression of official forgiveness, the Corporation commissioned
a bust of Lane from the Irish sculptor Albert Power: the bust was sta-
tioned in solitary splendor in the gallery's final room, surveying the
walls whose emptiness made a statement even stronger than the Lutyens building would have made. The "continental paintings" entered
into modern Irish collective memory as national treasures kept from
their rightful owners. The empty room was a reminder of unfinished
national business. In Grace Gifford's drawing the collection had been
an elephant without a house; now the house was ready, but the elephant wasn't there. This was the gallery Yeats visited, thinking not of
the Renoir and Manet that should have been there but (as usual) of
the illustrious dead: Synge, Lane, Lady Lavery, Lady Gregory.

1.8. The empty room. This is the "Lane Room," kept empty for the missing thirty-nine paintings until their partial return in 1961. The bust of Lane by Albert Power, commissioned by the Dublin Corporation, sits like a tutelary deity surveying the space that is its special preserve. Permission of the Hugh Lane Municipal Gallery of Modern Art, Dublin. Originally printed in *Municipal Gallery of Modern Art and Civic Museum Dublin* (Dublin: Browne and Nolan Ltd., 1933).

The loud message of the silent room was heard. Just as in 1950 the Stone of Scone was stolen from Westminster by Scottish students and driven to Scotland, so in 1956 (on April 12, near the time of the fortieth anniversary of the Rising) confiscated Irish national property, a Lane painting, was stolen by two Irish students, one of them an IRA member. And so once more the Lane paintings were associated with conflict around the point of transference, generating a story with distinct narrative appeal quite independent of its connection with the controversy. It made headlines in the *Irish Times* and the *Times* (London), and at least three versions of it have been recorded by the proud perpetrators.[85] The more radical of the two students, Bill Fogarty, attended veterinary school at the time, and the first telling of the story appeared in *Pegasus: Magazine of the Veterinary Students' Union*, just after the Irish Department of Agriculture's full-page advertisement for "Remedies for Cattle and Sheep Affected with Stomach Worms, Hoose and Fluke." Juxtaposed with articles on the cattle of Ireland, euthanasia, and Dún Aengus, Fogarty's "Coup de Tate" makes the Lane paintings seem intimately part of the physical world of Ireland.[86]

In this case it was Berthe Morisot's *Jour d'été* that suffered in the national cause. The theatrical pleasure Fogarty took in the logistics of the heist is clear in the "map" of the Tate Gallery's first floor, including "area patrolled by attendant," "doorman," "revolving door," and the "two detectives" sitting outside in a car.[87] A 1976 interview also indicates the fun of planning the heist: "We cased the joint for a few days," Fogarty says of the Tate Gallery.[88] And how did they know that "the gallery would be understaffed" that day? From "information" they received: "I cannot reveal the source."[89] When Fogarty and his companion in theft, Paul Hogan, took the painting from the wall, "the chain fell off with an awful bang. . . . I stuffed the chain in my pocket."[90] They had a reporter ready outside to record the event and publicize it in England and Ireland. After the theft the students issued a statement that read in part, "the authority for this action is the codicil to the will of Sir Hugh Lane, dated February 1915, bequeathing the 39 treasures to the City of Dublin. This action has been taken in the Irish national interest."[91] Both the Irish government and Dublin Corporation issued statements saying they would refuse the painting and return it to the Tate if it ever got to Ireland. Speaking in the 1976 interview, Fogarty said that "the present Irish government is no better than the government which wouldn't then stand up for the Lane pictures when we *got* one of them, it was *ours*, and they wouldn't even have it! They didn't want it; it was a hot potato."[92] The news was so hot that headlines about it took over the space most London papers had reserved for photographs of Grace Kelly arriving in Monaco to marry Prince Rainier.

How like Desdemona's handkerchief in this respect: they stole it; they didn't know what to do with it; Ireland wouldn't take it; they gave it back. As Beerbohm and Gifford had intuited visually, it was impossible to give these paintings away. It was even impossible to stash one of them. According to Fogarty, "We really didn't have good planning for what to do afterwards. We fully expected to be caught in the act. . . . We were more surprised than any to get away with it."[93] They got it to Mary O'Riordain's London flat, and as Paul Hogan tells the story, they left the painting out in the hall and went in to broach the matter carefully with Mary. "Have you ever heard of someone

1.9. The theft of a Lane painting. On April 12, 1956, Grace Kelly arrived in Monaco on the USS *Constitution* to marry Prince Rainier, who left the harbor in his yacht to greet her, but the lead headline in the next day's *Irish Times* went to another woman in another boat. On the same day, two Irish students stole one of the thirty-nine contested Lane paintings, Berthe Morisot's *Jour d'été*, on behalf of "the people of Ireland."

called Hugh Lane?" Paul asked her. "No," said Mary. They told her the story of the paintings kept from their rightful Irish owners, and she responded, "Well, that's awful! that's terrible!" "I'm glad you feel that way," said Paul, "because one of them is outside on the landing."[94] Even after Mary agreed to take it in, there were problems, as Bill told the story, because

> it was put under a bed, and then there was some kind of a party going on that night, some friends of theirs descended on the place, and everybody was drunk, and people were falling on the bed, and I was rather worried that the bed was going to collapse and smash the painting.[95]

How curious to think of those well-dressed women in their little row-boat on that calm *jour d'été*, their pensive faces gazing in different directions, hidden under the bed at a noisy drunken party. Like Morisot's *Sur le balcon*, the scene represents female interiority, the thoughtful gaze of the woman who is gazed at by the painting's viewer. But what did that matter to Fogarty, to Hogan, the two galleries, or the two governments? In the interview Fogarty refers to the paintings' provenance in abbreviated form: "some by Renoir, some by others, including Morisot, this girl." The painting was pure loot. It's the same problem as in 1913, in the Gifford cartoon: "Where now will I house him?" There's no place to put it, so they have to get rid of it. It was transported in brown paper to the Irish embassy in London, which returned the painting to the Tate.

Global Goods

> Exquisite critic, connoisseur of art!
> Whose generous uncompleted codicil
> Just failed for legal reasons to impart
> The spirit of thy patriotic will[.]
> Thy will that these French pictures should adorn
> The Dublin of thy dedicated life
> Was almost of its generous meaning shorn
> By Courts of Law and Parliamentary strife.
> But understanding, kindly common sense
> Has done what other forces failed to do,
> Has bridged the gulf where ritual found offence
> Made Dublin now thy pictures['] rendezvous.
> >   So the elite of Dublin here tonight
> >   Welcome thy generous gift with rare delight.[96]
> >   *(Hector Hughes)*

However difficult it was to give the thirty-nine paintings away, it was always easy to welcome them back to Ireland. They were welcomed over and over again: the history of the Hugh Lane Municipal Gallery of Modern Art is marked by *céad míle fáilte*. The paintings that Lane had selected for the brand new gallery in Clonmell House on January 20, 1908, were welcomed by Alderman Tom Kelly (who presided and praised Lane's energy and dedication), William Orpen's brother, the artist R. Caulfield Orpen, and the lord mayor, who officially declared the gallery open. Resolutions of thanks of various kinds were then moved by Rev. Dr. Mahaffy, Rev. T. Finlay, S.J., the Earl of Drogheda (who thanked the lord mayor and was seconded by Sir Thomas Drew and Stephen Gwynn), Sir Walter Armstrong (who thanked Kelly and was seconded by Sir Frederick Falkner), and then Kelly again, who thanked everyone for thanking him.[97] Twenty-five years later, on June 19, 1933, the Municipal Gallery of Modern Art, in its new and permanent quarters in Charlemont House, Parnell Square, was officially opened, and Tom Kelly—now identified as chairman of the Lane Bequest Committee—again presided, reminding those present that he had presided twenty-five years earlier. Another lord mayor (Alfred Byrne) declared the new gallery open, and, speaking in Irish, Eamon de Valera praised both Lane and the bequest committee. Taking part in the thanking ritual were Alderman Clark, Mary Kettle, T.C., Dermot O'Brien, the curator of the gallery John J. Reynolds, Sarah Cecilia Harrison, and John Keating. It was on this occasion that the bust of Lane was unveiled by R. Caulfield Orpen, who had also been present on the first opening of the gallery. The unveiling took place in the Sir Hugh Lane Room, the empty room that was ready to welcome the paintings.[98]

The movement of the thirty-nine paintings that began on July 31, 1913, when Lane so unceremoniously swept them up from Clonmell House and moved them to the Mansion House, began again in great ceremony on February 16, 1961, as twenty of them, at least, were officially received on loan from the trustees of the Tate. "END OF A CONTROVERSY," screamed the headlines, and "HOME AT LAST."[99] Was it really these national treasures, on which so much seemed now to depend, that Mr. Jones had said he wouldn't hang in his back kitchen, and Mr. Quaid had bid goodbye to with an angry "Let them go"? A gala occasion, worthy of crown jewels or some central, sacred national symbol, celebrated the arrival of the paintings. Back in Dublin at last were the arms of Mme. Gonzales, once so admired by George Moore. No longer shameless and shocking, they formed a focal point for an enormous national ritual. De Valera was again present—as were about seven hundred other people—when the Right Honourable the Lord Mayor of Dublin, Councilor Maurice E. Dockrell T.D., accepted the pictures "on behalf of the Citizens of Dublin" from the Taoiseach, Sean Lemass, who had received them from the British government. The lord mayor closed his remarks with the sonnet of welcome written by Hector Hughes, an MP sympathetic to the Irish request for the paintings. The concern that Irish worthiness of the great occasion be evident to the world was also reflected in a cartoon of the time that showed a harassed mother scolding her slovenly children with the words, "Come in owa that an' behave yerselves! Yous are nice people for the Lane Pictures to be returned to!"[100]

The Lane Gallery's archives reveal the exquisitely detailed protocol for the party that night: the front of the gallery was floodlit, and six members of the Fire Brigade, wearing newly designed uniforms, attended because the fire alarm had been switched off for the duration of the reception. Members of the gallery staff were asked to work overtime, and "all attendants," said a specially prepared memo, "should be specifically instructed *not* to partake of *any* refreshments during the course of the Reception." This was the new Ireland of the 1960s, taking its public role in international matters very seriously. The person delegated to announce the names, stated the memo, should have the "ability to read names in Irish or other languages and a strong cultivated voice."[101] On this state occasion, the guests included "members of Dublin Corporation in their robes, members of An Chomhairle Ealaíon, members of the government and of the Council of State, the Diplomatic Corps, former Ministers of State, the heads of government departments, the Board of Governors of the National Gallery of Ireland, members of the Cultural Relations Committee, members of the Royal Hibernian Academy, the Irish Exhibition of Living Art" as well as the Catholic and Protestant archbishops of Dublin, the chief rabbi, and those who had worked for years to negotiate the loan, Lord Moyne, the Earl of Longford, and Thomas Bodkin, who were all given honorary Doctor of Laws degrees by the National University of Ireland at the end of the week.[102]

Bill Fogarty arrived at the gallery that night but was refused admission to the reception.[103] His impatient militant tactics had not got the collection back to Ireland, though they had got one painting to the symbolic Irish space of the Irish embassy in London. The method that proved effective was less interesting and less theatrical, and it took ten years. The dispute had been officially brought to the attention of the British government after several years of private correspondence that began in 1949 when Lord Moyne wrote to Thomas Bodkin about the controversy, saying that he supported "of course the Dublin side, as any impartial person must who goes into the facts." But the time seemed never to be right for publicizing the issue: would

" Come in owa that an' behave yerselves ! Yous are nice people for the Lane Pictures to be returned to ! "

1.10. The return of the paintings. Charles E. Kelly of *Dublin Opinion* appeared to believe that the Lane paintings might have an elevating effect on Irish children. Many cartoons respond to the announcement of an agreement between the National Gallery (London) and the Municipal Gallery of Modern Art (Dublin) to share the paintings (1959) and to return half of the collection to Dublin (1961). Department of Early Printed Books and Special Collections, by permission of the Board of Trinity College Dublin and by permission of Frank Kelly. Cartoons from December 1959 (309) and January 1961 (359).

" I'll take you home an' you won't see the Lane Pictures at all!"

the "memory of Irish neutrality" damage their case? or Ireland's pre-
cipitate exit from the Commonwealth in 1948? or the "present ten-
sion over Partition"? In 1956 Lord Moyne and Bodkin (by now
"Bryan" and "Tom," after so long a correspondence) were organizing
high-power prandial politics at the Athenaeum, and soon after, with
the help of Lord Longford, Prime Minister Macmillan was approached
on the subject.[104] It took until November 1959 for the first in the series of agreements, ratified by the two governments, to be reached.

The "elite of Dublin," in the words of the sonnet, were celebrating
a complicated plan: the collection was to be divided in half, and for
twenty years the Municipal Gallery (Dublin) and the National
Gallery in London would exchange halves every five years. Thus each
city would have access to the entire collection, but not at one time.
Subsequent agreements have increased in mathematical complexity
and in acknowledgment of the Irish claim: in 1979 a fourteen-year
agreement lent thirty paintings to Dublin and left eight in London,
with Renoir's *Les Parapluies* spending seven years in each city. Then
in 1993, a twelve-year agreement put twenty-seven paintings in
Dublin for twelve years and four in London; the remaining eight are
divided into two groups of four, each group spending six years in one
city and then six years in the other.[105] As the current director of the
Hugh Lane Municipal Gallery of Modern Art, Barbara Dawson, put it
diplomatically, this agreement "took into account the desire of the
Irish public for increased access to the Lane bequest."[106]

Hugh Lane has been dead for ninety years, and William Martin
Murphy for almost as long (he died in 1919). Lady Gregory died in
1932, and Thomas Bodkin in 1961. Bill Fogarty died in 2001.[107] The
sonnet to Lane was written by an Englishman. Whatever anger fueled
the original controversy, in any of its various manifestations, has long
since died down. In fact it would be appropriate to say that the Lane
controversy no longer exists in its original form, although Irish articles about the *Lusitania* always speculate about what Lane paintings may have been languishing at the bottom of the sea off the coast
of Cork for most of the twentieth century. The issue lives on only in
the series of complicated arrangements for sharing the collection.

How then should the former "Lane controversy" now be seen? Although there is no consistent ideological significance to the thirty-
nine paintings, they have continuing power. Their cultural identity is
complex, and it ought not now to be seen in an Irish context but in an
international one. The nationalistic Stone-of-Scone model has been

replaced by another, the continuing redistribution of global goods. An empty room is being prepared in the new Acropolis Museum for the Parthenon (aka the "Elgin") marbles. The current heir to Jacob Goudstikker's collection of paintings, bought by the Dutch government from the Nazis and never returned to the family, has suggested that a special room be set aside for the Goudstikker paintings. In 1992 the controversy over the $45 million spent by the Spanish government on renovations to the Villa Hermosa in Madrid to hold the Thyssen art collection finally died down, as did the aesthetic dispute between the donor's wife and the architect over whether the floors should be marble or wood. The Holocaust Art Restitution Project of B'nai B'rith keeps extensive records on the works of art taken from Jewish people by the Nazis and now in the hands of museums, governments, and private owners, who bought them from the Nazis. The $40 million collection belonging to the Austrian Rothschilds, confiscated by the Nazis but finally returned to the family by the Austrian government in 1998, was sold at auction in 1999. Think of all the items continually being passed from hand to hand, from tribe to nation to government to tribe, booty confiscated by explorers, returned to "the people," reconfiscated by museums; Jewish money in Swiss banks; Native American bones in the Smithsonian Museum in Washington. Think of the whole planet from this point of view: skeletons, sculptures, altars, artifacts, scattered all over the face of the earth, perpetually claimed and reclaimed, bought and sold and returned by someone, sometime, for some reason or other. As high culture or national totemic objects, the thirty-nine Lane paintings are Ireland's tiny but valuable pieces of these continually circulating goods.

The Man Who Died for the Language

Rev. Dr. O'Hickey and the Irish Language
Controversy, 1908–9

Is minic a bhris béal duine a shrón.
It's often a person's mouth has broken his nose.

The granite statue of Dr. Michael O'Hickey in Carrick-on-Suir, County Tipperary, shows him with his arms folded across his chest, a gesture that might be read as defiance, obstinacy, or determination. When Cardinal Ó Fiaich unveiled the statue in July 1988, he put it in the most positive light: the statue revealed the man as "dolúbtha, dochorraithe" (unyielding, immovable) and—a wonderful word for O'Hickey—"soléite," readable. The man who refused to retract the strong language he had used against his ecclesiastical superiors had addressed them openly, honestly, directly. He was incapable of hiding his feelings. In the cardinal's kind words, O'Hickey's stubbornness and outspokenness were transmuted to integrity and idealism.[1]

Like the bust of Lane commissioned by the Dublin Corporation, the statue of O'Hickey came with an implicit message of apology: from the people of his native Carrick, who had done little to commemorate him in the seventy-two years since his death, and from the Irish Church, represented by the Archbishop of Armagh, Cardinal Ó Fiaich. " 'I AM HERE TO AMEND A WRONG,' SAYS CARDINAL" ran the headline in the *Nationalist* (Clonmel).[2] What could this roughhewn nationalist priest, whose passion for the Irish language drove him to defy the bishops and lose his teaching position at Maynooth, have in common with a titled Protestant dandy art connoisseur? Statuary and posthumous apologies indicate deeper connections between Lane and O'Hickey, whose controversies have attracted entirely different audiences. In the famous section on Ireland in *Autumn Journal*, Louis MacNeice might have been writing about the disillusion both men felt with their cultural projects:

> . . . one feels that here at least one can
>   Do local work which is not at the world's mercy
> And that on this tiny stage with luck a man
>   Might see the end of one particular action.
> It is self-deception of course.[3]

Precisely the kind of thwarted Irish idealists MacNeice was thinking of, Lane and O'Hickey flourished in the years of high cultural nationalism, the first decade of the new century. Each man gave himself with single-minded devotion to his own component part—painting, the Irish language—of the Irish renaissance. The beginning of 1908 saw the opening of the Dublin Municipal Gallery, established by Lane, and the end of the same year saw O'Hickey engaged in the "compulsory Irish" campaign, a drive to make fluency in the Irish language a requirement for entrance to the new National University, established by Parliament in August. On the "tiny stage" of Dublin, doing his own kind of "local work," Lane was unable to "see the end of one particular action," although his vision has been more or less accomplished by others since his death in 1915. And although on the tiny stage of the National University the Gaelic League won an Irish-language requirement, O'Hickey was dismissed from the chair of Irish at St. Patrick's College, Maynooth, for his outspoken engagement in that campaign.

The hatreds and behindbacks of the day attached themselves to O'Hickey as they had to Lane, and he himself became the center of a controversy, a spinoff from the larger controversy over compulsory Irish. Viewed in terms of their dramatis personae, the controversies over the thirty-nine Lane paintings and over O'Hickey's dismissal from Maynooth look very much alike: both involve uncompromising visionaries, insulted corporate bodies, intense public debate, partisan newspaper coverage, the sudden premature death of the man at the center of it all, martyr-making machinery (memoirs, poems, occasional pieces) and a legacy of idealism, a long period of dormancy, a statue, and an apology from the offended corporate body. Both controversies extended over most of the twentieth century, and neither is entirely stabilized: agreements over the division of the contested paintings are regularly revised, and in certain quarters opinion about O'Hickey is still passionate—on both sides. O'Hickey and Lane surely share the same space in the next world, accompanied by other high-minded visionaries, the kind of men whom Oscar Wilde was thinking of when he said of Parnell, "The greatest men fail, or seem to have failed."[4]

The Reverend Dr. O'Hickey (1861–1916) had been a parish priest in Scotland before returning to his home diocese of Waterford and Lismore in 1893 to become diocesan inspector of religious instruction. He had been involved in the controversy over the status of Irish in the intermediate school system (1899–1902) but had been absent from public debate for six years when he was invited to address the issue of compulsory Irish in 1908. A former vice president of the Gaelic League and now professor of Irish, he responded with an energetic passion directed at the supposed "enemies" of the language. In letters, pamphlets, and a talk to seminarians at Maynooth, O'Hickey reviled the clerical senators of the new university, whom he expected to vote against the Irish language requirement. Refusing to resign his position at St. Patrick's College, Maynooth, when requested to by the bishops, then appealing his dismissal to the Holy See for six long years, losing his case in Rome, and dying in November 1916, not long after his return to Ireland, Dr. O'Hickey embodied the spirit of rebellion of the times.[5] But it was a rebellion directed against the Church, not the British Empire. In June 1910, just after O'Hickey had left for Rome, the senate of the university, by a vote of 21 to 12, passed the recommendation "that the Irish language should be an essential subject for matriculation" beginning in 1913.[6] Much pressure had been put on the senators by the Irish County Councils: 18 threatened to withhold scholarship funds unless the requirement were passed.[7]

The commotion over O'Hickey himself was not to end so happily or so quickly. To the official Church he seemed disobedient; to those outside it he became heroic, a breaker of taboos. To a public of nationalists, Irish speakers, dissident clergy and religious, and those temperamentally impatient with institutions and authorities, the raw hostility of O'Hickey's speeches and writings was inspiriting. The very fact of his exile from Maynooth proved the extent of his dar-

2.1. Dr. Michael O'Hickey (no date). The serious expression shows the earnest and idealistic "priest of blameless life," as his colleague at St. Patrick's College Rev. Walter McDonald called him. Photo by permission of Siobhán O'Hickey; courtesy of Mícheál Briody.

ing: he took risks and failed. A nationalist defending the Irish language, a priest defying the Catholic Church, O'Hickey offered the vicarious experience of rhetorical license to admirers as ideologically incompatible as Patrick Pearse and Sean O'Casey. Separated from the controversy over matriculation in the National University, the controversy over O'Hickey's dismissal became a meeting ground for different ideologies. His work for the language had long inspired loyalty and friendship in Eoin MacNeill, who organized a testimonial meeting on his behalf at Dublin's Gresham Hotel. His troubles with the hierarchy of the Irish Church and the administrators at Maynooth drew the support of his good friend and colleague Walter McDonald, who painstakingly rehearsed O'Hickey's legal case in four chapters of *Reminiscences of a Maynooth Professor.*[8] W. P. Ryan's popular newspaper *Irish Nation and Peasant* celebrated O'Hickey as the hero of a more activist and nationalist church. In the pages of *An Claidheamh Soluis,* Pearse praised the intensity and sacrificial nature of O'Hickey's nationalism. In *Drums under the Window* O'Casey, a Protestant hostile to the absolutes of nationalism and religion, idealized O'Hickey as a high-minded independent soul who fought corrupt authorities.[9] And in the 1980s, the poet Michael Coady's interest in O'Hickey as part of the repressed history of Carrick-on-Suir led ultimately to his rehabilitation.

Not, then, for any single ideology, not simply for his linguistic nationalism, or his defiance of the bishops, or his insistence on faculty tenure, but for his unsilenceability, O'Hickey became a heroic figure to many of his contemporaries and to those who heard his legend later. Culture wars were fought through him, and his pamphlet *An Irish University, or Else* belongs to the category Stephen Greenblatt defined as literary works that "situate themselves on the very edges of what can be said at a particular time and place, that batter against the boundaries of their own culture."[10] A landmark in the cultural politics of the Irish language, the book consists of a collection of letters written on behalf of compulsory Irish and a talk O'Hickey gave on the subject to the students of the Maynooth literary society.[11] The copy of that pamphlet in Maynooth's Russell Library has been read carefully and shows almost literally what the Church's boundaries were. Its margins are dotted with the sign and initials of Michael Cardinal Logue, Primate of All Ireland: + M.C.L. on the bottom right of page 9, + M.C.L. on the top left of page 10, two + M.C.L.s on the left of page 31, two on the right of page 32, and others throughout the

Irish-Ireland invaluable and never-to-be-forgotten service. I do not think he will now blench, nor disappoint the hopes which I, and I think all Irish-Irelanders, repose in him. As for the other Clerical Senators, I shall say nothing farther than to recommend them to your earnest prayers.

The Senators, who are members of the Coiste Gnotha of the Gaelic League, will, I suppose, fight this battle to a finish,—at all events, let us hope so. Some of them have wobbled a good deal, but I trust they have now been got to toe the line. If, last Summer, when this question was prominently before the public, they had not been so credulous and confiding, if they had not been quite so intent upon crushing a minority, and had taken the measures which they were urged to take to educate and organise public opinion, there would be no such crisis as we are now face to face with. It required almost an earthquake to awaken them to the realities of the situation; the earthquake arrived in due course. Dr. Delany made his famous speech.

Let us hope for the best. But let us be prepared for the worst. It has been said that our first duty is to make the University a success. No. Our first duty is to make it Irish; and, if we cannot make it Irish, to abandon it to its fate. The treachery of those who show themselves false to Ireland at this juncture must never be forgotten whilst a solitary fragment of the historic Irish Nation remains. Sir Jonah Barrington has preserved for us a Black-list of those who voted for the infamous Union passed

—" by perjury and fraud,
By slaves who sold their land for gold,
As Judas sold his God."

A similar Black-list of the recreant Nationalist Senators must be preserved that, in after times, all men may know who were the false and vile, in a supreme crisis of Ireland's fortunes, and who the leal and true.

2.2. The "objectionable" lecture. When Dr. O'Hickey was summoned by Cardinal Logue to the board room at St. Patrick's College, the bishop of Galway, according to O'Hickey's account, "read the passages which had been marked in the pamphlet, first the passages from the lecture, and afterwards the passages from the letters. When each passage had been read, his Eminence . . . briefly commented upon it." The pamphlet from which he read, with the cardinal's initials marking the "objectionable" passages, remains in Russell Library. Permission of Russell Library, St. Patrick's College, Maynooth.

thirty-two pages of the book. The mark of Cardinal Logue appears on every page, objecting here to "a passage of brutal insult," there to a "disrespectful and insulting tone," and everywhere to language "calculated to stir up a spirit of rebellion against Ecclesiastical authority in students being educated by the Bishops." The cardinal's little marks of anger represent the lines drawn to contain the disrespect and insults of a rebel priest. This is the copy read by the Trustees of Maynooth College when they decided to ask Dr. O'Hickey to resign from the chair of Irish on June 22, 1909.[12]

The Church, the University, and the Gaelic League

The same spirit of condemnation animates the margins of Russell Library's copies of *An Claidheamh Soluis.* Researchers interested in the 1908–9 controversy over compulsory Irish need not scan every column of every page looking for material, pausing over rich irrelevancies like the electric bill sent—in the Irish language—to the provost of Trinity, who refused to pay it unless it was in English.[13] The bishops have done the work for us: every article connected to the debate is surrounded by large X's. When the issue of clerical involvement in the debate is discussed, the number of X's is greater, and episcopal anxiety is visible; seven X's call attention to the letter titled "The Bishops and the Gaelic League."[14]

The culture wars generated by Dr. O'Hickey took place in the context of other culture wars of long standing. Ever since the establishment of the three Queen's Colleges at Cork, Galway, and Belfast in 1845, the bishops had wanted a university in Ireland administered by Catholics for Catholic students. The Catholic University, with John Henry Newman as its famous first rector, had been founded in 1851, and its major constituent college, University College in Dublin, had been run by the Jesuits under Dr. William Delany since 1883. But the board of examiners that granted degrees to its students formed part of the Royal University (as the Queen's University had become in 1880). The Catholic University did not have the funds, the powers, or the status of the Protestant University of Dublin (known as Trinity College). The Irish Universities Act of 1908 transformed the system of universities in Ireland: the Royal University was dissolved. Queen's College in Belfast became Queen's University; the Queen's Colleges of Cork and Galway, together with University College of the old

Catholic University, became the new National University of Ireland. St. Patrick's College, Maynooth, the Catholic seminary where Dr. O'Hickey was professor of Irish, had been a constituent college of the Catholic University; in 1910 it became a "recognized college" of the National University. It was the senators of the National University, of whom five were clerics, whose vote would determine the requirements for matriculation. With the collective memory of a half century's struggle to secure their own university, the bishops naturally wanted to ensure those votes made the new university Catholic in its curriculum and its atmosphere.

At this time, the Catholic Church in Ireland was not known for its openness to new thought. In 1904 the Maynooth-trained radical priest and novelist Gerald O'Donovan, a Gaelic League colleague of O'Hickey's, had left the Church, finding it incompatible with the spirit of cultural nationalism he had encouraged.[15] (It was for the new cathedral in his parish in Loughrea, County Galway, that Lily Yeats and the women of Dun Emer workshop had embroidered banners.) In the previous half century the Church had come to resemble the British Empire in its rigid hierarchical administrative structure. In the years following the Great Famine, Cardinal Paul Cullen had "whipped the Church into line with Roman discipline."[16] He raised funds, built churches, developed the Catholic secondary school system in Ireland, and emphasized the subordination of priests to their bishops. Cullen made the Church into the kind of institution that someone like O'Hickey could rebel against. When O'Hickey called the culturally conservative Church hierarchy "West Britons," he was not far from the anticlericalism of the Christmas dinner scene in *A Portrait of the Artist as a Young Man.* Mr. Dedalus refers to Archbishop Walsh as "Billy with the Lip" and Cardinal Logue as "the tub of guts up in Armagh," and Mr. Casey ("with slow scorn") adds "Princes of the Church," no doubt thinking of the prosperous churchmen comfortably entrenched in their new buildings and offices, enjoying the extent of their power.[17]

The Gaelic League, founded in 1893, inspired all Cardinal Logue's anxious X's in the margins because its energy, youth, and general impatience with the tired old ways were a disruptive force. Perhaps because the bishops were, as W. P. Ryan put it, more remote from social and intellectual realities than the priests, more inimical to nearly all things distinctively Irish; perhaps because the Gaelic League, which organized the campaign for compulsory Irish, represented "a critical

and challenging outlook," a progressive, quasi-revolutionary force
threatening to the autocratic habits of the episcopacy; perhaps because of the highly charged nationalist rhetoric of the young priests
who addressed Gaelic League meetings all over the country; perhaps
because Dr. O'Hickey had in fact spoken in "language . . . wanting in
reserve and moderation" about Church authorities, the bishops felt
affronted by the League.[18] "Things have come to a pretty pass," Cardinal Logue wrote in exasperation to Archbishop Walsh of Dublin,
"when the Bishops of Ireland cannot regulate the discipline of their
ecclesiastical college without being subjected to abuse from these
people. I think the heads of the Gaelic League should be called to an
account and given clearly to understand that they cannot be permit-
ted to ride roughshod over ecclesiastical authority in this country."[19] He
also suggested that if the bishops were to "prohibit" *An Claidheamh
Soluis* "in their several dioceses it might bring those Gaelic League
people to their senses."

Although Dr. O'Hickey linked his passion for compulsory Irish
with the Gaelic League campaign, he was not himself present at the
League meetings where his words, read aloud by other people, were
greeted with thunderous applause. He reached even more people on
the days following the meetings, when the letters that had been read
aloud were printed in newspapers. As printed copy, he was ubiquitous, speaking through paper all over the country. Even when his
name was not before the public, his words were: he had been writing
anonymous pieces on the issue even before the League's campaign, in
the spring of 1908, and he published more anonymous essays the following spring. O'Hickey was not unlike Sean O'Casey's elusive and
disturbing Father Ned, who is never seen on stage (in *The Drums of
Father Ned*) and has always just left the place where his effect is being
felt. Everywhere he stirs up a quasi-revolutionary excitement he can
never quite be held accountable for.[20] The letters, pamphlets, and
statements O'Hickey published in 1908 and 1909 could not all, during his lifetime, be attributed to him, but posthumous identification
of them shows that he was never silent.[21]

O'Hickey's temperamental affinity for diatribes on paper was
strengthened by his faith in the power of an educated, reading Irish
public, people who would form their own opinions based in part on
what they read in newspapers. The literate public had grown since
Young Ireland days, and, as O'Hickey knew from his work in
parochial education and from his Gaelic League experience, its mem-

bers read newspapers, books, and pamphlets, especially cheap ones. (O'Hickey's pamphlets cost only a penny each.) Of course the large, long, noisy meetings held on behalf of compulsory Irish also helped create and change opinions. But the great number of newspapers—the *Irish Nation and Peasant, Sinn Féin,* the *Irish Citizen, An Claidheamh Soluis,* the *Freeman's Journal,* to name only a few national ones, and countless local papers—answered a need and created a market.

An Irish University, or Else—

In one of his earlier polemical works on the language, *The Irish Language Movement: Its Genesis, Growth, and Progress* (1902), O'Hickey had explicitly linked the note of aggression with the sudden success of the Gaelic League. Addressing an audience of Irish people in Liverpool, O'Hickey talked about the slow growth of the League in its early days: "The old stock arguments, that Irish was an ancient language, that Irish literature was one of the oldest vernacular literatures in Europe, that Irish from a philological point of view was not inferior in value to Sanskrit . . . did not impress the public mind . . . for some reason or other they left the popular imagination untouched."[22] What was it, then, that suddenly created a buzz about the Gaelic League and made it exciting and popular? O'Hickey mentions his own lecture "The True National Idea," in which he "endeavoured . . . to show how closely the Irish language was bound up with the traditional nationality of our people, and how vital was the one to the very existence of the other." Once he had linked the language with nationalist politics, things picked up, because "angry protests came from all sides." Anger, as O'Hickey explains it, was the indicator of success, and he focuses with pride on an occasion when Dr. Mahaffy, the notorious provost of Trinity College, forsook the lecture he was supposed to give in order, O'Hickey says, "to take me to pieces."[23] He had engaged the enemy: the success of the League was assured.

Read in the light of his rhetoric in the compulsory Irish campaign, this early talk reveals already the way public discourse about the Irish language was, for O'Hickey, inextricable from tropes, metaphors, and the fundamental idea of warfare. To be in combat was to be successful. The original members of the League "clearly grasped that the bat-

tle should be fought around Irish as a spoken tongue." And "Even for
those who have to bear the brunt and fury of the fight," O'Hickey announced, "it is a joy to live in these days to see the Gael resurgent."[24]
But the joy he felt may have been somewhat dampened by 1908, because the great battle for the language had been extended to St.
Patrick's College, Maynooth. The college's administration was not
fighting on the same side as the League: a ruling by the Trustees in
1904 allowed bishops to excuse certain students from entrance examinations in Irish. Over the next two years someone at Maynooth
leaked information to the nationalist press about the increasing numbers of students excused from Irish. In 1906 President Mannix accused O'Hickey of talking to the press, but he denied doing so, nevertheless asserting his right so to talk if he wished.[25] After that
contretemps Mannix replaced Mahaffy in O'Hickey's mind as the
chief antagonist of the national language: he was, O'Hickey wrote
Maurice Moore, "rabidly, fanatically opposed to essential Irish."[26]

Although most of the rhetoric in the compulsory Irish campaign
was charged with the territorial drive to mark the university as Irish,
some people did actually use those "old stock arguments" dismissed
as unimpressive by O'Hickey. Opening the new session of the Gaelic
Society at Trinity College on November 17, 1908, Frederick Ryan insisted on the importance of the language to Trinity during the Renaissance, pointing out that students were penalized after 1627 for
being absent from their Irish prayers and that a book of the New Testament was read in Irish over dinner every night.[27] Following Ryan
that night, Eoin MacNeill reminded his audience that "Ireland was
the one country in Europe containing a wide and copious early tradition and literature which stood outside of the pale of the Roman Empire, the one country in Europe whose institutions were not deeply
affected and changed by Roman civilisation."[28]

Only ten days after the meeting of the Trinity College Gaelic Society came the meeting that would lead Dr. O'Hickey out of Russell Library at St. Patrick's College, where he had been binding the O'Curry
collection of Irish manuscripts and nursing his anger at Mannix, and
into the fray. The fateful first meeting of the Gaelic Society of the
Catholic University College at St. Stephen's Green on November 27,
1909, set the terms for all the subsequent debate in the compulsory
Irish controversy. The presence of the Very Reverend William Delany,
S.J., president of the college, turned a pep rally into a debate. His participation gave the West Briton "enemy" a name and a face, un-

leashed the angers of the language supporters, and (so that one clerical academic could answer another) inspired the invitation to Dr.
O'Hickey for the great meeting at the Rotunda scheduled for December 7. As Dr. Delany, according to his biographer Father Thomas Morrissey, accompanied the speakers to the Aula Maxima and was about
to leave, Agnes O'Farrelly "pressed him to stay and encourage them
by his presence even though he took no part in the proceedings." He
stayed. After a few speakers had presented the argument for compulsory Irish, Dr. Delany spoke, according to his biographer, "in an unscripted response" and "strung his arguments together as he
spoke."[29] When he said that he wanted the Irish language, history,
and archaeology to "hold an honoured place in the curriculum," he
was greeted with applause. There is no record of audience reaction to
Dr. Delany's arguments against compulsory Irish, such as that an
Irish requirement might send non-Irish-speaking Catholics to Trinity
College; that the Irish to be taught must be "not the Irish of the fair
or market, but the Irish of scholars"; and that much scholarly work
on dictionaries, grammar, and manuscripts must be done "before
Irish could be used as an instrument of culture."[30] But here, at least,
the thinking of the opposition was articulated.

In an equally "unscripted" response, Patrick Pearse, headmaster of
the newly opened St. Enda's, stood up and said that although he "acknowledged the good work which Father Delany had done for Irish,"
nevertheless his "speech showed that there was a fight before them."
The chairman of the event, Eoin MacNeill, stood to reply to Dr. Delany, and Delany interjected comments at the end of every point.
When MacNeill said, "Father Delany refused his assent to the part of
the paper which said Irish should be an essential subject," Delany interjected, "An essential subject, and that now. Everything else I am
heartily with." When MacNeill asserted he believed that "a good and
cultivated knowledge of the Irish language and Irish history" was essential for educated Irishmen, Delany added, "So do I." And when
MacNeill said that no "form of education for Ireland" was national
that did not include the Irish language, Delany put in, "Certainly."
But MacNeill closed his speech *as Gaeilge,* thereby excluding from
the community of listeners the president of the college in whose
great hall he spoke.[31]

Dr. Delany, wrote Pearse in *An Claidheamh Soluis,* "is an old man
and we have no hopes of converting him to our ideas. He was old
when the Gaelic League was born."[32] The struggle to control the new

university was in part a generational struggle between those senior ecclesiastics who wanted a "Catholic" university and the more secular forces of the Gaelic League, a younger, louder, well-educated, and impatient generation that wanted an "Irish University, or Else," and that filled meeting halls around the country in the following months, cheering on essential Irish, listening sometimes until almost midnight. To some of those supporters, Dr. Delany represented all the tyrannical forces in the entire history of Ireland, as the hate mail he received made explicit:

> Reverend Father, is it not delightful how the movement is shaping in the new university? There is one invariable law of history: whenever nationalism is opposed by clericalism (in the absence of external protection) clericalism goes to the wall. Of course, Irish studies will be absolutely deadly to your ascendancy. The history of Irish land and language is a constant record of clerical hate of Ireland. Priests cursed Tara and destroyed the national unity. Priests fastened the English yoke on the Irish neck, and gave the clanlands to the Norman adventurers. Priests sold the parliament. Priests killed the language and preached in English—such preaching!—to Gaelic congregations. Priests killed Parnell. Yes, you do well to fight against Irish studies. But the jewel of the business now is that *now* you must fight in the *open*. No getting behind the Castle now. . . . It is you alone who have to operate the whole show in your own pious university, now that you have it.[33]

This anticlerical harangue is worth considering because it taps the same sources as Dr. O'Hickey's writings. Despite its simplistic historiography and crude expressions of anger, this letter shows the passions that were provoked in the essential Irish campaign. No wonder the young priests who supported the movement were "muzzled," as W. P. Ryan put it, when they spoke in such company.[34]

Dr. O'Hickey's extravagant, bellicose letters, read aloud at meetings throughout the country, expressed in more formal prose, more precise historical references, and less naked hostility some of these same feelings. He became a hero of the compulsory Irish campaign not because he offered it new ideas but because he expressed what many people already thought. The discourse of militant nationalism was in his every word, and his voice—or at least his rhetoric—was ubiquitous. His rousing words (read aloud by Douglas Hyde) were

heard at the meeting that kicked off the whole campaign, the Gaelic
League meeting at the Rotunda on December 7, 1908, where Hyde,
MacNeill, Arthur Griffith, and others addressed a crowded meeting
that lasted four hours.[35] Later in December his voice was heard in
Limerick, in a letter read aloud by Fr. Wall; in letters read in Cork,
Castlebar, Athlone, and Waterford; and, most dangerously, in
Maynooth, where he spoke in person to the literary society and im-
plicitly attacked the president of St. Patrick's College, one of those
clerical senators on whose vote so much depended.

"Even in the Clerical Senators as a body," O'Hickey said to the students at Maynooth, "I can repose little or no trust; although I cannot
possibly imagine how any body of responsible Irish ecclesiastics
could embark upon a more foolish or reckless course than to take
sides in this instance with the enemies of Ireland." His talk ended
with a threat:

> The treachery of those who show themselves false to Ireland at this
> juncture must never be forgotten whilst a solitary fragment of the his-
> toric Irish Nation remains. Sir Jonah Barrington has preserved for us a
> Black-list of those who voted for the infamous Union passed
>
> > ". . . by perjury and fraud,
> > By slaves who sold their land for gold,
> > As Judas sold his God."
>
> A similar Black-list of the recreant Nationalist Senators must be pre-
> served that, in after times, all men may know who were the false and
> vile, in a supreme crisis of Ireland's fortunes, and who the leal and
> true.[36]

The lines O'Hickey quoted come from the first stanza of John O'Hagan's poem "The Union," which continued:

> By all the savage acts that yet
>   Have followed England's track:
> The pitchcap and the bayonet,
>   The gibbet and the rack.
> And thus was passed the Union,
>   By Pitt and Castlereagh.
> Could Satan send for such an end
>   More worthy tools than they?[37]

For O'Hickey, the patriotic binarisms of poems such as this one formed a natural discourse for the defense of Irish culture. But to quote them in reference to Monsignor Mannix to the students of Mannix's own college constituted a direct challenge to the authority of his employer. The language he had used of the Protestant Mahaffy in 1902 had been mild compared to this talk of people being "false and vile."

But aggression was his muse. Dr. Delany, according to O'Hickey's opening sally in the campaign, spoke for "the Catholic West Briton faction," and, he concluded, "it is war between Ireland and West Britain. If we are defeated in the first battle, the fight must still go on."[38] The note of exhilaration sounds through all Dr. O'Hickey's writings in the controversy as his imagination invokes hostile confrontations of the past. As the clerical senators are attacked in the guise of the Saxon tyrant, the prose becomes charged with excitement. His letter to Patrick Bradley, read aloud at the great meeting at the Rotunda, ended with an invocation of the Manchester Martyrs: "God defend the right, and God Save Ireland!" His letter to Father Wall in Limerick compared those who opposed essential Irish to the Soupers, "who stooped to 'Sell their souls / For penny rowls, / For soup and hairy bacon.'" Approaching the blasphemous, he added, "Far more squalid . . . would be the apostasy which is at present being urged upon Irishmen."[39] To Father Forde in Athlone, O'Hickey invoked the story of the defense of Athlone against Godert de Ginkel, when the men at the bridge fell to the Williamite forces: "In other and more strenuous days there was little welcome in Athlone for Ginkel and his myrmidons, little enthusiasm for the cause they represented. That to-day there is quite as little appreciation of the West Britons to be found there, not a whit more enthusiasm for their opportunist, reactionary, obscurantist proposals, seems equally evident. The spirit of the men who held Athlone Bridge 'in the brave days of old' is manifestly not extinct."[40]

Writing Father Forde again after the bishops issued their statement of January 20 suggesting that essential Irish, "instead of being a help, would be a hindrance to the language movement," Dr. O'Hickey wrote, "but with or without the help of their Lordships, 'on the cause must go.'"[41] As Fr. Forde no doubt recognized, his correspondent was quoting T. D. and A. M. Sullivan's song about the Manchester Martyrs:

> Never till the latest day
> Shall the memory pass away

Of the gallant lives thus given for our land;
    But on the cause must go,
    Amidst joy, or weal, or woe,
Till we've made our isle a nation free and grand.
    "God Save Ireland!" say we proudly;
    "God Save Ireland!" say we all.[42]

The campaign for the Irish language requirement, in Dr. O'Hickey's vision of it, was indistinguishable from the cause of Irish nationalism, about which there not two acceptable opinions. Writing to Father Wall of Limerick, Dr. O'Hickey closed his letter comparing the supporters of essential Irish to the Jacobites in the siege of Limerick: "The men and women who defended the walls, and perished gloriously in the breaches, of your ancient and historic city in bygone days, fought not for a cause nobler nor yet more sacred." When his own native Waterford County Council passed a resolution supporting the cause, Dr. O'Hickey wrote the editor of the *Waterford News*, praising the council by invoking the "men who smashed the power of the Beresfords," the powerful Waterford Protestant family famously defeated in the 1826 election.[43] In O'Hickey's excited imagination, every city in Ireland, at this "supreme crisis" of the nation, was engaging in the most important battle of its history.

It was these letters that were collected in *An Irish University, or Else*. Its central trope was the direct, hostile confrontation with the enemy, and the clerical senators were that enemy. Even the "or else" of the pamphlet's title conveys the defiantly bellicose tone of its prose. No wonder Cardinal Logue found so much to annotate. With the color in his style, the Young Ireland poetry, the vivid allusions to the high drama of Irish history, the *amplificatio*, the flourishes, Dr. O'Hickey had reached the nationalist public over and over again. The letters were read at huge meetings, they were printed in local papers, and they appeared in pamphlet form in the late winter of 1909. He was the man of the hour, and now he, too, found a place in a ballad, "an tSean Bhean Bhocht agus na hEasbuig" (the "Poor Old Woman," i.e., Ireland, and the bishops, to the tune of "Oh the French Are on the Sea"):

See O'Hickey in Maynooth,
Our brave advocate of truth;
Fighting for the Poor Man's Youth,
    Says the Sean Bhean Bhocht.[44]

The "brave advocate of truth" had spoken words that other, less foolhardy priests privately admired. "You have unfortunately for yourself been guilty of the one offence for which there is no forgiveness," one of O'Hickey's clerical friends said to him after he was asked to resign. "You have . . . criticized some of the Bishops, and thereby you have ruffled the feelings and outraged the dignity of the entire body. That is not to be tolerated. What a pity they are unable to charge you with some really serious offence."[45] How else could a compulsory-Irish campaigner have sounded? When O'Hickey was called before the officials at Maynooth in June 1909, Cardinal Logue pointed out that Douglas Hyde had spoken on behalf of Irish, but in language "worthy of a gentleman."[46] O'Hickey doesn't say what speech Logue was alluding to, but in his words at the great Rotunda meeting, Hyde had certainly not attacked the Catholic clergy when he spoke. "National Ireland was now on its trial before the world," Hyde was quoted in the papers as having said, and

> They must establish a University that would strike the imagination from the first, which from the first would rouse a pride of race in the people that attended it, and which would command the attention of all classes in Ireland . . . the Gaelic League and the new University must make up their minds to voice the older civilisation of Ireland. . . . Some saw this very plainly; others saw it dimly; others again . . . were jealous of the old Irish race. They would have the confederation of Kilkenny over again, and if they had, then he stood by Owen Roe (loud applause).[47]

The cautious Hyde could sound rousing without offending anyone, calling for solidarity rather than antagonism. But an offensive and antagonistic style was central to O'Hickey's mission, a mission that demanded the precise words that he used. As he affirmed in his apologia, the defense intended to explain his position to the world after his death,

> I regret nothing that I have written in my pamphlet; I withdraw nothing; I apologize for nothing. It is all true. . . . What I have written, needed to be written to save the nation from a huge and grievous blunder. Every line and paragraph of it I felt it to be my duty to write. In similar circumstances of national peril, I would write every word of it again; there is not a word or phrase which I would change.[48]

Violent Language, Golden Pen

In the summer of 1909, after O'Hickey had refused to resign his chair but before the trustees dismissed him, he sent a series of letters to Liam Bulfin, the nationalist writer whose daughter would later marry Maud Gonne's son. Bulfin had begun a correspondence that O'Hickey evidently found comforting and sympathetic, because he responded with detailed accounts of the actions taken against him by the Trustees of Maynooth. One revealing letter shows how O'Hickey thought about what was happening to him during his own supreme crisis. "Thanks for your letter," O'Hickey began.

> If I were in any wise in need of sympathy, messages like yours would be a great comfort and stay at present; but I do not at all feel crushed nor depressed. I have endeavoured to do my duty, and to stand for the rights of my colleagues in Maynooth, of my brethren in the priesthood, and of the Irish Catholic laity. From the outset, my resolution was taken that, be the consequences what they might, I would retract nothing, admit nothing, apologise for nothing. I could, at any time, have got off with a lecture (even after the full meeting of the Trustees) by expressing a regret which I did not feel, and which I could not express honestly or without doing violence to my conscience.

"Their Lordships" the bishops and archbishops, he continued,

> have not got much glory out of this affair. In every way in which a priest may legally and becomingly do so, I shall fight this thing to the end—not for my personal interests, but for many other interests. As far as I am concerned, I do not mind leaving Maynooth. I owe it nothing. I think it owes me a good deal; for I have given to it for 13 years every ounce of energy I possessed. No doubt my work was primarily for the language and the nation, but Maynooth reaped the glory. Should I have to go (as, of course, I shall), I shall be just as happy on the mission, if not more so; and as for money, well I have never known a priest to die of hunger yet; and one who is prepared to work for the people can calmly face the future anywhere. If their Lordships are not at present more ill at ease than I am, they are to be envied. When they tackled the grandson of a United Irishman, who was not unacquainted with the interior of a British dungeon, and the son of a

Young Irelander and a Fenian—well, they were, as the Yankees say,
"up against a very serious proposition," were they not?[49]

The rousing tones and bracing metaphors of O'Hickey's public pronouncements sound through this letter to one person. The language
of aggression gradually evolves, in the course of the letter, into a nationalist discourse, as O'Hickey comes to identify his own cause with
the cause of the Irish language. The discourse blends the cause of
O'Hickey into the cause of Ireland and therefore gives O'Hickey the
high moral ground against the Trustees. At the beginning he distin-
guishes three groups for whose rights he is fighting: "my colleagues
in Maynooth," "my brethren in the priesthood," and "the Irish Catholic laity." Soon he defends the position he spoke up for in terms of
his duty "as an Irishman." Then he ascribes his powers of resistance
to his political inheritance: he is "the grandson of a United Irishman . . . and the son of a Young Irelander and a Fenian."[50]

To modern ears the rhetoric is inflated, the high moral ground too
emphatically claimed. But O'Hickey's contemporaries saw his controversy as he did, and their comments register a passionate sympathy with his resistance to episcopal power. "Here was a priest of
blameless life," wrote his colleague Walter McDonald, prefect of the
elite postgraduate Dunboyne Establishment at Maynooth. O'Hickey
was "successful as a professor, transparently honest, dismissed for
acts which even his greatest enemies admitted were performed by
him . . . from a keen sense of patriotic and religious duty. If he could
be dismissed for such a cause, which of us was safe? . . . The position
of the whole staff was at stake."[51] The Trustees did not have the right
to dismiss a chaired professor without indicating in writing precisely
how he had violated the statutes under which he was hired.[52] In fact
they were unable to find those statutes when O'Hickey wrote from
Rome requesting them. The laity, too, as O'Hickey anticipated, identified with his struggle; he would have appreciated the private correspondence of the Moynihan brothers. "What do you think of the
bishops' treatment of Dr. O'Hickey?" Michael Moynihan wrote his
brother John after the call for O'Hickey's resignation. "I hope time
will prove that they have overreached themselves. I wonder how will
Dr O'Hickey take it—in the approved saintly fashion, that is, with
humility, or in a manly way, with indignation."[53] During the period
of his controversy, December 1908 through August 1909, O'Hickey
provided, *pro bono publico*, the vicarious experience of rebellion

against the bishops. To those who followed the trajectory of his public life, he was indeed heroic.

In January 1909, at the first expression of episcopal anger, Dr. O'Hickey had taken on himself the qualities of the heroes his imagery celebrated. His rhetoric had created, in his own life, the polarized situation its allusions invoked: subtly, the issue shifted from the value and significance of the Irish language to the permissibility of speech itself. After O'Hickey's own bishop, Richard Sheehan of Waterford, wrote him on behalf of the Episcopal Standing Committee that the bishops "take exception to the language" in his letters as "wanting in reserve and moderation," O'Hickey responded, "Of course, I take no further part in the Irish controversy" and announced "I at once and cheerfully acquiesce in the wishes of their Lordships." But he didn't exactly acquiesce, and he wasn't cheerful. Writing in response to Bishop Sheehan, he defended his right to speak even as he purported to obey:

> Restraint and moderation of language are relative things. Language which in one case and set of circumstances might be quite unjustifiable, in different circumstances might well be not only warranted, but actually called for. That the language I have used was in no way too strong for the occasion that called it forth, I am convinced. . . . By the part I have taken in this controversy, it is my profound conviction that I have done the College and the Catholic Faith as well as the cause of Irish nationality a service.[54]

As the last sentence of this passage makes clear, O'Hickey was beginning to see that rhetorical license had become a cause worth fighting for. His unrestrained language served the college by insisting on the free speech of faculty members, and the Catholic faith by showing the limits of episcopal power.

At the same meeting their lordships had issued a statement on compulsory Irish. "Whether it be good for the Irish language movement, and good for the New University," they noted, "to make Irish compulsory is a question for fair argument." But, the statement added, "It is quite possible that in existing circumstances compulsion instead of being a help would be a hindrance to the language movement. It certainly would drive away from the University not a few students who if once brought under the influence of the Gaelic School of a Constituent College would grow up good Irishmen."[55] In

spite of their anticompulsory view, the bishops nevertheless looked
forward to "the day when the Irish Language will again be spoken
throughout the country and will in consequence become largely the
medium of instruction in the Constituent Colleges." In those colleges now, however, their lordships hoped to see "bright centres of
Gaelic study." As Mícheál Briody put it, the bishops "were not opposed to Irish: they were opposed to being opposed on the question of
compulsory Irish, or indeed on any major issue."[56]

Given their lordships' preference for submission in all areas of doctrine and policy, it was not entirely clear to language activists what,
under the circumstances, "fair argument" meant. Out in Galway,
George Moore's brother Colonel Maurice Moore, at a meeting of the
Coláiste Chonnacht, decided to propose a resolution on behalf of
compulsory Irish, but Archbishop Healy refused to allow it. When
Moore reminded him that "the bishops say that it is a matter for fair
discussion," His Grace said "It was a matter for fair discussion before
they spoke, but not since."[57]

St. Patrick's College Maynooth could not be muzzled. Believing, no
doubt, that compulsory Irish was still a "question for fair argument,"
the Maynooth students who had heard Dr. O'Hickey quoting John
O'Hagan's "The Union" sent a telegram to a meeting of students in
favor of essential Irish at the Mansion House on February 8. "Columban League Maynooth are in complete sympathy with fellow-
students' demands for compulsory Irish in the National University,"
they wrote. Like O'Casey's Father Ned, O'Hickey was invisibly present where youthful excitement was manifest. Maynooth was well
represented that night. The graduate students of the Dunboyne Establishment also sent a telegram: "Uncompromising we stand for compulsory Irish."[58] For these gestures of support, all the students were
punished at the time O'Hickey was asked to resign. As he wrote to
Maurice Moore, "The entire Committee of the League of St. Columba
were deprived of the orders to which in the ordinary course of things
they would have been entitled—the President of the League (the most
distinguished student probably in the College) being deprived of
priesthood. . . . they violated no rule, nor were they in anywise guilty
of a break of discipline. But they expressed themselves publicly in
favour of a measure to which the President is well-known to be rabidly and unreasoningly opposed."[59] The administrative council of
the college recommended in addition "that the Dunboyne priests be
withdrawn by their Bishops; that all newspapers be removed from stu-

dent libraries; and that the activities of student societies be suspended until their rules were revised." The Visitors accepted the recommendations.[60]

During the winter of the compulsory Irish controversy, W. P. Ryan in the *Irish Nation and Peasant* gave almost daily updates on the status of priests who spoke on behalf of the language requirement. "Ennis Priests Not Muzzled" read one headline; "The Suppression of the Rev. Dr. O'Hickey" read another.[61] A brief news item read, "Father Wall, of St. Munchin's College, Limerick, has been 'muzzled,' we understand, in connection with the Irish-in-the-University discussion. Thus there is a very notable addition to the series that already contained Canon MacFadden, Dr. O'Hickey, Father Forde, and the priests of St. Jarlath's."[62] But muzzling didn't stop the printing presses, and rebellion continued on paper. As Ryan wrote in February,

> the Standing Committee intervened and stopped his letter-writing. And lo! straightway from the busy printing press there comes a 32-paged pamphlet entitled "An Irish University, or Else—" . . . a penny will secure plenty of "material" without the slightest possibility of episcopal censure or displeasure. Suppressed, Dr. O'Hickey yet speaketh. Or if you like to say he is silent, his silence can be felt— acutely, expressively, and impressively felt. All Ireland can hear him thinking, as in folk-lore privileged people hear the grass growing.[63]

In that last sentence, Ryan seems to be suggesting a role for O'Hickey in the popular imagination something akin to that of the "drunken priest" figure Lawrence Taylor writes about, who wanders through the countryside "after being 'silenced' by the bishop," curing and blessing with the water from holy wells, freely using his magical powers to perform miracles now that he exists outside "the *smacht* [rule, regulation] of the bishop."[64] Dr. O'Hickey was not a drinker, but the analogy emphasizes his continued popular support despite— even because of—episcopal suppression. O'Hickey as represented by Ryan has an intuitive, quasi-magical connection with "All Ireland." The publication of his pamphlet *is* his magic, and because of it people can "hear" him even though he has been "silenced." All Ireland is specially attuned to O'Hickey, because he is a people's hero: through his thinking Ireland is given access to another realm of being.

Ryan was right that people could hear O'Hickey even in his silence, as the availability of private correspondence now confirms. When

O'Hickey was first silenced, Michael Moynihan wrote to his brother John of his concern that this "patriotic priest" had "tamely . . . allowed himself to be suppressed by his bishops." Yet two sentences later he writes, "Did you see Dr. O'Hickey's letters on the subject [of compulsory Irish] yet? If they are not on sale in Tralee, I will take them home with me." In June, Michael wrote again, "it is impossible to say what Dr. O'Hickey will do as regards his dismissal, but it is certain that, whether openly or not, he will show a spirit equal to the circumstances."[65] The brothers were following the drama as it unfolded in the pages of Ryan's newspaper, emotionally involved as the values they cherished were attacked in and defended by O'Hickey. Ryan's "All Ireland" extended even to Brazil, where the British consul Roger Casement, not yet the center of his own controversy, heard O'Hickey thinking: "We must try to help the O'Hickey Memorial by the way," he wrote. "That is a disgraceful thing the dismissing him from the Chair of Irish in the Irish College because he stuck up for the language he is paid to teach."[66]

In his anonymously published pamphlet, *The Irish Bishops and an Irish University* (1909), O'Hickey challenged the bishops directly, without Young Ireland poetry, as if knowing now that his true subject was the political tyranny of the bishops, not the cultural tyranny of West Britain. "Outside the sphere of faith and morals," he wrote, "the Bishops as such have no official authority whatsoever; no right to command the obedience or to bind the consciences of Catholics." Now O'Hickey was no longer writing from his political unconscious: "In Ireland historical causes have given the Bishops more political power, more influence in civil and social affairs, than their Episcopal brethren possess in any part of Catholic Christendom. In view of their recent pronouncement, it has become necessary to ask seriously, though regretfully, whether it is well that they should continue to wield such exceptional adventitious power."[67] In the essay's peroration, the "muzzled" O'Hickey speaks as Romeo, of all people, addressing the woman he loves. Like all good Irish cultural nationalists, O'Hickey could quote Shakespeare without feeling disloyal, and the woman in question is a moribund Juliet ni Houlihan. "Courage, old land!" he apostrophizes,

> Thou art not conquered; beauty's ensign yet
> Is crimson in thy lips and in thy cheeks
> And death's pale flag is not advanced there.[68]

To quote such a passage at such a time implies that his love has been thwarted, that he cannot rescue the woman to whom he has long devoted himself, and that the "enemy" is about to win. The scene of hostile confrontation is gone because he has been removed from the battlefield, the war of words. Unable to speak his cause aloud in public, he chooses an allusion that places him in a tomb, without hearers. It is an ominous, pre-apocalyptic passage, entirely lacking the exhilaration and energy of O'Hickey's previous writings. This is the allusion of a person unable to act.

In all his flamboyant Irish historical references, the encounter with the enemy involved emotional excitement or physical activity, holding the bridge at Athlone, defending the walls of Limerick, forming "a solid phalanx on Ireland's side."[69] What O'Hickey met with, in his own great encounter, was an *explication de texte*. All the rebellion was in that one-penny pamphlet. On Ordination Sunday, June 20, O'Hickey was summoned to the board room where the Visitors to the College were meeting. There, after some preliminary conversation, Cardinal Logue began to speak of *An Irish University, or Else*.

> A lecture which I had delivered to the students, their Lordships considered particularly objectionable. In that lecture, his Eminence added, I had criticised some of the Bishops, and spoken disrespectfully of the President of the College, whom I was bound to respect and obey. He then referred to a speech made by Dr. Hyde in favour of compulsory Irish, the language of which he described as worthy of a gentleman. . . . The Bishop of Galway read the passages which had been marked in the pamphlet, first the passages from the lecture, and afterwards the passages from the letters. When each passage had been read, his Eminence . . . briefly commented upon it.[70]

Asked if he wished to make a statement, Dr. O'Hickey said only that he had very little to say beyond confirming that he had written the passages and adding, "I still believe that I was undoubtedly justified in writing everything I have written; and, having written it, I am, of course, prepared to take the consequences."

With those lines O'Hickey seems to have silenced the bishops: "When I had finished nobody spoke. For what seemed a considerable time, there was silence." Cardinal Logue then—as O'Hickey tells it—addressed the Visitors:

—I suppose, your Lordships, we can do nothing further in this matter
at present. There was no response. As the silence was beginning to be
painful, to relieve it I said:

—I suppose, your Eminence, I may go.

—I suppose so, replied his Eminence. Thereupon I proceeded to leave,
but, just as I had reached the door, the Cardinal again spoke:

—Just a moment, Dr. O'Hickey. Their Lordships sent for you to afford
you an opportunity of making any statement you might wish to
make. To which I replied:

—I am very grateful to your Eminence and to their Lordships, but I
have nothing to add to what I have already said. I then left the Board
Room.[71]

Whether or not Logue and O'Hickey actually said "I suppose" back
and forth to each other three times can never be known, but the account definitely captures the stress level of the meeting and the contrast in negotiating styles. Logue and their lordships patently wanted
O'Hickey to acknowledge that the offending passages were offensive,
to apologize, and to promise silence and obedience in the future.
Their lordships may have had in mind the example of Father George
Crolly, a mid-nineteenth-century professor at St. Patrick's College
who, under compulsion, had written a letter of submission and a formal retraction of his doctrinal errors.[72] Retraction was impossible for
O'Hickey; it would have constituted infidelity to his most cherished
ideals. He believed his tropes and metaphors, and modeled the encounter with his employers on the defiant heroics of Irish rebels over
the centuries. The silence that was so painful to O'Hickey must have
been a stunned silence.

Summoned to the board room on June 22 for the meeting of the
Trustees, and informed that the Trustees had before them "a resolution depriving him of his chair," O'Hickey was invited one final time
to make a statement to their lordships. He said: "Your Eminence, I
have little to add to what I said when I appeared before the Visitors.
The writings complained of I published in the discharge of what I felt
to be a duty. For any sacrifice the discharge of that duty may entail I
am prepared. *Whatever may befall me, I cannot play false to my conscience nor to Ireland.*"[73] Given O'Hickey's construction of his role
in the compulsory Irish controversy for the previous six months, the
situation clearly required a speech from the dock. The words sound
so stilted and generic that they seem to have been memorized for a

part in a play, but they are what O'Hickey said, as the minutes of the Trustees meeting report also. Perhaps, like "I love you," a speech from the dock is always a quotation also. And like all those who speak from the dock, O'Hickey was addressing an audience beyond the bishops, an audience who would need to read the speech because they were not there to hear it. Clearly O'Hickey's formal refusal to retract his writings marked, for him, a particular stage in the rebel's trajectory. On July 29 the Trustees met again, and Dr. O'Hickey was dismissed from the chair he had refused to resign.

In spite of O'Hickey's fear (expressed to Liam Bulfin) that people would "shirk this fight," that they would not "rally round" a priest who had been "struck down in the name of discipline," he drew indignant expressions of support and contributions to his defense from far-flung members of the Irish diaspora, their names and locations listed in the columns of *Sinn Féin* and the *Irish Nation and Peasant*.[74] Five days after the dismissal, a meeting with a "large attendance, including a number of ladies" was held in the Gresham Hotel to thank Dr. O'Hickey for his services and to "take steps to present him with a suitable testimonial," because he would no longer draw a salary from Maynooth. Eoin MacNeill chaired the meeting and delivered the fundraising speech. With an eye, perhaps, on the future support of the bishops for the language issue, MacNeill based his appeal on loyalty to a fellow worker, keeping the O'Hickey controversy distinct from issues of patriotism and linguistic nationalism:

> He had good reason to know that Irish public opinion regarded the dismissal of Dr. O'Hickey as a most deplorable thing. [Hear, hear.] But now there were some people saying that they who were banded together in the cause of their national language ought to stand aside and remain silent and without action. . . . If that were to happen, then they, too, would be disgraced. . . . There he was; he had fought their fight; he had been struck down, no matter by what hand. Should they stand by motionless and in silence and leave him to his fate? If they did they need never face another fight nor look for respect or sympathy from any man in Ireland. [Hear, hear.] They stood by the man who had stood by them. [Applause.] . . . Let people say what they liked, they would not see a man whom all who knew him knew to be an upright, conscientious man, loyal to his convictions, a priest among priests, an Irishman among Irishmen—they would not see him deserted on the roadside. [Applause.][75]

With an intuitive understanding that O'Hickey's contribution to the cause had been textual, Liam Bulfin, speaking for the Irish community in Buenos Aires, announced that "at a banquet recently held in Buenos Ayres steps were taken to present Dr. O'Hickey with a gold pen, and it would be one of the pleasantest acts he had ever performed to present the pen to that gentleman. [Applause]."

The Relic

Having defied the enemy and delivered a speech from the dock, O'Hickey had become the Irish hero of his own metaphors and allusions. Following the paradigmatic hero's life, he obliged by becoming a martyr. "Today," Pearse wrote of Dr. O'Hickey in *An Claidheamh Soluis* after the meeting with the Trustees, "he has earned a new fame and a new title to love and veneration. There is not a hamlet in the Gaedhealtacht, there is not a city in Ireland or Britain or America or Australia in which brave and patriotic and religious Irishmen will not bless the Irish priest who dared to meet tyranny face to face, answering it back with words as proud as its own."[76] Certainly people from all over contributed to the testimonial fund, but by the time O'Hickey returned from Rome in the summer of 1916, after six years of legal procedures had failed to overturn his dismissal, other martyrs (Pearse chief among them) had displaced him in the popular imagination.[77]

Although Pearse may have exaggerated the duration of interest in O'Hickey, the veneration remained alive unofficially. According to Séamus Ó Maoleóin, his mother had O'Hickey's photograph in her prayer book "until the day she died." Under it she had written, "Sagart Gaelach a dúnmharaíodh ag easpaig ghallda na hÉireann"— "Irish priest who was murdered by enemy bishops of Ireland."[78] At the local level, in Carrick-on-Suir, where O'Hickey had been born and where he was buried, he remained a focus of ambivalent reverence for a small number of friends, and so it was that Carrick became the site of his triumphal posthumous return in the 1980s. Like so much else in his public life, this stage of O'Hickey's career was text-driven, and by a text whose material existence was for a long time its defining characteristic. Whether the words of this 147-page manuscript were written with that gold pen can only be surmised, but the pages themselves were sacralized. Even the very envelope was kept intact for sixty-three years, as the only copy of the 1909 "Statement concerning the Dismissal of Rev. Dr. O'Hickey from the Irish Chair, St. Patrick's College, Maynooth" was passed from one Carrick native to another. It was less a text than a relic.

The odd story of the manuscript's survival sounds like the plot of a play Lady Gregory might have written in, say, 1903 but then thought better of and thrown out before beginning *Spreading the News*: it has so many local characters and so much improbability that it could pass as the creation of a Protestant revivalist writer.[79] Through a sequence of events that can only be called hokey, the manuscript emerged into general view in 1973 from under the shop counter of Bourke's Drapery, Main Street, Carrick-on-Suir, where it had been carefully placed by Hugh Ryan, a shop assistant and a collector of local history and lore. Ryan had been given the manuscript a few years earlier by Paddy Nolan, who had found it in the midst of rubble while doing construction work in Murphy's Medical Hall (now Meade's Medical Hall) across the street. The pharmacy had been the former home and office of Dr. Philip Murphy, a general practitioner, Gaelic League member, and friend of O'Hickey's who died in his nineties in 1970.

In November 1973 Monsignor Mac Fhinn had just finished his biography of O'Hickey and wanted a picture of the O'Hickey family gravestone at the Franciscan Friary cemetery in Carrickbeg, so Michael Coady, at the request of Mac Fhinn's publisher's wife, Bríd Bean Uí Éigeartaigh, went to photograph it. Naturally, Coady's trip to the cemetery did not go unobserved. A day or so later Ryan sent for Coady to find out why he had been taking the photograph and why he was interested in the long forgotten O'Hickey. When Coady told him about the biography, Ryan said, "I have something here which might interest you," and pulled the manuscript out from under the counter. The biography was at the printers already, but Coady telephoned Bríd to stop the presses. Perhaps, as W. P. Ryan had written years earlier, "All Ireland heard him thinking," and some intuitive collective working of the spirits of Paddy Nolan, Hugh Ryan, Michael Coady, Bríd Bean Uí Éigeartaigh, Monsignor Mac Fhinn, and the recently dead Dr. Murphy made the book turn up, as Coady put it, "at the precise time that an opportunity had finally come around to put it into print and on the record." Or perhaps, as Coady also suggested, O'Hickey was directing the whole thing from the grave whose headstone had been photographed.

Whatever the hidden cause, all the people involved did exactly what they should have done both singly and collectively, so that the relic became a matter of public historical significance. The pages so carefully preserved proved to contain O'Hickey's apologia, a detailed account and defense of everything that had happened between O'Hickey and his ecclesiastical superiors during the essential Irish controversy. In its pages O'Hickey legitimized himself with implicit comparisons to famous martyrs of Western history: he invoked Joan of Arc (beatified in 1909), who had been "sent to the stake by the Bishop of Beauvais and other Anglicised French Prelates and ecclesiastics."[80] And he ended with the words of Socrates to the judges who had just condemned him: "I would very much rather defend myself as I did, and die, than as you would have me do, and live."[81] It was this self-defense—or, to be precise, the discovery of the defense—that led indirectly to O'Hickey's rehabilitation by the archbishop of Armagh and primate of all Ireland, Tomás Cardinal Ó Fiaich. The manuscript's recovery brought O'Hickey once more within the "*smacht* of the bishop," because the local relic became the means of reconnecting him with the institutional Church. With the help of the people of Carrick, his manuscript brought him in 1988 what it could not have in 1909.

The gesture of pulling the manuscript out from under the counter symbolically enacted the return of O'Hickey to the collective consciousness of Carrick-on-Suir: it happened when everyone was ready. O'Hickey's rehabilitation was managed cautiously, with tactful awareness of the uncomfortable and ambivalent feelings he provoked. Some members of his own family were embarrassed about him: "We were never anti-Church!" was usually the indignant response of his niece Mary Murphy (née Hickey) when the subject of her uncle came up.[82] An obstinate man who fought the bishops and lost was not a figure to be proud of; he had returned to Carrick a failure, his new bishop had never seen fit to employ him anywhere, and he had died before he had the time to do anything at all, however simple, that might have seemed useful and redemptive.[83] In the oration delivered at O'Hickey's grave after the weekend of Dúchas (heritage) with which the Gaelic League honored O'Hickey in 1985, Michael Coady carefully acknowledged his own participation in the town's silence. He decontextualized O'Hickey's conflict so that it did not seem disobedient or shameful; it was heroic, a matter of "universal questions concerning freedom of thought and expression within any institu-

information leaflet

O'HICKEY MEMORIAL SCULPTURE
Dealbh Chuimhneacháin Uí hIcí

published

On the occasion of the Official Unveiling
by His Eminence Cardinal Tomás Ó Fiaich,
Archbishop of Armagh and Primate of All Ireland:
Sunday, 24th July 1988

In iothlainn Dé go dtugtar sinn.

Micheal Ó hIcí agus a aintín, Bean Uí Bhriain

> "It was the reading of an essay of Thomas Davis, by the banks of the silvery Suir, that awakened within my breast the longing to master our native tongue, and the ambition, Providence so willing, to do one man's work for its preservation."

2.3. The rehabilitation of Dr. O'Hickey. This is the cover of the leaflet printed on the occasion of the unveiling of the statue of O'Hickey in Carrickbeg. Leaflet courtesy of Michael Coady, who organized the fundraising for the statue and the ceremonies at the unveiling.

tional structure, be it college, or university, or Church." The idea of
erecting a statue of O'Hickey, the ultimate reconstruction of the
man, was presented as a testimony to qualities that were almost
saintly: "Let us raise to O'Hickey a worthy and well-made monument, not fruitlessly to prolong an old controversy, but as some small
acknowledgment and recompense in his own place . . . no man ever
can malign his holiness, his zeal, his patriotism, his integrity, his
courage."[84] Like Ryan, MacNeill, and Pearse before him, Coady urged
his audience to reward the values from which they derived vicarious
benefit. The local community functioned in 1985 as the nationalist
one had in 1909, offering the populist base for O'Hickey's reputation.

But the local collective memory that was re-creating O'Hickey to
present to the larger world had been insulted and disgraced also. Carrick, too, required rehabilitation. Rather than being flattered by
O'Casey's chapter on O'Hickey, Carrick was ashamed, because
O'Casey had claimed that the funeral (which he had not attended)
had been small.[85] "When he was put under the sod," O'Casey wrote,

> there was no Hyde, Mac Neill, Oona Fearally, Edward Martyn, in
> freshly-made suits of mourning marching down to Carrick Beg to
> murmur a last farewell to one of Ireland's greater dead. They stayed at
> home. No Drum Taps beaten, no Last Post sounded; only the caw-caw
> of many a crow flapping a dark wing through a grey sky. No sermon;
> no band of students chanting sad melodies . . . nothing here but a tiny
> band of friends, shivering in the centre of a cold, damp day, a little in
> from a lonely road alongside the noisy sullen Suir, led by the coura-
> geous Dr. McDonald, to see their comrade safely sheltered in his last
> home.[86]

No matter that in November 1916 MacNeill was in prison for his part
in the Rising and that O'Hickey himself thought the Suir a beautiful
river, recalling reading Thomas Davis "by the banks of the silvery
Suir."[87]

Given the sixty-one members of the clergy mentioned in the contemporary newspaper account, the five family members designated
"chief mourners," nine members of the Gaelic League from neighboring areas, and the custom of joining a funeral during its walk
through the town, O'Casey's "tiny band" was more likely a few hundred. The paper notes that "many other priests wired expressing in-
ability to attend" and that "there was a very large attendance at the

interment." The Gaelic League activist and writer Agnes O'Farrelly, a close friend of Dr. O'Hickey's who did in fact attend the funeral, would no doubt have been offended by O'Casey's emphasis on her absence: hers is the first name mentioned after that of the bishop's, and she also sent a wreath. Douglas Hyde, though not present, sent one of the "large numbers of handsome wreaths."[88]

In his graveside oration urging the erection of a statue, Coady offered a revisionist interpretation of the funeral:

> It was not a mere handful which gathered about this grave on that day of the funeral. . . . High Mass was chanted beside here in St. Molleran's church. The bishop presided and Walter McDonald was the chief celebrant. Many of the clergy from all over the diocese were present, together with various representatives from the University, from academic life, and from the Gaelic League. There too, of course, were O'Hickey's own grief-stricken people, and a great throng of the people of Carrick.[89]

The official ceremonies for Dr. O'Hickey's rehabilitation on July 24, 1988, were composed of three separate rituals, performed in a sequence that built up to the speech of Cardinal Ó Fiaich.[90] The Liturgy of Reconciliation (led by Father Michael Mullins of St. John's College, where O'Hickey had been ordained) around O'Hickey's grave reconciled O'Hickey and the people of Carrick to each other, confirming the value of the hero for the community and the community for the hero. Coady's list of the people there ("a great throng . . . distinguished ecclesiastics, academic figures . . . members of the O'Hickey family, Irish language organisation and local community") so closely echoes his revisionist characterization of the funeral that the liturgy must also have been perceived as a second, more affirmative funeral. Then "the assembly proceeded to the site of the Memorial, where His Eminence Cardinal Tomás Ó Fiaich . . . performed the unveiling" of Cliodna Cussen's statue.[91] Ó Fiaich praised O'Hickey's "unvarnished directness . . . his lack of ambivalence—nothing hidden within him which he did not reveal," and the rebel priest became a local saint.

In words that were consciously and deliberately ritualized, Ó Fiaich undid what Logue and Mannix had done: "As the eighth successor of Dr. Mannix as President of Maynooth and the fifth successor of Cardinal Logue as Archbishop of Armagh, I have inherited the mantle of those responsible for removing him from his Chair. I have come along

2.4. The granite man. The simple, elegant statue by Cliodna Cussen, standing high above the river Suir, looks east, says the leaflet, "towards the sunrise and the hope of a new dawn for Ireland, towards Waterford where O'Hickey was ordained, towards Rome where he sought redress of his grievance, towards the village of Portlaw where he died." Photo credit: Michael Coady.

today to make amends, and to show that Dr. O'Hickey is still honoured in Maynooth College and by the Irish Church." Because Ó Fiaich was also a passionate and assertive language activist—indeed a rowdy one in his younger days—his act of devotion to O'Hickey honored and sanctioned the very energies his predecessors had punished. Ó Fiaich was in the perfect position to bless and forgive everyone, to say of all the 1909 controversialists, "Go dtuga Dia maithiúnas dóibh go léir agus luach saothair síoraí ar neamh."[92]

Thus after a long wait was Dr. O'Hickey welcomed back to the official Church through the agency of his own manuscript, the relic whose retrieval from the dust of history was made possible because his words were sacralized by a few people in Carrick, even those who didn't read them. Yet although the Archbishop of Armagh, the successor of Cardinal Logue, ritually reconnected the priest in his local place with the national ecclesiastical center and installed him as a figure of popular devotion, O'Hickey remains in uneasy relation to Maynooth. In the official history of St. Patrick's College published seven years later, Monsignor Corish does not mention the rehabilitation and cites approvingly Leon Ó Broin's comment that the Trustees "were entitled to be aggrieved at the leading part one of their priests and professors took against them."[93] But the disapproval of official Maynooth is balanced by the heritage book on sale in the college bookstore there. Innocent of academic or ecclesiastical politics, it makes the proud claim that "in the domain of Gaelic literature Maynooth has always been in the forefront . . . the first pamphlet of the Gaelic League came from the pen of Father Michael O'Hickey, the then Professor of Irish there."[94]

Ceist na Teangan

Although stubbornness, Dr. O'Hickey's great-niece tells me, runs in the family, Dr. O'Hickey's "unbending, immovable character" was culturally significant, a characteristic that was praised, punished, recorded, remembered, and finally represented in granite.[95] Much is visible in miniature in the essential Irish controversy of 1909, as, at those crowded noisy meetings that lasted until late at night, the new state was emerging in debate, defiance, and "adversarial Irishness." In spite of the Standing Committee of the Bishops, the university was claimed on behalf of the Irish language, and in its victory the Gaelic

League showed its populist strength. Other priests were "muzzled," as Ryan's *The Irish Nation and Peasant* made clear, and certainly other priests tangled with the bishops. But Dr. O'Hickey was one of those who break rather than bend, and in his breaking the divisions of his time are made manifest. If he had been a compromiser, if he had used "the language of a gentleman," if he had decided to apologize, we would not know at precisely what point the discourses of the two major native institutions, the Church and the Gaelic League, parted company; nor would we know what the bishops sounded like when they spoke as if *ex cathedra* in the board room at Maynooth.

Viewed with hindsight, the O'Hickey controversy can be seen to exist in the overlapping histories of the Church, the state, and the language. Cardinal Ó Fiaich's apology to Dr. O'Hickey was only one of many public apologies made by the Church as its moral authority began to weaken in Ireland and elsewhere toward the end of the twentieth century. When the counterhistory of the Catholic Church in Ireland is written some day, much of it will be seen to coalesce around Dr. O'Hickey. It will include Hanna Sheehy Skeffington's rebel uncle Father Eugene Sheehy, the "land league priest"; Gerald O'Donovan, whose novel *Father Ralph* tells the story of his leaving the priesthood; Professor Walter McDonald, whose theological scholarship disturbed the Maynooth authorities; Father Michael O'Flanagan, who encouraged his Sligo parishioners to steal turf; all those "muzzled" priests made famous in the pages of the *Irish Nation and Peasant*; and perhaps Father John O'Reilly, whose name was on the sixty-three-year-old envelope and who had evidently been reading O'Hickey's "Statement" out in Carna, County Galway.[96] O'Hickey family folklore claims that his friend Sister Otteran was asked to leave her convent in Scotland because of an angry letter, defending O'Hickey, that she sent to President Mannix.[97] These stubborn, maverick priests and religious are usually studied separately, but their hidden networks, as they are brought to light, will create a more complex view of the institutional Church.

A secular iconoclastic tradition also constellates around O'Hickey, one that includes people like Sean O'Casey, Sean O'Faolain, Frank O'Connor, Owen Sheehy Skeffington, and Noel Browne. Frank O'Connor, complaining in 1942 about the "grip of the gombeen man, of the religious secret societies," felt the lack of some "idealistic opposition which would enable us to measure the extent of the damage."[98] O'Hickey's legacy was exactly such "idealistic opposition."

Sean O'Faolain wrote only a few years later that "all one's sympathies, mine do at any rate, will go out to that courageous man Dr. O'Hickey, Professor of Gaelic at Maynooth, who was sacked by Maynooth in 1909 because he fought openly for the introduction of compulsory Irish in the National University."[99]

And finally, when the history of language politics in Ireland is written some day, this controversy will find its place in the swirl of passions for getting Irish into school curricula, before the history notes the later and equally great passions for getting it out, as well as battles over Irish in courts, on signs, on television, and in the speeches of government officials. If he were alive now, Dr. O'Hickey would no doubt be reading Nuala Ní Dhomhnaill's poems, and the title "Ceist na Teangan" would certainly catch his eye. There Ní Dhomhnaill uses the great Mosaic trope of nineteenth-century Irish political rhetoric to focus attention on the Irish language.

> Cuirim mo dhóchas ar snámh
> i mbáidin teangan
> faoi mar a leagfá naíonán
> i gcliabhán
> a bheadh fite fuaite
> de dhuilleoga feileastraim
> is bitiúman agus pic
> bheith cuimilte lena thóin
>
> ansan é a leagadh síos
> i measc na ngiolcach
> is coigeal na mban sí
> le taobh na habhann,
> feáchaint n'fheadarais
> cá dtabharfaidh an sruth é
> feáchaint, dála Mhaoise,
> an bhfóirfidh iníon Fharoinn?
>
> I place my hope on the water
> in this little boat
> of the language, the way a body might put
> an infant
>
> in a basket of intertwined
> iris leaves,

its underside proofed
with bitumen and pitch,

then set the whole thing down amidst
the sedge
and bulrushes by the edge
of a river

only to have it borne hither and thither,
not knowing where it might end up;
in the lap, perhaps,
of some Pharaoh's daughter.[100]
        (Translation by Paul Muldoon)

The poem reclaims from militant nationalism the Old Testament paradigm of liberation, using it to signify a cultural struggle occurring in a place apart from the violence and controversies of the public political arena. Saving the language, in this trope, begins in a hidden world of maternal love, an alternative to the realm of bureaucratic discourse in which the abstract "question of the language" remains a matter of partisan political argument, *as Béarla.* Ní Dhomhnaill focuses on the part of cultural change that is accidental, unchartable, mysterious, a permeation of enemy territory rather than an attack or a position paper. Pharaoh's daughter will be charmed into helping the cause by the attractive vulnerability of a baby: "And when she had opened it, she saw the child: and, behold, the babe wept. And she had compassion on him." Avoiding entirely the agonistic segment of the story, Ní Dhomhnaill shows a contact made by floating, not fighting. Accustomed as he was to polemic, campaigns, and debates, Dr. O'Hickey might not agree with an outcome so dependent on the fortuitous. But he might be interested to contemplate how culture can be transmitted independent of institutions; and he might also consider how by routes just as indirect and as lucky, his own writings on the language question survived to find an audience.

3

The Shewing-up of Dublin Castle
Lady Gregory, Shaw, and *Blanco Posnet*, August 1909

Gheibheann cos ar siúl rud éigin.
A moving leg gets something.

John Campbell Gordon, Lord Aberdeen, Viceroy of Ireland, was a collector of jokes. Categorized according to ethnic group, nation, and class, the jokes in his collection *Tell Me Another* are so politically incorrect that there is almost an innocence about them. Those in the chapter "Specimens of Irish Wit" make it difficult to believe that this was the man who presided over colonial rule in Ireland at the height of cultural nationalism (he was viceroy from 1906 to 1915 as well as in 1886). Here's a sample joke from his collection: two men, he says,

> were brought before a magistrate for fighting in the street. As the evidence against one of them was not conclusive, the order was given for his release, and the magistrate was about to inflict a fine on the other, when the man who had been liberated addressed the magistrate thus:
>
> "Shure we were not fighting when the Polis tuk us."
> "What were you doing then?" said the magistrate.
> "We were just trying to separate one another."[1]

To the title *Tell Me Another*, the contemporary reader might be tempted to respond: Don't. With their anecdotes about Scottish clergymen and Bishop Wilberforce, or what the author's second cousin

Admiral So-and-So said to Lady So-and-So in 1863, the jokes must have seemed a bit musty in 1926, when the book was new. Evidently Lord Aberdeen did not bear Lady Gregory any permanent ill will for her triumph over the Dublin Castle bureaucracy and Aberdeen himself in 1909, because he sent her a signed copy of the book when it came out. In return, Lady Gregory sent him some jokes she had collected, which were, she confided in her journal, "better worth telling" than the ones in the book. Other, even better ones she decided to "keep for my own possible use."[2]

The great encounter of August 1909 between Lady Gregory and Lord Aberdeen, the Abbey and the Castle, over the production of Bernard Shaw's banned play, *The Shewing-up of Blanco Posnet,* overlapped with the O'Hickey controversy for several weeks. On July 6 Lady Gregory was writing Shaw, "I don't think anything could show up the hypocrisy of the British Censor more than a performance [of *Blanco*] in Dublin," while a week later Bishop Sheehan met Dr. O'Hickey for lunch at the Gresham Hotel and attempted to persuade him to resign his chair.[3] As the phase of O'Hickey's controversy visible to the Irish public was ending, with a testimonial meeting for O'Hickey chaired by Eoin MacNeill on August 3, the visible phase of the *Blanco* controversy was just beginning. On August 5 an *Irish Times* article was headed, "Mr. Shaw's Prohibited Play. Is There an Irish Censorship?"[4]

No apologies or statues appear in the *Blanco* narrative because it did not endure long in popular memory. No sudden eruptions of emotions are involved, no ruined lives, no bitterness—or not too much— and no unresolved issues to burden the next generation. The whole thing was over in twenty days. But both controversies were constructed by their chief participants, Lady Gregory and Dr. O'Hickey, out of the same materials, the discourse and the iconography of Young Ireland. "I look to Miss Augusta to buy all my Fenian books," said the old bookseller in Loughrea, who sold the young Augusta Persse (born in 1852) "the paper covered collections of national ballads, *The Harp of Tara, The Irish Song Book,* and the like."[5] She was given *The Spirit of the Nation* as a birthday present by a sister who took the precaution of inscribing in it Samuel Johnson's maxim, "Patriotism is the last refuge of a scoundrel," but it was too late to change her ways.[6] O'Hickey, born eight years later, was reading Thomas Davis and growing up in a family with a rebel flag from 1848 in its possession.[7] While O'Hickey was hearing about his United

3.1. "They are defying the Lord Lieutenant." The lord lieutenant (also known as the viceroy) was, as he pointed out to Lady Gregory, "the King's representative" and so could not go "against the King." Left to right: Lord Aberdeen, Queen Mary, King George V, Lady Aberdeen. Permission of The Marquess of Aberdeen.

Irishman grandfather and the "interior of a British dungeon," and about the more recent adventures of his Young Ireland father, Lady Gregory was hearing from her nurse Mary Sheridan about the escape of the rebel Hamilton Rowan.[8] In her essay "The Felons of Our Land" (1900) Lady Gregory celebrated the poems and ballads that ring through O'Hickey's prose.[9]

Certainly between the Protestant daughter of a Big House and the Catholic son of a strong farmer many differences loom, but they were close contemporaries, and the angel voice of Thomas Davis sang round both their beds; their imaginations were charged with the same ballads, the same symbols, the same stories. When, then, Lady Gregory was given the opportunity of fighting Dublin Castle directly, she shaped and designed the controversy as she had shaped and designed her plays *The Rising of the Moon* (1904) and *Gaol Gate* (1906), forming it out of the images, tropes, and quotations inherited from a century of demotic nationalist culture. She saw her controversy, as Dr.

3.2. Lady Gregory. Lady Gregory enjoyed the "fight with the Castle," as she called it, over Shaw's play *The Shewing-up of Blanco Posnet* and wrote triumphantly about it in her 1913 book *Our Irish Theatre*. Her diary entries about her visits to Dublin Castle authorities (published in *Shaw, Lady Gregory, and the Abbey: A Correspondence and a Record*, edited by Dan H. Laurence and Nicholas Grene) give more details than her book. Photo credit: *Irish Times*.

O'Hickey saw his, as an enactment of nationalist resistance in the cultural sphere. The Abbey for Gregory, like the university for O'Hickey, was a site to be maintained as national, a small patch of Irish independence that would represent "the idea of a culture that has not yet come to be in political terms."[10] Gregory's personal encounters and public jousting with Aberdeen sound (in her records of them) like a comic version of O'Hickey's encounters with Cardinal Logue, the tyrant of the old guard who is given, *malgré lui*, the role of the enemy of Ireland. Whatever nationalist credentials Aberdeen and Logue might have claimed, their rearguard functions in their respective controversies made such an identity inevitable. Both controversies were duly and thoroughly recorded in the private papers of their protagonists, with an eye to future publication. Newspapers reported the progress of both affairs as if they were all-Ireland finals. The *Blanco* controversy, however, never became at all personal, as Lord Aberdeen's gift of *Tell Me Another* to Lady Gregory seventeen years later suggests. He thought of her as a friend. And because she knew she was fighting an ancient decrepit bureaucracy, not a personal antagonist, Lady Gregory's tone never ceased to be ludic. This was sport, and she would win the game.

To some extent both Gregory and O'Hickey provoked their controversies and set them up as nationalist happenings: O'Hickey quoted inflammatory poetry ("by slaves who sold their lands for gold / As Judas sold his God"), applied it to his employer, and then published his speech twice; Lady Gregory advertised the production of a play censored in England. They were asking for trouble. But Gregory and Shaw welcomed the controversy with joy as the opportunity of a lifetime. When Gregory wrote Shaw on August 12 that a Belfast newspaper had noted about the production "probable interference of the Lord Lieutenant," she added, "but that is too good to be true." And Shaw echoed her excitement: "Your news is almost too good to be true."[11] The dynamics of this controversy were not determined by uncontrollable feelings: artifice was everything. It was a genre in which Shaw and Gregory both were already experts; now they were co-authoring a controversy, carefully, artfully, strategically putting it together. It would include their public statements, Abbey Theatre press releases, and private meetings with the undersecretary and the viceroy; much behind-the-scenes politicking with journalists, with Castle society people and their friends; and of course the play itself, *The Shewing-up of Blanco Posnet*, whose production, rehearsals, and opening night were so much more exciting than its script.

The ability to taunt and tease and play games with one's opponent, as Gregory and Shaw knew well, derives from the awareness of controversy as a special kind of performance, not ordinary life. The controversy was itself the play they were staging. Instead of seeing the play in the foreground, the controversy in the background; instead of seeing the play as primary and the controversy as secondary, they saw the controversy and the play in the same plane, as equally important, both forms of expressive behavior, both forms of theater. Like plays, controversies constitute a tradition themselves: they have a history and refer back to previous controversies. They have their own traditions, customs, and allusions. If as a sequence they form traditions, then controversies are intertextual: they refer to one another, copying rhetorical styles, modes of conflict, and expressive behaviors such as hissing, heckling, throwing vegetables at the actors, or the antiphonal singing of political songs. All these actions are copied from previous controversies, a theatrics of protest handed down because controversies are modeled on, and are the model for, other controversies.

The Genealogy of the *Blanco* Controversy: England

For Gregory and Shaw, the meaning of the *Blanco* controversy, as they tried to shape it, would derive from its place in a sequence of previous controversies. It was created for particular audiences for whom it would have particular meanings. One of those audiences was English: *The Shewing-up of Blanco Posnet* had been written with the design of provoking a controversy to test the English censorship laws. Shaw had been waiting over ten years for just the right circumstances. In a letter of 1897 to his boyhood friend Edward McNulty, Shaw contemplated a possible site for the performance of *Mrs. Warren's Profession*, an "immoral" play and unlikely to be licensed, its author noted, because the subject was a "procuress." To secure a copyright performance, Shaw wanted to get the play put on "out of the Lord Chamberlain's jurisdiction," and Ireland, he wrote, "is in that happy condition. What censorship there may be there—from the Castle or elsewhere—I don't know."[12]

The law governing British theatrical censorship originated in 1737, when Sir Robert Walpole, irritated by caricatures of himself in plays by John Gay and Henry Fielding, sent the Stage Licensing Act through Parliament. The measure required submission of plays to the Lord Chamberlain for licensing a fortnight before opening performances and granted him power to deny licenses without giving any reason and to issue fines. Nor was there any procedure for appeal. The act established the office of the notorious examiner of plays, the actual censor. But theaters in Ireland were not within the examiner's jurisdiction. In every Irish city except Dublin, theaters came under municipal control; in Dublin (according to a 1786 law passed by the Irish parliament) theaters could be established only by royal letters patent. The examiner of plays derived his authority from Parliament, but the royal letters patent grounded the Dublin theaters in the authority of the British monarch and hence of the viceroy (also known as the lord lieutenant) in Dublin.[13]

Throughout his career as a dramatist Shaw had been lobbying against stage censorship. He had followed with interest the hearings in the House of Commons of the 1892 Select Committee on Theatres and Places of Entertainment. His good friend the theater critic William Archer had testified against censorship then, but Archer's was a minority position. After *Mrs. Warren's Profession* was denied a license in 1894, Shaw fought the censorship in letters to newspapers and in articles, while also mobilizing the members of the Society of Authors. In the spring of 1909, stage censorship was at last the subject of parliamentary inquiry. Anticipating the hearings of the Joint Select Committee of the House of Lords and the House of Commons on the Stage Plays (Censorship), Shaw engaged his antagonist by writing two plays that were refused licenses. In one of these plays, *Press Cuttings*, a Prime Minister Balsquith engages in cross-dressing. Shaw's teasing was in high gear; "one can hardly avoid concluding," observes Samuel Hynes, "that Shaw had written both plays as intentional exercises in examiner-bating."[14]

Blanco, however, was designed as a subtler provocation: this "sermon," as Shaw's subtitle calls it, tantalizingly uses what the censor considered blasphemy to express its religious vision. With the figurative clarity of an American *Everyman*, *The Shewing-up of Blanco Posnet* dramatizes the conversion of a thief who gives his stolen horse to the mother of a dying child. Set in a mythical Wild West, *Blanco* features as its chief authority a benign and charitable sheriff. The play ends with a comic feast in the local saloon. The script includes a cavalier allusion to the Almighty, which is immediately censored by the

3.3. Bernard Shaw on the bench at Coole, 1915. Shaw is writing another play on his lap-top, perhaps *O'Flaherty, V.C.* (1915), whose scene, he wrote to Lady Gregory, "is quite simply before the porch of your house." Photo by the Hon. W. F. Bailey; Bernard F. Burgunder Collection, Cornell University.

hero's hypocritical brother. Encoded within *Blanco* is the story of its own purposes, the testing of the state's goodwill toward an offending subject:

> BLANCO: . . . He hasnt finished with you yet. He always has a trick up His sleeve—
>
> ELDER DANIELS: Oh, is that the way to speak of the ruler of the universe—the great and almighty God?
>
> BLANCO: He's a sly one. He's a mean one. He lies low for you. He plays cat and mouse with you. He lets you run loose until you think youre shut of Him; and then, when you least expect it, He's got you.
>
> ELDER DANIELS: Speak more respectful Blanco—more reverent.[15]

The play was not only an open challenge to the censorship but an advance quotation of it, integrating into the drama the conflict between impertinent author and upright censor. In case the examiner was too dense to notice it, Shaw has Elder Daniels say, "Speak more respectful." The other passage intended to awaken the attentions of the examiner occurs when Blanco says of the local whore, "I accuse the fair Euphemia of immoral relations with every man in this town."[16] By contemporary standards this "obscenity" is not even noticeable, and even by 1909 standards it is pretty mild, but the point was to include a few, just a few, offensive phrases. The genius of the play lay in its inclusion of the minimum number of offensive phrases necessary to provoke the examiner, in a story otherwise pious and unsubversive.

Carefully attended to, the plot can be understood as a fantasy of reconciliation with authority, embodying the naughty misfit's wistful longing to be accepted by society. Judged "not guilty" by the Sheriff, a wise figure whose authority is never challenged, Blanco preaches a sermon on the mystery of God's workings in human affairs. Because the child dies in spite of Blanco's donation of the stolen horse, Blanco is "shewn-up" by the deity: "I played the rotten game," he announces, "but the great game was played on me; and now I'm for the great game every time." Enemies shake hands, and the men adjourn to the saloon, where Blanco stands the drinks.[17]

Like Dick Dudgeon of *The Devil's Disciple* (1897), Blanco is a "bad" brother whose eccentric good deed saves him from punishment and binds him to the community. For Shaw, the American setting of both plays provides an almost mythic realm whose apparent classlessness makes visible in pure form the confrontation between delinquent subject and state authority. The challenges of characters like Dick Dudgeon and Blanco Posnet reflect Shaw's own status as dissident. *Blanco* was his move in the strategic game the state had been playing since it began to censor stage plays 172 years earlier in response to Henry Fielding's provocations. And Fielding had been responding to Walpole.

But this larger drama was taking place in England, not in the tolerant West of Shaw's imaginings, and the plot of *Blanco* did not accurately predict the play's reception. Shaw's reputation for subversion made everything he did seem dangerous, and in the spring of 1909 he was censored repeatedly. The examiner of plays, George Alexander Redford, did not share the Sheriff's generous tolerance for unconventional virtue. In May *Blanco* (already in rehearsal with Herbert Beerbohm Tree in the title role) was refused a license. Shaw derived great pleasure from the news (in late June) that Beerbohm Tree had been knighted and, the same day, the news that *Press Cuttings* had also been denied a license. "It only remains," Shaw wrote to the *Times*, "for the King to make me a duke to complete the situation."[18] Curiously enough, Edward VII did not confer a dukedom on Shaw, but the state was in continuous relationship with the theater that spring and summer. The hearings of the Joint Select Committee were a diligent, determined, bureaucratic attempt to find out precisely what, if anything, was naughty about the theater, and to what extent the populace should be protected from it. Bishops, theater managers, playwrights, and officials of various kinds answered the questions of Lords and Commons.

The testimony of the examiner himself, Mr. Redford, revealed perfectly the nature of the enemy Shaw and other progressive thinkers were up against in the England of 1909. His vague, inane, and uninformative answers made clear why so innocuous a play as *Blanco Posnet* had been forbidden: he didn't get it. Was he somehow, magically, created by Kafka? Had Beckett or Pinter managed to write his lines? Redford was inarticulate about what exactly the examiner of plays was looking for when he examined plays:

> CHAIRMAN (HERBERT SAMUEL): On what principles do you proceed in licensing the plays that come before you?
> WITNESS: Simply bringing to bear an official point of view and keeping up a standard. It is really impossible to define what the principle may be. There are no principles that can be defined. I follow precedent.[19]

Robert Harcourt, the most dedicated anticensorship member of the committee, attempted to drive home a point that troubled many of its members. He asked, "You do not think that some of these plays which have been abused on the ground that they deal with serious subjects are less harmful than some of the lighter comedies that have been licensed?" And Redford responded, "It seems to me that this is touching on the question of being a critic. I have no critical view on plays at all. I simply have to maintain a standard."[20] When Hugh Law put before him an obvious contradiction between two decisions, Redford pointed out that they were eight or nine years apart. Law continued, "And in that time your mind had developed?" And Redford said, "My mind, if you are speaking of my individual mind, was probably always the same." When Lord Gorell suggested that a committee of appeal might be useful in cases when a license was denied, because "one man's opinion may not agree with the opinion of everybody else," Redford replied, "I should have no fear of my judgment being reversed. It never has been reversed." In later questioning Redford acknowledged that he had himself authored a few plays, but they had not been performed. His previous occupation had not had anything to do with the theater: "I was a bank manager," he said, a sentence that was to reverberate soon in Dublin Castle.[21]

All the theatrical luminaries of the day made appearances before the committee—W. S. Gilbert, James Barrie, Granville Barker—and were questioned at length. When Shaw's turn came, he argued sensibly that the stage should be accountable to the law, not to an arbitrarily chosen individual, and should come under the same regulations that protect or prosecute the speech of ordinary citizens. Shaw also made the case for the "conscientiously immoral" play and argued eloquently for its production: "I think that the danger of crippling thought, the danger of obstructing the formation of the public mind by specially suppressing such representations is far greater than any real danger that there is from such representations. The real difficulty, of course, is not to suppress such representations, but, on the contrary, to bring them about."[22] The committee did not wish to accept as much of Shaw's immoral mind as he wished to offer. When he asked that his eleven-thousand-word statement on censorship be read into the transcript, the committee (having first cleared the room and met privately) abruptly refused: "The committee, after deliberation, have decided that it would not be permissible to print the statement as part of the evidence." Then, as if nothing out of the ordinary had happened, the chair took up the interrupted conversation: "I think you were saying . . ."[23] When Shaw returned six days later for a second round of questioning, he was dismissed before he could open his mouth. The most illustrious playwright of the day was silenced by the state before he could complete his testimony on censorship, and the members of the committee, lined up in a row, made a little ceremony out of returning to him their unread copies of his statement.

The Genealogy of the *Blanco* Controversy: Ireland

Thus *Blanco Posnet* in England derived its meaning from the strategic game of theatrical censorship that had been played for almost two hundred years: with two plays and his immoral testimony in the spring of 1909, Shaw had staked out a provocative position. In Ireland *Blanco* found its place in a sequence of Abbey Theatre controversies whose terms were entirely different. There, the Abbey directors wanted to publicize and (with the help of a good controversy) to dramatize the theater's nationalist credentials. The names of the patrons who had answered Lady Gregory's solicitation in 1897 for the Irish Literary Theatre, the Abbey's predecessor, did not have a very revolutionary ring ("Lord Dufferin, Viceroy of India and Canada . . . Lord and Lady Ardilaun, the Duchess of St. Albans"), though the supporters did include Maud Gonne and the Fenian John O'Leary.[24] With its first production, Yeats's *Countess Cathleen* (1899), the Irish Literary Theatre had angered the Catholic Church hierarchy with the story of starving Irish people selling "souls for gold." And in 1907 the Abbey lost much remaining nationalist support over the performance of J. M. Synge's *Playboy of the Western World*, which was considered an "unmitigated, protracted libel" on Irish country people and inspired riots that have become legendary.[25] As Nicholas Grene has shown, the location of sex and violence in the sacred West of Ireland made *Playboy* particularly offensive to nationalists. The play violated the clear ideological distinctions that required Mayo women's beauty to be nonsexual and Mayo men's violence to be rebellious, not murderous. Both narrative and language offered a "deeply disturbing affront to the middle-class nationalist community whose self-image depended" on clear moral categories.[26] Moreover, the Protestant background of the three Abbey directors (Yeats, Gregory, and—in 1907—Synge) exacerbated the apparent insult: "Coded into that antagonism," writes Grene, "was a subtext of sectarian suspicion."[27]

The Abbey's record was not one of "unmitigated" attacks on church and nation: in *Kathleen ni Houlihan* (1902) Lady Gregory and Yeats had written the most powerful version of the summons to rebellion heard on the Irish stage, a drama Adrian Frazier calls "incendiary folk theatre."[28] And Gregory's *Rising of the Moon* (1907), in which an Irish police sergeant allows a rebel to escape, was so permeated by nationalist ballads it would have warmed the heart of Dr. O'Hickey; during the Black and Tan Terror it was considered seditious.[29] In the 1909 "fight with the Castle," as Lady Gregory styled it later, the Abbey of course staged for the viceroy and his attendant officials the drama of its own cultural independence. But another audience, those Dubliners who, in Yeats's phrase, had "hated *The Playboy of the Western World*," was even more important. With all the publicity it could summon, the Abbey was displaying its nationalism for those ultra-nationalists who remembered the police summoned to eject the *Playboy* rioters and the Trinity students singing "God Save

the King" to drown out the rioters singing "A Nation Once Again."
The controversy was a message for them. To make that message unmistakably clear, the construction of the *Blanco* controversy as an
answer to the *Playboy* controversy is emphasized in Lady Gregory's
book *Our Irish Theatre*. Chapter 4 is called "The Fight over *The Playboy*" and chapter 6 "The Fight with the Castle."

Transported to Ireland, the "American" *Blanco* would take on a
kind of Irish coloration; the nut-shucking of the opening moments
would have to be changed to apple-paring, because Irish nuts were not
ripe in August.[30] Although *Blanco* had not been composed for Irish
performance or for abetting the Abbey's nationalist reputation, the
kinglessness of the frontier world in which Blanco is accepted made
(in Ireland) an implicitly anticolonial statement. But that Shaw
should have been the means by which the Abbey acquired an aura of
nationalist dissidence was hardly predictable. When Gregory first en-
countered Shaw in March 1897, he was responding with confident
hyperbole to a talk on Irish actors given at the Irish Literary Society
in London: "The Irish nation is effete," he announced, "and as to saying there are good Irish actors, there are not, and there won't be until
the conditions in Ireland are favourable for the production of drama—
and when that day comes I hope I may be dead."[31] In 1904 the Abbey
did not produce Shaw's *John Bull's Other Island*, his first Irish play,
because (so its author insisted) the work was hostile to the "neo-
Gaelic movement."[32] An international socialist, Shaw nevertheless
understood the necessity of nationalism: "A healthy nation is as unconscious of its nationality as a healthy man of his bones," he wrote
in one of the many prefaces to *John Bull*. "But if you break a nation's
nationality it will think of nothing else but getting it set again."[33]

In June 1909, however, Gregory and Yeats's *Kathleen ni Houlihan*
softened Shaw up. After a London performance by the Abbey Players,
Shaw said to Lady Gregory, "When I see that play I feel it might lead
a man to do something foolish."[34] She seized the moment, inviting
Shaw to become the third member of the Abbey directorate, joining
herself and Yeats and replacing Synge, who had died in March. Although Shaw did not accept the invitation—*Kathleen* did not lead
him to be that foolish—he did offer the Abbey *Blanco*, which had
been denied the Lord Chamberlain's license only weeks earlier.[35] It
was a brilliant move to contest two sites at once: the banality of the
"blasphemous" passages, once publicized, would reveal the inanity of
the English censor; and a successful performance in Ireland would

dramatize Irish cultural and administrative autonomy. *Blanco* provided precisely what was needed: a play that would offend the censor in England but not the audience in Ireland.[36]

Encounters with the Viceroy

When Dr. O'Hickey was given his final chance to make a statement to their lordships the bishops, he gave his miniature speech from the dock: "Whatever may befall me, I cannot play false to my conscience nor to Ireland." Had he been coached by Lady Gregory in his controversy, he might have avoided martyrdom and survived in good health to serve Ireland in other ways. But in June 1909, while he was making his last stand in Maynooth, she was on tour in England with the Abbey Players, and then visiting Bernard and Charlotte Shaw in Hertfordshire. When Lady Gregory, summoned to Dublin Castle for the first time, confronted authority in the person of the undersecretary, Sir James Dougherty, he began the conversation by saying, "Well?" to which Lady Gregory replied, "Are you going to cut off our heads?" Sir James must not have liked her attitude, because he responded, "This is a very serious business."[37] Throughout the controversy Lady Gregory mocked the Castle's seemingly superior political power, playing the role of rebel in a manner that was taunting but also "very serious." Face to face with the enemy, she was cool, detached, ludic. Lady Gregory and Shaw used the same agonistic metaphors O'Hickey did, but they used them in quotation marks. Whereas O'Hickey seemed to feel, and certainly inspired, all the belligerence of his figures of speech, Gregory flaunted them with a deliberate display of skill. This was not life or death: it was public relations.

Even before Gregory set foot in the Castle, she had begun constructing the controversy in her discourse. At the first hint of some kind of trouble, she wrote Shaw, "Blanco is our best cheval de bataille, and I am glad we had it first." As her phrasing and metaphor make clear, the controversy is not the accidental, secondary, and unfortunate result of the play: the play is the means by which the controversy can be provoked. "It is great fun," she continued,

> the respectable Lord Aberdeen being responsible, especially as he can't come to see it, as vice-royalty doesn't like the colour of our carpets. . . . One of the Belfast papers in its notice that *Blanco* was to be

performed put as a heading "Probable interference of the Lord Lieutenant" but that is too good to be true—we could raise a great cry of
injustice to an illtreated son of Erin if this were done.[38]

And Shaw wrote back, echoing her words and tone:

Your news is almost too good to be true. If the Lord Lieutenant would
only forbid an Irish play, without reading it . . . forbid it at the command of an official of the King's household in London, then the green
flag would indeed wave over Abbey St, and we should have questions
in parliament and all manner of reverberating advertisement and nationalist sympathy for the theatre.[39]

They are talking in quotation marks, using even in private correspondence a discourse designed to associate their opposition to Dublin
Castle with popular nationalism. Later, in mid-controversy, Shaw,
too, began quoting patriotic songs, in this case "The Wearin' o' the
Green." "If we can only fix the suppression of the play on the King,
then 'if the color we must wear be England's cruel red,' we perish gloriously."[40] Shaw's and Gregory's way of perishing gloriously was
different from O'Hickey's: they meant to survive.
    The Abbey patent was not, of course, unconditional. Like patents
for other Dublin theaters, it forbade "profanity or impropriety of language," "indecency of dress," "offensive personalities or representations of living persons," "Exhibition of Wild Beasts," "misrepresentation of sacred characters which may in any degree tend to expose
religion or bring it into contempt," and "anything calculated to produce riot or breach of the peace."[41] What was unique to the Abbey
patent was its specification that the plays produced take up Irish subjects and encourage dramatic art in Ireland. Lady Gregory, as paten-
tee, had the legal responsibility for seeing that the theater abided by
the terms of its patent. The final clause vested power in the lord lieutenant to declare the patent null and void. Theaters in all other cities
in Ireland were under municipal control, but the situation in Dublin
was different: the lord lieutenant, Lord Aberdeen, he of the 1926 joke
collection, had in his hands the power to destroy the Abbey Theatre.
The accidents of Irish theatrical history made it possible for the
Abbey to do what no other theater in Ireland could do: represent its
resistance to censorship as resistance to colonial authority.
    When Lady Gregory wrote Shaw before the first of her visits to
Dublin Castle, the anticipated encounter set off in Shaw's imagina-

tion the possibility of martyrdom—as, indeed, a similar encounter had in O'Hickey's. The visits are morphologically similar: O'Hickey in the chamber of the trustees of Maynooth spoke in the tradition of Robert Emmet or the Manchester Martyrs, and writing his "Statement concerning the Dismissal . . ." he had invoked Saint Joan and Socrates. Anticipating Lady Gregory's visit to Dublin Castle, Shaw wrote her: "Threaten that we shall be suppressed; that we shall be made martyrs of; that we shall suffer as much and as publicly as possible. Tell them that they can depend on me to burn with a brighter blaze and louder yells than all Fox's martyrs."[42] Perhaps a hint of *Saint Joan* (still thirteen years off) lurks in Shaw's metaphor, but the plan of course was not that they actually become martyrs but that they use the idea of martyrdom as a threat. Shaw means that their response to assertions of power will be to stage a media event. All the Gregory–Shaw tropes insist on a contest to be engaged in publicly: "cheval de bataille," "raise a great cry," "the green flag would indeed wave," "all manner of reverberating advertisement." Without the newspaper culture of turn-of-the-century Dublin, this feat would have been impossible. Each move in the game, all the players knew, would be reported daily by nationalist and unionist papers. In fact the undersecretary implied it was the newspapers that got the Castle involved in the first place. "We would not have interfered but what can we do when we see such paragraphs as these," Sir James confided in Lady Gregory, showing her a clipping from the *Irish Times* with the heading, "Have We a Censor?"[43]

And so, in her four encounters with Castle officials, Gregory (accompanied by Yeats, the other Abbey director, on three visits) spoke her lines with the confidence that the private conversations would have public "reverberations." Her detailed records of the conversations make clear that she sought to dramatize as an ideological opposition what the Castle authorities imagined only an anomalous disagreement. Deliberately and playfully transgressive, she indulged in the strategies necessary to discover the extent of her power. Her provocative beginning ("Are you going to cut off our heads?") had been met with a rebuke. At the end of her fourth visit she flaunted a misquotation from Parnell: "Who shall set bounds to the march of a Nation?"[44] While quoting the most famous Irish home-rule leader in the face of the undersecretary for Ireland may not have been quite so daring as, say, citing Bernadette Devlin McAliskey to Margaret Thatcher, the line still had an insubordinate air about it.

Yet both the undersecretary and the lord lieutenant were Home Rulers and Liberals; they did not consider themselves hostile to the more benign forms of Irish nationalism. That a titled Protestant would not be more sensitive to their predicament never ceased to puzzle them. "You have put us in a most difficult and disagreeable position by putting on a play which the English Censor objected to," complained Sir James. And later: "It is very hard on the Lord Lieutenant, you should have had more consideration for him." "It *is* hard on him," answered Gregory, "for he can't please everybody." In their second meeting (August 14) Sir James implored Gregory and Yeats to "save the Lord Lieutenant from this delicate position." As if unaware that he was dealing with a deliberate act of resistance, albeit only cultural, he added, "You defy us, you advertise it under our very nose, at the time everyone is making a fight with the Censor." When Sir James suggested a private performance of the play, and Gregory said Shaw explicitly objected to that course, the undersecretary "moaned, and said, 'it is very hard on us.'" Sir James must have been almost in tears when he pleaded, "Oh, Lady Gregory, appeal to your own common sense." When Gregory, mindful of mentioning the players and their needs, asked to know as soon as possible if the Abbey would lose its patent, so she could find them other employment, Sir James "threw up his hands and said, 'oh my dear lady, but do not speak of such a thing as possible.'" To which Gregory responded, "Why what else have you been threatening all the time?"[45]

The men in the Castle appeared to assume that in spite of her rebelly talk, Lady Gregory—a titled Protestant, after all—was one of their own. Certainly Gregory suggested that class alliances carried some weight when she shared a little joke with Sir James about Redford's stupidities. Citing one of the examiner's sillier objections in the past, she said, "How can we think much of the opinion of a man like that?" And Sir James replied, "I believe he was a Bank Manager." Mr. Redford never knew that his recent conversation with the Joint Select Committee, in fact one of his more direct answers, had constituted part of a minor coded exchange between a "Sir" and a "Lady" who considered themselves his intellectual superiors. Sir James also appeared to believe that Gregory might have some social interest in the Aberdeens, but there he was wrong: "Stay and you will probably see Lady Aberdeen also," he urged Gregory on August 14. Lord Aberdeen's letter to Gregory assumed that women behave in a predictably female way: "Perhaps I may be forgiven for expressing the belief that when, at the first interview with Sir James Dougherty, you indicated a disposition to change the piece, it was an instance of that 'women's wit,' or *instinct*, which somehow seems often the guide to the best course more surely than some of the *processes* which are supposed to be more *regular*, and more characteristic of the other sex."[46] Aberdeen praised female "instinct" at the expense of male rationality to encourage what he wrongly took to be Gregory's compliancy, just as she herself played on a common class background ("How can we think much of the opinion of a man like that?") to encourage in Sir James a supercilious view of the examiner. But the appeal to caste or to gender did not change anyone's mind about the fundamental issue of English authority in Ireland.[47]

The biggest shock to the viceroy must have been Gregory's refusal of his proffered cup of tea. Of sacrifices in the name of Irish independence this one may not rank very high, but its significance lies equally in Gregory's refusal to act respectful and in her use of this unwitnessed nationalist gesture four years later, in her book on the theater. There she says that her "conversation with the King's representative" must be kept secret and that she can "only mention external things":

> Mr. Yeats, until he joined the conference, being kept by the secretary, whether from poetical or political reasons, to the non-committal subject of Spring flowers; . . . the courtesy shown to us and, I think, also by us; the kindly offers of a cup of tea; the consuming desire for that tea after the dust of the railway journey all across Ireland; our heroic refusal, lest its acceptance should in any way, even if it did not weaken our resolve, compromise our principles.[48]

Those "principles" were of course anti-imperialist. The invisible quotation marks around *heroic*, like the snatches of ballads quoted in Gregory's and Shaw's letters, show how Gregory constructed even the smallest gesture of the controversy in imitation of Irish nationalist resistance. Here she maintained an unrecorded tradition of refusing to drink imperialist beverages, a custom also followed by Constance Markievicz, who would not drink the king's health with her sister Mabel's British in-laws, and (much later, in 1948) John Costello, the Taoiseach, who refused to drink the king's health in Ottawa because the Canadian government had forgotten to toast the health of the president of Ireland.[49] Gregory knew intuitively the kind of gesture to make and to cite in allying herself with popular nationalism.

At the same time, in the same conversations, the representatives of the state attempted to ally themselves with the Abbey Theatre. In their tacit emphasis on allegiance to class as a means of solving the absurd bureaucratic mess the silly London censor had got them in, the Castle officials represented poor Aberdeen as a censor *malgré lui* and, indeed, a theatrical sort of person himself. If Lady Gregory played Hamlet in the court of King Claudius, using the theater as a site of resistance, then as the pathetic agent of the king, Lord Aberdeen was a reincarnation of Polonius. "My lord, you played once i' th' university, you say?" Hamlet asks Polonius, who answers, "That I did, my lord, and was accounted a good actor." Aberdeen protested to Gregory, "You must not think I am a sour faced Puritan, I am very interested in the drama. In fact at Oxford it was often said that that would be my line. My Grandfather also, though considered so strict, went so far as to take a part in plays under a pseudonym. So you see I have a great deal of sympathy with you." The week before, Sir James had defended the viceroy to Lady Gregory along similar lines: "He is a supporter of the drama. He was one of Sir Henry Irving's pall bearers." Lady Gregory's genius compelled a Home-Rule, theater-loving lord lieutenant to threaten the theater and defend the king. Trapped between the state apparatus he did not fully support and the dissident artists amused by his feeble attempts to sympathize, the viceroy felt obliged to prevent the performance of *Blanco,* he said, only "because of the courtesies of officials toward one another; and I as the King's representative cannot go against the King."[50]

In the midst of all this moaning and groaning and dear-ladying and offering of cups of tea and theatrical reminiscing by Aberdeen and Dougherty, Gregory tried to find out the precise nature of their authority, something they did not know themselves. The threat conveyed by the crown solicitor at the Castle to Gregory's solicitor, Dr. David Moore, had been strongly worded: the lord lieutenant was "entirely opposed to the play being proceeded with and would use every power the law gave him to stop it." When Gregory asked, "May I be told on what clause of the Patent we are to be suppressed?" Aberdeen read "passages against indecency, blasphemy and disorder but could not say on which count we were charged, except that there was one against riot being stirred up, and he thought there might be a riot." As Gregory pointed out, the previous Abbey riots had been caused by radical nationalist organizations, especially Sinn Féin, and Sinn Féin had this time explicitly requested its members not to "play the Castle game" by inciting a riot.[51]

By August 20 the nature of Dublin Castle's authority became clear, when the testimony of the chief clerk of the Irish Office before the Joint Select Committee was reported in the *Times* of London. Sir James had asked the clerk, Thomas LeFanu, to "steer clear" of all discussion of *Blanco*, but that topic was precisely what the committee members wanted to hear about. The starchy Lord Newton asked, "In the case of the play which it is intended to produce during Horse Show week, there is nothing to prevent that play being produced, whether the Lord Lieutenant approves of it or not?" And LeFanu answered, "I think no legal steps could be taken. Unless it is done in a friendly way I think there would be no power to stop production."[52]

While the Abbey directors were happily anticipating a media event, deciding to "die gloriously" if they forfeited the patent, the Castle officials suffered a more gentlemanly anxiety about the exposure of viceregal interventions. Sir James thought for a moment that the Abbey would politely postpone the production until after the Joint Select Committee had finished its hearings, but he misunderstood his opponents:

> GREGORY: Of course we should have to announce at once that it was in consequence of the threatened action of the Castle we had postponed it.
> SIR JAMES: Oh you really don't mean that, you would let all the bulls loose, it would be much better not to say anything at all or to say the rehearsals took longer than you expected.
> GREGORY: The public announcement will be more to our advantage.
> SIR JAMES: Oh that is dreadful.[53]

When, at their last meeting—just before Parnell was introduced into the conversation—Sir James uttered his final threat, that the Abbey "would be just as much attacked as [we] would whatever happened," Gregory taunted him in French: "après vous." The second language of the educated Anglo-Irish elite was used in the service of the *cheval de bataille*.

The public positioning of state and artists gave the Abbey the opportunity to represent itself as a citadel of resistance. The Castle authorities began this process with their August 20 letter to the Abbey, released to the press (along with Gregory's private response to the letter) and published in the Dublin *Evening Telegraph* and numerous other papers. The letter reiterated that *Blanco* violated the terms of the original patent by not being Irish enough and that "His Excellency . . . has arrived at the conclusion that in its original form the play is not in accordance with the conditions and restrictions contained in the Patent as granted by the Crown." Apparently His Excellency also felt bound to "call your attention . . . to the serious consequences which the production of the play in its original form might entail," and he would regret taking any action that "might result in depriving the Society, that has already done good work for Irish dramatic art, of the means of prosecuting a worthy enterprise."[54] The unionist *Irish Times* termed this a "precautionary notice." If the first performance of *Blanco Posnet* "leads to an immediate disturbance, or is followed by any public complaints of a representative character, His Excellency will be in the position of having forewarned the company of any action which he may think it necessary to take."[55]

Now the Abbey directorate could "blaze" and "yell" and wave the green flag. The public display of nationalism was, after all, the whole purpose of the controversy for Gregory and Yeats. "If our Patent is in danger," their statement began,

> it is because the English censorship is being extended to Ireland, or because the Lord Lieutenant is about to revive, on what we consider a frivolous pretext, a right not exercised for 150 years, to forbid at his pleasure any play produced in any Dublin theatre, all these theatres having their Patent from him. We are not concerned with the question of English censorship, but we are very certain that the conditions of the two countries are different, and that we must not by accepting the English censor's ruling, give away anything of the liberty of the Irish theatre of the future.[56]

To speak of "the Irish theatre of the future" was to talk, if not altogether to think, like Patrick Pearse at St. Enda's school, opened only a year earlier, where all classes were taught in the Irish language; or like Constance Markievicz with her Fianna, advertising that very August for boys "willing to work for the independence of Ireland"; or like Eoin MacNeill and O'Hickey arguing for Irish to be required for entrance to the new National University. The institutions of an independent Ireland were emerging in the rhetoric and bravado of 1909.[57]

Behind the rhetoric, in their private conversations, Gregory and Yeats had determined, like O'Hickey, that they could not play false to their consciences or to Ireland. From her solicitor Gregory learned that the penalty for putting on a play despite an official order to desist was £300. Believing that they were about to receive an order "forbidding the performance of the play," the Abbey directors had to decide what to do. A few sentences in *Our Irish Theatre* offer a brief glimpse of Yeats and Gregory, walking through the Dublin streets at night, confronting the fact that they might lose their theater:

> We knew that we should, if . . . this threat were carried out, lose not only the Patent but that the few hundred pounds that we had been able to save and with which we could have supported our players till they found other work, would be forfeited. This thought of the players made us waver, and very sadly we agreed that we must give up the fight. We did not say a word of this at the Abbey but went on rehearsing as usual. When we had left the Theatre and were walking through the lamp-lighted streets, we found that during those two or three hours our minds had come to the same decision, that we had given our word, that at all risks we must keep it or it would never be trusted again.[58]

Their genius was to light on just the right public discourse—"the Irish theatre of the future"—to link their own quarrel with the larger national quarrel. Their luck was that, as LeFanu had said in London earlier that very day, the lord lieutenant "had no power to stop the production."

This was Shaw's controversy too, of course, and the nature of his grievance was different. His responses to the episode as it unfolded did not have the populist ring of Lady Gregory's. In phrases like "the Saxon tyrant," his quotation marks are darker and stronger. Ever the intransigent subject but not the people's representative, Shaw responded as one personally attacked, ridiculing and embarrassing the Castle officials. (He did not receive a signed copy of *Tell Me Another* in 1926.) Although he was on holiday in the west of Ireland at the time, he insisted on staying away from Dublin, participating exclusively through the printed word. The Castle's "precautionary notice" had been published along with a letter from Gregory to Sir James stating that certain passages in *Blanco* had been removed "in deference to His Excellency's opinion."[59] Gregory had (with Shaw's permission) agreed to delete the phrase "immoral relations" but balked when Aberdeen suggested that the phrase "dearly beloved brethren" might "offend the susceptibilities of the Church of Ireland." We must, she argued, "have some respect for our audience and not treat them as babies."[60] Gregory considered the change a mere sop to the viceroy, but the word "deference" was too much for the author. "The play," Shaw announced in a letter written to Yeats for distribution to the Dublin papers,

> will now be given exactly as written by the author without concessions of any kind to the attacks that have been made upon it, except that to oblige the Lord Lieutenant I have consented to withdraw the word "immoral" as applied to the relations between a woman of bad character and her accomplices. In doing so I wish it to be stated that I still regard those relations as not only immoral but vicious; nevertheless, as the English Censorship apparently regards them as delightful and exemplary, and the Lord Lieutenant does not wish to be understood as contradicting the English Censorship, I am quite content to leave the relations to the unprompted judgment of the Irish people. . . . in point of consideration for the religious belief of the Irish people the play compares favorably with the Coronation Oath.[61]

Naturally this move required one to counter it. In an interview Lord Aberdeen was questioned about the deletion of the word "immoral": " 'The sentence', said His Excellency, with the slightest touch of temper, 'in Mr. Shaw's letter on the matter is an absurd and rather gross misrepresentation of my views regarding this particular feature of the play.' " The interview, originally printed in the *Evening Telegraph*, was copied by the *Irish Times*. But the next day, underneath a letter from Lady Gregory in the *Irish Times*, the following item was printed: "The Reported Interview with the Lord Lieutenant: We are requested to state that the report of an alleged interview with the Lord Lieutenant in reference to Mr. Shaw's play is entirely unauthorized."[62] His Excellency apparently regretted displaying that "slightest touch of temper," and the *Irish Times* respectfully (but tardily) attempted to deprive the whole exchange of validity. With such a wonderful controversy, who could need a play? With Gregory hammering away at "English censorship" and "Irish theatre," and Shaw hitting the members of Parliament and the viceroy with the word "immoral," newspaper readers could see an exciting drama unfolding in the papers every day, artists fighting the government for the sake of revolutionary social changes.

"They are defying the Lord Lieutenant"

Revolutionary social changes can, on occasion, be constructed of un-likely materials. The simple political binarisms of the discourse Gre-gory and Shaw had chosen to use, the deliberately provocative sound bites, did not fit precisely the more complex social reality of the events so represented. The discourse of the *Blanco* controversy came from Young Ireland, from *The Spirit of the Nation,* from the Fenians, from the books that Dr. O'Hickey and the young Augusta Persse read. But the audience for the play was in large part composed of people so "West Briton" that they were unionist. "There is very heavy book-ing," the Abbey secretary reported to Lady Gregory a few days before the opening night. "First class people, a great many from the Cas-tle!"[63] When Sir James warned Gregory that "Dublin society will call out against us if we let it go on," she could reply, "Lord Iveagh has taken six places." What, Dublin's richest unionist? Impossible: "For that play?" Sir James asked in amazement.[64] Of course that was the audience required; Lord Iveagh and five friends were not likely to throw potatoes or stinkbombs at the actors or cause a riot. A good-mannered audience was what was needed.

The audience was put together with as much care as the play itself. The play had been written for the sake of provoking an English con-troversy; its Irish production had been designed to provoke an Irish controversy; and a particular kind of audience was required to show up the viceroy, the examiner, the Lord Chamberlain, and the king, the whole silly decaying royal apparatus of containment. Shaw em-ployed the Fabian technique of "permeation," by which one or two members of a powerful corporate body are befriended and encouraged to influence their associates. He enlisted the aid of his friends Gilbert Murray, Regius Professor of Greek at Oxford, and his wife, Lady Mary Murray. Gilbert Murray's supportive letter, which Shaw passed on to Lady Gregory, read in part:

> This is perfectly monstrous about the Dublin Castle officials: fla-grantly unjust to you and insulting to the intelligence of those who have any serious interest in Literature and Drama. I think, and my

wife, whose tastes are severe, agrees with me, that the condemnation of Blanco Posnet is one of the most utterly unintelligent things in Redford's record.[65]

After the successful first performance Shaw wrote Murray,

> You have contributed very materially to the Dublin victory. The real point at issue was not the liberty of the stage or the merits of Blanco, but whether Lady Lyttelton, the wife of the Generalissimo, would come with her party. The fate of the Castle hung on that; and Lady L. at first said she could not possibly bring her young people to a wicked play or bring a blush to the cheek of the military. An unscrupulous use of your letter and Lady Mary's verdict decided the struggle. I sent the letter to Lady Gregory; Lady Gregory planked it down confidentially on Lady L's dressing table; and Lady L. took her Bible & hymnbook and brought her whole flock to the play with military honors. Down came the Castle flag; Charlotte was overwhelmed with invitations to the Vice Regal Lodge.[66]

Lady Lyttelton was the wife of General Sir Neville Lyttelton, commander in chief of British forces in Ireland, the man who would be charged with putting down the kind of rebellion present in Lady Gregory's metaphors. Her presence at such a daring event was even more significant than Shaw mentions: one of the victims of the notorious 1882 Phoenix Park murders in Dublin, Lord Frederick Cavendish, had been married to Sir Neville Lyttelton's sister Lucy. The Murray ménage offered the perfect team to bring the state over to the side of the artists, because *she* was the Earl of Carlisle's daughter, and an Earl of Carlisle had been viceroy of Ireland in the mid-nineteenth century; and *he* was a playwright, translator, and professor at Oxford (where, as we know, Lord Aberdeen's acting career did not quite get off the ground). In a letter written several months later, making the case that Gilbert Murray should be invited to membership in the Dramatists' Club, Shaw argued on the basis of "the social influence he has through his marriage with Lady Mary." The connection with an earl's daughter, Shaw emphasized, would "attach us to that big nerve system of the general social world."[67] Of course Lady Gregory was also part of that "big nerve system," and the few degrees of separation from Lady Mary to Lady Gregory to Lady Lyttelton helped the most radical dramatist of the day show up the lord chamberlain and helped

the Abbey make a statement of nationalist defiance. The Abbey Theatre on the night of August 25, 1909, seems to have been filled with
people observing the audience: were not they more important than
the play? The Abbey's patent, after all, depended on their behavior.
Walking through those lamp-lit streets five days earlier, Gregory and
Yeats had decided to risk the patent, the theater's whole future, for
the sake of fidelity to the players and to the nationalist principles on
which the Abbey was founded. The audience that saved the theater
constituted, in fact, the theater that night. Joseph Holloway, the
Abbey architect and Dublin's most faithful playgoer, noted the buzz:
the actresses Sarah Allgood and Maire Walker had "caught the excitement as well as everyone else and wondered what the night would
bring forth." A crowd was assembling outside before the doors
opened, and

> many sought admission in vain and lingered on all the night about the
> Vestibule in the hopes of getting in. . . . The people came pouring in
> from the time the doors were opened. All artistic, literary and social
> Dublin passed in a rapid succession . . . John McCormack . . . George
> Russell ('AE') . . . William Orpen . . . Sheehy Skeffington . . . Mrs.
> Shaw, W. B. Yeats, Lady Gregory, R. Gregory . . . Lords and ladies were
> present a galore, and many "nice people with nasty ideas" had come
> on the off chance of hearing and seeing something strongly unpleas-
> ant. These were doomed to disappointment as Shaw's play proved a
> sort of sermon set in vivid melodramatic frame.[68]

It was an event produced by hype and inspiring further hype. Lily
Yeats attended the play with her brother Jack and sister-in-law Cottie
and saw outside "such a crowd—motors, Cabs, carriages police & a
big buzzing crowd of onlookers." She had been asked to save a fourth
seat for Shaw's aunt, but "Willy came & whispered Shaws Aunt is so
intoxicated that Mrs. Shaw will not let her out of the house." At
Willy's request, Lily gave the extra seat to Lord Dunsany, one of those
many "lords and ladies" noted by Holloway.[69]

The curtain-raiser was Gregory and Yeats's *Kathleen ni Houlihan*,
and Lily noted that "a lady near us broke down at the end & sobbed."
Probably it was not Lady Lyttelton, but obviously *Kathleen* was intended to rub some of its nationalism onto *Blanco Posnet*. Lord Iveagh
and his six, Lord Dunsany, and Lady Lyttelton and her flock applauded
a play dramatizing the apotheosis of nationalist sacrifice before they

FORBIDDEN IN ENGLAND, PRODUCED IN IRELAND.
BERNARD SHAW'S "THE SHOWING UP OF BLANCO POSNET," AT THE ABBEY THEATRE, DUBLIN.

3.4. Scenes from the first production of Shaw's *The Shewing-up of Blanco Posnet*. According to Lily Yeats, the performance on opening night "went with great go all through and got a great reception." The original captions identify the photos: "(1) the trial of Blanco Posnet for horse-stealing: the scene in the primitive court-house. (2) Mr. Fred O'Donovan as Blanco Posnet, and Miss Sarah Allgood as Feemy Evans. (3) Mr. Fred O'Donovan as Blanco Posnet, and Mr. Arthur Sinclair as Elder Daniels. (4) Blanco addressing the crowd in the court-house: 'I'm for the great game every time.'" Photo credit: Dan H. Laurence Collection, Archival and Special Collections, McLaughlin Library, University of Guelph. Photo by Lafayette. The original copy is in the National Library of Ireland.

applauded a play banned by the Lord Chamberlain. *Blanco* "went with great go all through and got a great reception," wrote Lily to her father. "The English press men made a bolt for the door where the post-office had messengers waiting to take the telegrams."[70]

Like Holloway and Lily Yeats, Lady Gregory was also observing the audience, and she appropriates their behavior for her controversy:

> The play began, and till near the end it was received in perfect silence. Perhaps the audience were waiting for the wicked parts to begin. Then, at the end, there was a tremendous burst of cheering, and we knew we had won. Some stranger outside asked, what was going on in the Theatre. "They are defying the Lord Lieutenant" was the answer; and when the crowd heard the cheering, they took it up and it went far out through the streets.[71]

"Defying" may seem a hyperbolic or even a romantic word to use, when all the lord lieutenant did was bluff and issue a "precautionary notice." And were the lords and ladies really "defying" or simply happily applauding the inoffensive end of Horse Show week's most notorious event? But "You defy us," Sir James had complained to Lady Gregory, and in the context of the Abbey's defiant press releases the performance constituted genuine resistance to attempted censorship. In Gregory's description, the crowd in the streets, those people who had not even seen the play, participate vicariously in defying the lord lieutenant. When they start cheering, the defiance shifts from the stage to the streets. The applause of the stylish audience gets transformed into the seditious cheers of the crowd outside, and it is not the end of the play but the Abbey's triumph in the controversy that is being cheered. "Glorious reception splendid victory where is the censor now," read Gregory and Yeats's telegram to Shaw, a message they naturally shared with the *Irish Independent*.[72]

After the performance, Gregory continued to construct the event in Young Ireland style: what is political resistance without a ballad? She wrote Shaw that she had been "teaching our actresses tonight the old song of 'The Lower Castle Yard,'" a ballad about a nationalist "bard" of the 1850s, Jimmy Nugent, whose political poems involve him in trouble with Dublin Castle officials.[73] After a trial in which he is found innocent, the man prints poems that get his enemies removed from office. Although the ballad (in a version printed in the *Irish Times* in 1915) shows the power of literature to create commotion and ruin political careers, it also shows the beginning of a beautiful friendship between the lord lieutenant and the poet:

> His lays they banished Eglinton
>   And tore Lord Derby down.
> Far, far from town, their grief to drown,
>   They took to drinking hard.
> While he tuk tay with Lord Carlyle
>   In the Upper Castle Yard.[74]

The realignments of power are such that the poet is invited to the Castle, where (unlike Lady Gregory) he drinks tea with the viceroy. And this viceroy was actually the great-uncle of Lady Mary Murray, whose approval of *Blanco* had served to link Dublin Castle society with defiant writers on this occasion. The ballad was in fact originally sung by its author, "Dr. Nedley," "at a dinner given in the Castle by Lord Carlisle, and was the means of procuring for its author the appointment of medical officer to the Dublin Metropolitan Police Force."[75] Lady Gregory celebrated the successful defiance of the lord lieutenant's threats with a ballad composed to gain the favor of an earlier holder of the office.

The triumphalist atmosphere, the jolly song, and the rebelly activity of ballad-singing obscured the many social connections between the opponents in the controversy: after all, Sir William Gregory, Lady Gregory's late husband, had been born in the undersecretary's lodge in Phoenix Park because his grandfather was undersecretary at the time. Yet the stark opposition made possible by the peculiarities of the laws governing theaters did not require permanent enmity; George Alexander Redford was not important enough to destroy Dublin Castle society. Lord and Lady Aberdeen were present at a dance given by Sir Neville and Lady Lyttelton on August 27.[76]

Once the theater had been liberated from the English censor and the Irish viceroy, the incident itself became contested, as a new series of press releases, editorials, and letters set differing ideological spins on the event. When the Abbey protested (this time in the Dublin *Evening Mail*) "against the grave anxiety and annoyance we have been put to by the endeavour to force an incompetent and irrelevant Censorship upon Ireland," one J. R. A. Moore responded in the *Irish Times*.[77] Yeats and Gregory, he pointed out, had "the privilege of producing, before crowded houses, a play which, in ordinary circum-

3.5. Dublin 1909 during Horse Show week. From the *Irish Times,* August 23, 1909. The advertisement for the first performance of *Blanco* appears on the same page as the notice of a ball (to be held the same night) patronized by the lord lieutenant and his wife, the Countess of Aberdeen. Reproduced by permission of the *Irish Times.*

stances, would have been produced before crowded houses else-where."[78] Moore was right: attempted censorship proved lucrative to its intended victims. With sold-out houses and renewed nationalist support, the Abbey did well. "It is a pity we had not thought in time of putting up our prices," remarked Gregory in her history of the the-ater.[79] The *Irish Times*, which had earlier called the play "the dra-matic event of the season," now blamed the Castle officials for allow-ing themselves "to fall into the trap so cunningly set for their unwary feet." The whole business had been an economic ploy, they main-tained, and as revenge the paper recommended that the censorship be strengthened by the addition of more and better play-readers and be extended to Ireland.[80]

The international array of reviewers that attended the opening night responded with counter-hype. "Nothing more flimsy can be imagined," wrote the young James Joyce, reviewing for the Trieste paper *Il Piccolo della Sera*, "and the playgoer asks himself why on earth the play was interdicted by the censor."[81] The *Irish Times* re-viewer pretended to be disappointed by the absence of the "dreadful things" he had been hearing about: "Last night we always seemed on the point of getting to these things but they never actually arrived."[82] In his journal Holloway noted that "all the audience at its conclusion wondered only why the censor vetoed it and put the bad name on it."[83]

Construction of the episode varied from colony to imperial power. Yeats wrote his father the gossip he had heard, that " 'no one at the Castle spoke to any other on that subject', it was too painful."[84] But the English did not seem overly distressed. At a dinner party given by Edmund Gosse in November 1909, Yeats was seated next to Prime Minister Asquith. "I see you've had a lively time over Shaw's play," observed Asquith to Yeats, "and that the state of things is so perfect in Dublin that we need not bring it under the censorship."[85] The episode did not stand in the way of the state's patronage of an Irish artist: within a year Yeats was offered a civil-list pension of £150 a year. His responses in interviews during the controversy had been tactful and banal: "The Irish public and the English public are alto-gether different. A play objectionable in one country is not objection-able in the other. The religions of the countries are different and the national characteristics of the countries are different."[86] This caution paid off: Yeats managed to defy the king's representative and to be awarded a pension from the king's privy purse. The after-hype of the

Blanco controversy may have helped Gilbert Murray's career also. Around the time Yeats was dining with Asquith, Shaw was writing to the playwright Arthur Pinero urging that Murray be invited to join the Dramatists' Club. That "big nerve system of the general social world" was actually (then as now) based on mutual need: politicians and aristocrats needed the glamour of artists as much as the artists needed the patronage and glamour of the powerful.

Over in France the militant nationalist Maud Gonne, not knowing of the pension to come, wrote to Yeats praising the radicalism of the whole gesture: "Delighted that you have made the viceroy ridiculous," she wrote days after the event, "& that once more you are at heart with our people. . . . At last the Abbey theatre has been definitely against the English government in Ireland." Gonne was also pleased that "German papers sent correspondents" so that it could be "known abroad that in art as well as politics Ireland is separate & distinct from England & ready to defy her on all occasions."[87]

The Legacy of *Blanco Posnet*

As the controversy around *Blanco* became one in the lengthening sequence of Abbey controversies, it formed part of a tradition that could be drawn on, used, and invoked to shape other controversies. T. S. Eliot says of literary tradition that it is "modified by the introduction of the new . . . work of art," and that the "complete meaning" of any subsequent literary work depends in part on its relation to tradition.[88] So with controversies. The dominant element in the legacy of the *Blanco* controversy seemed to be the idea that a truly delightful fracas could be engaged in, to the honor of playwrights and the embarrassment of officials. Shaw's composition of *O'Flaherty V.C.* in 1915 was inspired, or rather driven, by both the *Playboy* and *Blanco* controversies. It was his hope to have the physical violence of the one and the moral victory of the other, with the grand publicity of both.

Not only, then, was the controversy not secondary to the play: the play was clearly secondary to the mother of all controversies, which Shaw evidently desired. Designing a deliberately provocative play, Shaw wrote competitively against Synge, hoping for riots in the theater. The play's subject is an Irishman home on leave from the Great War, and Shaw wrote to Lady Gregory, "The picture of the Irish character will make the Playboy seem a patriotic rhapsody by comparison." Expecting the actor Arthur Sinclair to play the lead, Shaw wrote, "Sinclair must be prepared for brickbats." The play was set at Coole, and Shaw wrote Lady Gregory, "The scene is quite simply before the porch of your house." According to Shaw's summary of the plot, "The idea is that O'Flaherty's experience in the trenches has induced in him a terrible realism and an unbearable candor. He sees Ireland as it is, his mother as she is, his sweetheart as she is; and he goes back to the dreaded trenches joyfully for the sake of peace and quietness."[89] No doubt to ensure a good healthy riot, the script featured insults to many categories of people: landlords, women, Irish nationalists, and English patriots.

Shaw also anticipated a replay of the *Blanco* controversy: in the same letter he said of the play, "At worst, it will be a barricade for the theatre to die gloriously on." In a letter to Yeats he wrote, "It is by no means sure that it will be licensed in England; and a few preliminary trials in Dublin might do no harm."[90] Shaw's happy vision was of the completely offensive play, offensive to audiences and to civil and military authorities, and commotion everywhere, audiences rioting, Dublin Castle issuing threats, with Lady Gregory calm, smiling, and defiant throughout it all. Purporting nonetheless to believe that his play might be construed as part of the war effort, a patriotic gesture, Shaw subtitled it *A Recruiting Pamphlet* and wrote to Yeats, "It is written so as to appeal very strongly to that love of adventure and desire to see the wider world and escape from the cramping parochialism of Irish life which is more helpful to recruiting than all the silly placards about Belgium and the like."[91] After the first performance was announced, however, in November 1915, Dublin Castle intervened in the person of Undersecretary Sir Matthew Nathan, suggesting that the play be postponed. While all this was going on, Lady Gregory was in America with the Abbey Players, and Yeats wrote her that when he told Shaw they wouldn't fight the issue, "Shaw, I thought, was disappointed. He said, if Lady Gregory was in London, she would fight it, but added afterwards, that he didn't really want us to but thought you would do it out of love of mischief. I told him that was a misunderstanding of your character."[92]

Sir Matthew Nathan's letters make clear that it was precisely the license of controversy that Dublin Castle did not want. In 1915 recruitment in Ireland was not going very well, and the last thing in the world the civil and military authorities wanted was a riot in a theater on that account and a long newspaper debate kept alive by Shavian

provocation. Politely Nathan suggested that it would be better for all
parties involved if the play were withdrawn: "The representation of
this play at the present moment would result in demonstrations
which could do no good either to the Abbey Theatre or to the cause
that at any rate a large section of Irishmen have made their own."[93]
Outside of Dublin, aside from rumors that the play had been suppressed under the Defence of the Realm Act and a few newspaper interviews with Shaw, there was no public debate: the controversy had
been suppressed as well as the play. The first performance of the play
actually took place at the western front in 1917, with Robert Loraine
(Robert Gregory's commanding officer) in the title role; Robert Gregory played O'Flaherty's mother. On the actual field of battle, it was
beyond controversy.

After the creation of the Irish Free State and the consequent disappearance of the office of viceroy, it might seem that the sequence of
Abbey controversies of which *Blanco Posnet* formed a part had ended,
and that theatrical controversies in post-Treaty Ireland constituted an
entirely new sequence. Certainly the dynamic of the controversy surrounding Sean O'Casey's *The Plough and the Stars* was quite different, involving as it did not official censorship from a corporate body
but strong popular feeling, especially women's feeling, about the Rising. Any student of later Irish culture knows, however, that censorship did not stop with the Government of Ireland Act. The 1923 Censorship of Films Act and the 1929 Censorship of Publications Act,
and the presence of a government representative on the board of the
Abbey Theatre (by then the official National Theatre), more than
made up for the absence of the bumbling Lord Aberdeen and the pow-
erless Sir James Dougherty. And given the enormous authority of
John Charles McQuaid, the notoriously conservative Catholic archbishop of Dublin between 1940 and 1974, "a clerical nod was as good
as a wink," as Christopher Murray puts it.[94] The Dublin Theatre Festival of 1958 was killed entirely not because of any law or any public
debate about the merits of the plays, but because McQuaid simply refused to say the Votive Mass to open the festival. So much for
O'Casey's *Drums of Father Ned*, which was to have been performed
there—the play, it might be added, that was dedicated to Dr.
O'Hickey's friends Dr. Walter McDonald and Father Michael Flanagan. The accidents of theater law had made the *Blanco* controversy
take the form of nationalist resistance, but in fact the form of the

censorship conflict as Shaw saw it, the struggle between "immoral" writers and the state, proved more enduring.

The 1957 controversy over Alan Simpson's production of *The Rose Tattoo* by Tennessee Williams at the Pike during the Dublin Theatre Festival resembles the *Blanco Posnet* controversy morphologically to some extent and provides a glimpse of what *Blanco* might have looked like in a later Ireland. A play morally conventional and even religious, sanctioning faithful married love, caught the attention of the unsophisticated because of a detail that seemed naughty. *The Rose Tattoo* was objected to by the League of Decency because a contraceptive is dropped on the stage. Like Shaw's phrase "immoral relations," the dropped contraceptive does not function as an encouragement to sexual promiscuity: when the heroine, a Sicilian widow, sees the horrid thing, she "screams and abuses" the man who has dropped it. And also like Shaw's phrase, the contraceptive was in fact absent from the play: the Pike was unable to get one in either the Republic of Ireland or Northern Ireland, and the homemade substitutes they tried to use could not be properly kicked as required by the script. "Not dropping a non-existent condom might seem like a minor offense," as Chris Morash writes.[95] Nevertheless, the device was assumed to be on the stage, seeming (according to the League) to advocate "the use of birth control by unnatural means."[96]

Although the play received enthusiastic reviews, the festival patrons—the lord mayor of Dublin, Fianna Fáil, and Minister for Lands Erskine Childers—and the theater's producer, Lord Longford, all withdrew their support. Simpson was arrested and granted bail, and the play continued; one night Brendan Behan appeared in the audience and sang rebel songs. Refusing, like Lady Gregory and Yeats, to cease production, Simpson was tried for producing an indecent play. When the counsel for the state asked the prosecuting garda, "At this juncture in the play, was any object dropped on the stage?" the policeman said (in Hugh Leonard's transcription), "No. Dere was nothing dropped. But it was my dishtinct impression dat it was a contraceptive dat wasn't dropped." Although the High Court decided against Simpson, on appeal the case was returned to the Dublin district court, which found that the play had not been indecent.[97] But the Pike Theatre was ultimately ruined by the case: better to have as enemies the ineffective bureaucracy of Dublin Castle in its twilight than the police and the League of Decency in an independent Ireland.[98]

Viewed from the perspective of the suppression of O'Casey's "anti-clerical" play and the attempted suppression of the "indecent" *Rose Tattoo*, the *Blanco* controversy can be said to anticipate the struggle against theatrical censorship in post-Treaty Ireland. In their struggle with the viceroy, Gregory and Yeats were clearing a space and setting a precedent for the struggles of later Irish artists against the state. They were fortunate enough to win precisely because the enemy in their case could be identified with the colonial oppressor; they were able to get sympathy and support for the Abbey because they could make use of all those Young Ireland tropes. They could wave the green flag, threaten martyrdom, and have a grand time playing at being rebels. They were able to produce a play ridiculously charged with "blasphemy" and "indecency" because they could invoke "the liberty of the Irish theatre of the future" and claim the battle against censorship as a rebel's stand. In the independent Dublin of the 1950s, when that future was actually the present, the men and women of the theater did not have the same opportunity.

4

Hunger and Hysteria

The "Save the Dublin Kiddies" Campaign,
October–November 1913

Aithnítear an duine ar a dhéirc.
The person is known by the alms.

"ALLEGED KIDNAPPING" was the headline in the *Freeman's Journal* of October 28, 1913. A "respectably dressed" woman of forty-two, Kate Burke, had been charged with abducting ten-year-old Mary Barrett. Oddly enough, Mary had run home to tell her father that she had been kidnapped. In the presence of a magistrate, the father acknowledged that Miss Burke had not taken Mary. "And the only evidence you have is that the child told you she caught her by the arm?" "Yes," said Mr. Barrett. "It is a ridiculous charge, your worship," said Mr. Brady, for the defendant. "The woman lives with an invalid sister in the city, and was on the way to see one of the priests in Church Street. Barrett rushed out of a side street with a crowd of howling women after him, and frightened the life out of the poor woman. She never saw the child before. I think some people are going kidnapping mad." The magistrate agreed, dismissing the charge and remarking "that a sort of insanity was prevalent in the city at present."[1]

So indeed it was: many more than one person went "kidnapping mad." A barrister involved in another kidnapping case thought it sounded like something out of Gilbert and Sullivan.[2] A letter to the *Irish Times* advised that if "you are an old gentleman, and want to take your grandchild down to the country for a few days, you had better apply for police protection, if you do not want to be surrounded by a howling mob."[3] It was almost impossible to leave Dublin with a child in tow. Concerned that a charitable campaign organized by English socialists was a Protestant proselytizing scheme, Archbishop William Walsh had warned the "Catholic mothers of Dublin" not to part with their children "without security that those to whom the poor children are to be handed over are Catholics, or indeed persons of any faith at all."[4] Thus inspired, parish priests and mobs of supporters prowled the railway stations and docks, ready to rescue Catholic Irish children from the arms of the women who thought they were rescuing them from starvation, packing them off for a "holiday" with English families who would feed them. Helping a father put his own sons on the train at Dublin's Kingsbridge station, Frank Sheehy Skeffington, the noted journalist and pacifist, was beaten and stripped by an angry mob shouting, "Kill him! Kill him!"

All this hysteria formed part of the "Save the Dublin Kiddies" campaign, the episode that "raised the wildest emotions" of any during the five-month strike and lockout of the Irish Transport and General Workers Union, led by the labor organizer Jim Larkin.[5] The terrible poverty of Dublin, already the worst in Europe, grew worse during the strike: by October about 25,000 men were on strike and one-quarter of the city's population without regular income. The members of the ITGWU had gone on strike on August 26, 1913, in support of a hundred of its members locked out by William Martin Murphy's Dublin United Tramways Company. Over the weekend of Saturday, August 30, and Sunday, August 31, police baton charges killed two men and injured hundreds of others. By the end of September other unions had joined the strike. Larkin, arrested in early September for "sedition and conspiracy," was soon released and traveled to England, where he addressed huge gatherings about the Dublin strike.[6] At a meeting in London's Royal Albert Hall on October 10, Dora Montefiore (1851–1933), an active socialist, suffragist, and feminist who was also on the platform, heard "what straits the workers and their families were in, after seven weeks of slow starvation."[7] Montefiore did not let the grass grow under her feet: still listening to the speeches, she passed Larkin a note seeking his approval for her idea to board children of the striking workers with socialist families in England. She was said to have been inspired by a similar project organized by Margaret Sanger the previous year during the textile workers' strike in Lawrence, Massachusetts.[8] With his blessing, she set to work the very next day publicizing her campaign through the socialist paper the

Daily Herald, and by October 13 she already had over 110 offers of room and board for the "kiddies."

When, only ten days later, the plan was put into effect in Dublin, the ensuing hysteria took Montefiore and her helpers completely by surprise. Over a period of several days, beginning on October 22, outraged priests and angry mobs recruited by the Ancient Order of Hibernians grabbed many of the children from the hands of the social workers washing them at the Tara Street baths; pulled others off boats at the North Wall of the Liffey or off trains at Kingsbridge station; attacked anyone attempting to leave Dublin with a child; and marched triumphantly along the quays singing "Faith of Our Fathers" after each day's successful "rescues." Although eighteen children made it to Liverpool, plans for getting three hundred more out of Dublin were abandoned. Montefiore and her principal helper, the American Lucilla Rand, were arrested and charged with kidnapping; other lawsuits were brought against members of the belligerent mob at Kingsbridge.

In orations delivered by the curates and priests mobilized to rescue the kiddies, in spontaneous arguments, posters, and excited headlines, the Dublin children were variously described as being deported, abducted, kidnapped, evacuated, rescued, "souperized," or sold into the white slave trade. Although Catholic Emancipation, the legal liberation of Catholics from the final remaining penal laws, had been achieved in 1829, the aggressive proselytizing efforts of English Protestant Bible societies, especially in cities, continued well into the twentieth century. The socialists' appropriation of poor children—what the Dublin parish priests called "kidnapping"—seemed to constitute yet one more attempt to eradicate Catholic Irish culture. The threat of starvation and the eager charities of English people evoked the reviled famine-era practice of "souperism," when families were offered soup and thereby saved from starvation only if they agreed to become Protestants. The terms of debate had been set by Archbishop Walsh's letter of October 21, published in several newspapers:

> A movement is on foot, and has already made some progress, to induce the wives of the working men who are now unemployed by reason of the present deplorable industrial deadlock in Dublin, to hand over their children to be cared for in England by persons of whom they, of course, can have no knowledge whatsoever. The Dublin women now subjected to this cruel temptation to part with their

helpless offspring are, in the majority of cases, Catholics. Have they abandoned their Faith? Surely not. Well, if they have not, they should need no words of mine to remind them of the plain duty of every Catholic mother in such a case. I can only put it to them that they can be no longer held worthy of the name of Catholic mothers if they so far forget that duty as to send away their little children to be cared for in a strange land, without security of any kind that those to whom the poor children are to be handed over are Catholics, or indeed are persons of any faith at all.[9]

The archbishop's language was intended to scare: a phrase like "hand over their children" already sounded more desperate and absolute than the realities of the situation required. In the hope that their children might have food, clothing, and healthy surroundings, families had given signed permission for their children to stay with English and Scottish socialist families for a few months. The phrase "hand over" followed by "to be cared for in England" made England sound more foreign and remote than in this case it was. To say that the women were "subjected" to a "cruel temptation" of course condemned their decision as wrong and immoral, and to call the children "helpless offspring" implied that they were being sent away, handed over, for some terrible purpose. To be labeled by the archbishop of Dublin as "no longer . . . worthy of the name of Catholic mothers" was a serious insult.

Archbishop Walsh intended to imply (this is how his letter was interpreted) that the women behind the plan were Protestant proselytizers. To him, to the parish priests and the Ancient Order of Hibernians, the campaign resembled, or could be made to resemble, the sectarian struggles over "rescued" children common in nineteenth-century Dublin, London, New York, and other places, when Catholic and Protestant agencies fought to retain custody of orphaned children, especially those of mixed marriages. Although Walsh received private assurances from Montefiore herself and from Catholics in Liverpool that the eighteen children sent there were being visited regularly by priests and were going to Mass, and although the private letter he sent to Montefiore suggested that he knew that the children were not being turned into Protestants, his public utterances nevertheless insisted on the sectarian nature of the issue. The campaign was an effort, he announced to the St. Vincent de Paul Society, "to deport our Catholic children to England, and to place them in the homes, and under the guardianship, of persons for whose fitness to undertake the guardianship of Catholic children there is no guarantee."[10] Without labeling the host families proselytizers, in fact carefully stopping short of that identification, Walsh used ambiguous phrasing ("deport our Catholic children to England") that was deliberately inflammatory. His letter to Montefiore, by contrast, was dry, even witty: "If the motive which has inspired the scheme is a purely philanthropic one,—and I dare say you have been made aware of some sinister rumours to the contrary, that are afloat in Dublin . . ."[11] Indeed she was aware. Having read his letter, she wrote, "I felt it was no use wasting time over this obtuse prelate."[12] Each side called the other "obtuse": in a letter to the *Freeman's Journal* Montefiore was referred to in the phrase "well-meaning, though obtuse English philanthropists."[13]

Anna Davin has shown how, at the beginning of the twentieth century, children's health "took on a new importance in public discussion, reinforced by emphasis on the value of a healthy and numerous population as a national resource." Children, in this light, belonged "not merely to the parents but to the community as a whole"; they were "a national asset," "the capital of a country"; on them depended "the future of the country and the Empire."[14] Population, argues Davin, was "power." Although the Catholic Church in Ireland was not a nation, it functioned to some extent as a state within a state. A large part, perhaps the central part of its glory and power, was its huge network of social service institutions: orphanages, hospitals, asylums, primary schools, secondary schools, as well as the parish churches and convents that performed many state functions, such as feeding and caring for the local poor. Under the guidance of Cardinal Cullen in the greater prosperity of the post-Famine years, this network had expanded enormously. In so far as the Church's life and health were identified with and expressed through these institutions, "population" was indeed power.

The provision of nourishment, housing, and medical care to the poor, especially to mothers and children, was the area of greatest concern to those English women involved in the reform of social welfare. In the late nineteenth and early twentieth centuries, as Seth Koven and Sonya Michel have written, "women envisioned a state which not only had the qualities of mothering we associate with welfare, but in which women played active roles as electors, policy makers, bureaucrats, and workers, within and outside the home."[15] The

4.1. William Walsh, Archbishop of Dublin, in 1910. Archbishop Walsh's letter,
published in several newspapers on October 21, 1913, ignited the controversy
surrounding the "Save the Dublin Kiddies" campaign. Speaking of the plan to
send workers' children to live with families in England, he wrote, "The Dublin
women now subjected to this cruel temptation to part with their helpless offspring are, in the majority of cases, Catholics. Have they abandoned their Faith?
Surely not. Well, if they have not, they should need no words of mine to remind
them of the plain duty of every Catholic mother in such a case." Photo by
Lafayette. Printed by permission of the Dublin Diocesan Archives.

4.2. Dora Montefiore in 1920. The "Save the Dublin Kiddies" campaign of October 1913 was Dora Montefiore's idea. After she read Archbishop Walsh's letter to her recommending that she stop saving the Dublin kiddies, she wrote, "I felt it was no use wasting time over this obtuse prelate." Photo permission of Mitchell Library, State Library of New South Wales.

meaning that Koven and Michel ascribe to the term *maternalism*—concern for the values of "care, nurturance, and morality"—effectively characterizes the ideal functions of the Irish Catholic Church's welfare system as well. To a great extent Archbishop Walsh and Dora Montefiore were in the same business, performing state functions before the existence of a "welfare state."

Montefiore began her political life as a suffragist, involved in numerous organizations dedicated to women's and to adult suffrage in Australia (where she lived between 1874 and 1892, around the time of her marriage to George Montefiore in Sydney) and England. Moving beyond her original Liberal politics, she joined the Social Democratic Federation in the early years of the century, beginning the Women's Socialist Circles in 1904. According to Karen Hunt, Montefiore's main political interest was on "her own woman-focused socialism."[16] She had not been directly involved in working with children before. In her autobiography, Montefiore describes the sight of Dublin children rummaging hungrily through garbage: in the terrible circumstances of the strike and lockout, not every child was being fed. If the Dublin parishes were not taking care of everyone, if children were driven to eat garbage, there was immediate and urgent work for socialists to do. To Montefiore's internationalizing, anticapitalist sensibility, all the starving children of the workers were alike her concern, whatever country they lived in.[17]

But feeding was an intimate activity, closely related to the formation of identity. The myth of Persephone, whose consumption of six seeds of pomegranate gave her to the god of the underworld for six months a year, and the more recent folk memory of "souperism," indicate the great power ascribed to those who feed. Irish Catholic children fed by English Protestants would—this was the assumption—become English Protestants. However much Montefiore and her supporters denied any proselytizing purposes, a powerful symbolic logic suggested that the children's ethnic and religious identity would be transformed drastically if they were fed under the auspices of such a scheme, even if they stayed with Catholic families in England and attended Mass. Like the Lane paintings, which were French (for the most part) in origin, Irish when they were in the Dublin gallery, and English when claimed for the London gallery, the children had an identity vulnerable to sudden mutation. The paintings changed nationality according to where they were hung, the children according to who fed them. Although (unlike the paintings) the children were born in Ireland, their youth and helplessness made them appear more malleable: they could become anything.

The Dublin workers' children, then, represented an overlapping of two symbolic domains, that of the Irish Catholic Church and that of maternalist women, in this case socialists linked with the striking workers. The "Save the Dublin Kiddies" controversy was driven by issues of territory, space, and boundaries, boundaries that could be defined and reinforced only by the priests themselves. At every level, the symbolic conflict over control of the children—a physical custody that signified an ideological power—was expressed corporeally and gesturally: in the direct force applied by the priests against the women who were carrying the children away; in the processions of the Catholics around certain parts of Dublin and the marches of the strikers around others; in the struggles at the city's boundaries, the train stations and docks; and in the struggles on the trains and boats themselves that under these circumstances marked the national border between Ireland and England. If the children could not be gotten off the boats, then they would inevitably become Protestant and English. The logic was spatial: if the boat pulled away from the North Wall with Irish Catholic children on it, it had for all intents and purposes crossed the boundary of an ideological domain, and they were lost forever.

Sean O'Casey's description of this controversy in *Drums under the Window* gives a vivid sense of its physicality:

> Led by their clergy, the marchers, beerded nicely, and supportered [sic] by a good conscience, brandyshed sticks and cudgels, bottling their wrath with difficulty . . . drinkaway boys, and slugalowers marched past yodelling and godelling their war-chant,
>
>> Faith of our fathers, we will love
>> Both friend and foe in all our strife;
>> And preach it too, as love knows how,
>> By kindly words and virtuous life,
>
> adding sense to it by giving a knock to the head of a father trying to get his child out of mudesty into life, tearing skin from the face of a friend helping the father, and the shirts from the backs of any coming near enough to shout the slogan shame.[18]

One memory that has survived offers a child's version of this physical discourse: Paula Meehan's great-uncle Joseph Meehan, a young boy at

the time, remembered the large body of a priest blocking him as he
ran along the North Wall on his way to a boat for Liverpool.[19] Dora
Montefiore's autobiography gives another instance of the assertion of
territoriality as she attempted to board the train to the Kingstown
steamer:

> As I approached the carriage door a priest thrust me rudely aside, and
> held me by my shoulder. I told him he was assaulting me by laying his
> hand on me, and when he saw I was calm, but very much in earnest in
> the matter, he let me go. I again approached the door to speak to Mrs.
> Rand, when another priest flung the door back against me, hurting me
> considerably, and making me feel very faint.[20]

In this vignette, the Dublin priests literally function as tutelary figures, guardians of their territory, patrolling the boundaries—the
doors—to prevent strangers from carrying off their children.

The complex ideological antagonisms visible in this controversy
exist in a particular historical moment. Two years later, in the autumn of 1915 and winter of 1915–16, James Connolly would gradually reconcile his socialist beliefs with militant nationalism. By the
beginning of World War I, less than ten months later, the Catholic
Church in Ireland had become less actively hostile to socialism.[21]
And with the establishment of the Irish Free State in 1922, anxieties
about English Protestant encroachment on the Irish population
would take other forms: much of Irish legislation over the first ten
years of independence would be devoted to preventing English ideas,
books, and social practices from crossing the boundaries of the Free
State.

The Genealogy of "Save the Dublin Kiddies"

Two different traditions of child rescue are visible in the genealogy of
"Save the Dublin Kiddies." The two principal antagonists, Archbishop Walsh and Dora Montefiore, understood the history of the
controversy in different cultural contexts. In all his public pronouncements on the subject, Archbishop Walsh used language that
would evoke the classic rescue battles between rival Catholic and
Protestant charities common in nineteenth-century Dublin and

other cities. These conflicts, dating from a time of Protestant cultural hegemony, were in the minds of many people who wrote to the archbishop, such as Father John Brophy, a parish priest in Montreal, who told the children in his catechism class that "the little Dublin boys and girls fled in horror from those disguised wolves, when the mask was torn off, and turned back gladly to cold and hunger rather than risk their precious faith."[22]

Margaret Aylward, founder of the Holy Faith Sisters, recorded many such struggles in the papers of the (Catholic) Ladies Association of Charity, whose Dublin branch she set up in 1851. Her language sounds like Father Brophy's: in order to recover, or rather repossess, Catholic children, the Ladies went directly to the Protestant schools that "cover as the snares of the fowler, the face of the city." On one such visit, in 1856, the superintendent of the Protestant school called the police to arrest the Ladies, saying, "These Ladies are about to persecute our people; they are organising a persecution of Protestants." When the policeman asked for their names, one of the Ladies challenged him, saying, "What authority have you to ask them?" To this the superintendent replied, "Take them to the station-house; make a clean job of it."[23] In her work at St. Brigid's Orphanage, which she founded for this purpose in 1857, Aylward was herself on the cutting edge of rescue struggles. She records an 1859 incident in which a Protestant foster mother tried to prevent a Catholic biological mother from retrieving her children. The foster mother "sent out scouts and placed spies on the streets through which the children were expected to pass." However, the Catholic mother was too quick for the scouts and grabbed her children back. She made her getaway with the help of one of Aylward's Ladies, who had hired a car that "conveyed [them] to a place of safety."[24] In the famous 1860 case of the orphan Mary Mathews, child of a Catholic father and Protestant mother, Aylward endured a six-month prison term rather than reveal the whereabouts of the child to her widowed mother.

The Protestant opposite number to Margaret Aylward was the infamous Mrs. Ellen Smyly, founder of "Birds' Nest" homes in cities all over Ireland. Her religious aggressions were celebrated in the song "Come Pray with Mrs. Smyly," whose geopolitics contrasts the rich Protestant Merrion Square area, in central Dublin (home, in the mid-nineteenth century, to Oscar Wilde's parents), with the poor Catholic area, the Coombe, in the southeast of the city:

Come all good Christians I declare
Will you follow me down to Merrion Square
Where each murdering thief will get mutton and beef
If he prays with Mrs. Smyly.

Now Maisie Brown she was terrible poor
The neighbors said she was on the flure
Now she rides to hell in a coach and four
Since she prayed with Mrs. Smyly.

And Mary Bro she lived in the Coombe
She lived there in her little back room
Now she entertains in her own saloon
Since she prayed with Mrs. Smyly.[25]

As an Englishwoman offering food ("mutton and beef") and material comforts to impoverished Dublin children, Dora Montefiore inevitably appeared as the latest incarnation of Mrs. Smyly.

Listening to Jim Larkin's speech about the poor starving children of the striking Dublin workers, however, Montefiore had been thinking of quite another tradition, as her language suggests:

I have seen industrial troubles in every part of the world, and have noted how, during prolonged strikes or lock-outs, not only the children suffered severely, and often permanently in physique, but that mothers carrying still unborn babies, so starved themselves in their pitiful attempts to feed their growing children, that the babes born during or after the strike period were too often rickety and physically unfitted for the battle of life. . . . I felt, from what I had heard and read of the slums of Dublin and the abysmal poverty of its sweat workers, that if we could give the children a holiday from such surroundings and fill them with a vision of what life might hold in the way of cleaner and more hopeful environment, my colleagues and I might be the means not only of saving some of the children, who should be the hope of the race, but also of doing some constructive work for the future of organised industrialism.[26]

The vivid contrasts in Montefiore's imagery form part of a larger romantic discourse about the industrial city. Her thoughts combine contemporary eugenic discourses and William Blake's apocalyptic vision of the industrializing London of the late eighteenth century:

I wander thro' each charter'd street,
Near where the charter'd Thames does flow,
And mark in every face I meet
Marks of weakness, marks of woe.

. . . .

How the Chimney-sweeper's cry
Every black'ning Church appalls;
And the hapless Soldier's sigh
Runs in blood down Palace walls.

But most thro' midnight streets I hear
How the youthful Harlot's curse
Blasts the new born Infant's tear,
And blights with plagues the Marriage hearse.
                        (William Blake, "London")

Like Blake, Montefiore places a pastoral landscape in opposition to the urban one, "a holiday from such surroundings." Blake, however, did not set English social policy; nor did Dickens, who wrote a version of the blighted, impoverished urban child in *Bleak House.* But similar visionary notions of childhood form part of the genealogy of the progressive socialist thought fundamental to Montefiore's ideas.[27] From the German educator Friedrich Froebel (1782–1852), who founded the first kindergarten in 1849, came the idea that "garden" surroundings were beneficial to the development of children's cognitive powers. Froebel's ideas spread quickly through Europe, England, and America. Dickens visited a Froebelian kindergarten in 1855; in 1874 a Froebel Society was founded in Manchester, and the Froebel Educational Institute in 1892 in London. Progressive thought in the second half of the nineteenth century emphasized not only early childhood education but pleasant, nonpunitive educational methods and the education of children from all classes: Froebelian schools in Germany educated Jews and Christians together.[28]

The socialist reformer Margaret McMillan had been one of the earliest people to translate philosophical ideas of the child into socialist policy. She was especially famous for setting up the Deptford Camp School (which evolved from her Deptford Clinic) in South London around 1911. Soon after its establishment, she let some of the girls sleep in the garden and wrote about the "healing joy of such nearness to the earth spirit."[29] The "healing joy" of the outdoors had long been an aspect of children's rescue work. Margaret Aylward also considered the country a better place for the rearing of orphaned children, preferring "the seaboard, the hillside, the glen and the plain" to "the back lanes of the city."[30] A Fresh Air Association was founded in Dublin in 1885 (only eight years after its American counterpart) to send poor urban children recovering from illness to families in the country. In 1910 the appropriately named American education reformer Leonard Ayres published *Open Air Schools*, part of a larger campaign for hygiene and exercise. In McMillan's scheme, the children sleeping outdoors were working-class children for whom such an activity was part of a larger humanitarian and educational project. They were learning to keep themselves clean, to take care of their health, to read and write and gain basic cognitive skills. Drawing on Froebel and on the ideas of childhood that influenced him, and drawing on contemporary socialist thought, especially that of Henry George, McMillan believed that the camp school would reveal to politicians and to the poor themselves that "children's ill-health was not just in the way of things, but rather had causes: in dirt, poor housing; in the material conditions of life." She believed in the potential of the child and in the powers of soap, water, fresh air, and education to serve as agents of social mobility. Class was not a barrier; children could become anything; and humanitarian care and cultural makeovers could give them the advantages of the rich.

If "population was power" for humanitarian empires as well as for political ones, then Montefiore was clearly thinking of her empire when she hoped that by "saving some of the children" she might also be accomplishing "constructive work for the future of organised industrialism." But she was no Mrs. Smyly; she was not motivated by sectarian hatred. Nor was she stealing or abducting the children: she and her helpers accepted only children whose mothers had given signed permission and whose fathers had agreed to the temporary custodial shift. When Montefiore put her plan into action in Dublin, she was as shocked and indignant at its frustration as the nuns Linda Gordon writes about in *The Great Arizona Orphan Abduction*. In that 1904 episode, nuns from the New York Foundling Hospital traveled all the way to Arizona to give forty Catholic orphans, primarily Irish-American, to Catholic families in two small mining towns. The local padre, himself a French Catholic, gave the children to Mexican families who had been previously approved; but the towns' primarily

Protestant Anglo women were outraged that "white" orphans were being given to Mexican families. At their instigation, a posse was organized to retrieve the children from the Mexicans. The nuns were in shock, but Arizona was not New York. "A metamorphosis had transpired among these children," writes Gordon, "although they were themselves unaware of it. As the orphan train chugged across the Mississippi and the great plains, the children were bleached, as the Mexicans say, as they went. This transformation made their placements 'interracial,' or, as the Clifton Anglos said, 'half-breed.'" The categories Catholic–Protestant had been replaced by white–dark.[31]

Montefiore experienced a similar taxonomic shift. She thought she was "saving" poor children; she discovered she was saving Irish-Catholic children, and that for an English Protestant to "save" them was to "kidnap" them. In fact, as an English woman socialist and a Protestant widow bearing one of Europe's most prominent Jewish surnames, Montefiore fitted into so many threatening categories that one or two of them would have been enough to damn the whole operation. She was "blissfully unconscious of Irish clerical susceptibilities."[32] Energetic, efficient, determined, confident in her own humanitarian motives, Montefiore had not expected to be demonized. Unaware of or untroubled by the history of rescue conflicts, she went about her business in high gear: she wrote letters, contacted newspapers, made lists, and summoned help from her huge network of Labour friends to put the scheme into effect. She was shocked and appalled at the Dublin priests' response.

Soon Dublin's progressive intellectuals came to Montefiore's aid: Frank Sheehy Skeffington, Constance Markievicz, William Orpen. Bernard Shaw defended her in London and provoked a spin-off controversy when he spoke "as a Dublin man" to "apologize for the priests of Dublin."[33] George Russell (AE) spoke at the same London gathering as Shaw, along with James Connolly and Jim Larkin's sister Delia. Rebecca West attacked G. K. Chesterton, who had attacked Montefiore, and Yeats wrote to the *Irish Worker* complaining about the Ancient Order of Hibernians, the Dublin police, the Unionist press, the nationalist press, and "fanaticism" everywhere.[34] In a letter to Lady Gregory, Yeats cut to the quick: "Sooner or later we'll have to face the Catholics on the question of sex."[35] Montefiore gradually came to see the matter in a new light, and at the end of the pamphlet she wrote about her adventures in Dublin, *Our Fight to Save the Kiddies*, she allies herself with "all those who are fighting side by side to save the world from the combined sinister forces of capitalism and clericalism."[36]

Montefiore was truly from another world; Dublin was a foreign country to her, though she never knew it. No one gave her a map of the territory. Her innocence extended beyond the charity wars. Before leaving Dublin, Montefiore (according to the *Irish Times*) decided to send a gift to Jim Larkin, then imprisoned in Mountjoy. It was a generous notion to buy him a nice comfortable armchair, but it was not a good idea to buy it at Clery's, the large Sackville Street department store owned by none other than William Martin Murphy, the man against whom the workers were striking. "The armchair," wrote the paper, "was conveyed under police protection to Mountjoy and placed in Mr. Larkin's cell. But when the labour organiser received the label he ordered the chair to be removed at once. This was done."[37] The offending object was sent to Liberty Hall, its further history of no interest to journalists. The drama of the chair, like the drama of the kiddies themselves, lay in its sudden, surprising detour.

"Remarkable Scenes"

Montefiore did not go to Dublin until October 17, after she had received three hundred offers of housing for the strikers' children. With the help of Grace Neal, an experienced labor organizer, and Lucilla Rand, a young American friend with no hands-on political experience but much sympathy for the children, Montefiore set up operations in Liberty Hall, where Delia Larkin gave her a room. After a meeting with the locked-out workers' wives, the women collected names of mothers "anxious to take advantage of our offer." Pairing children with prospective hosts, making separate lists of places for boys and for girls, collecting clothing, they were busy and well organized. Women and children stood in line to sign up, the "crush . . . so great that often two or three mothers forced their way in," according to Montefiore's account. On Wednesday morning, October 22, as they prepared to send the first fifty children to their temporary homes, "we each had our apportioned work." Miss Neal "presided over a batch of volunteer workers at our room in Liberty Hall, who were sewing on to the children's new clothing labels bearing their names and addresses, and small rosettes of green and red ribbon." Mrs. Rand was at the Tara Street baths, just across the Liffey from Liberty Hall, where "a trained woman had been engaged" to wash the children's heads and bodies. Because the children came from tenements, where often seventy-five or a hundred people shared a single tap of running water and a single toilet in the yard or basement, bathing them before they traveled was necessary hygiene. It was standard procedure for social workers of the time. Montefiore herself was out on the town buying clothing, tickets, and food to sustain the children during their trip.[38]

Returning to Liberty Hall, she "heard the first news of trouble being made by the priests." She went immediately to the Tara Street baths, arriving around 10:30 to witness an adversarial encounter on a large scale, what the next day's *Freeman's Journal* called "Remarkable Scenes." There she perceived a "yelling, wailing, hysterical multitude" of children, parents, priests, and social workers, an "indescribable scene going on in the street":

> a surging crowd, some with us, some against us, beat up against the steps of the baths and was again and again pushed back by two red-faced, brutal-looking constables. Right inside the girls' side of the baths, where he had no business to be, stood a priest, who asked me what I was doing there. I told him I had come to help Mrs. Rand with the children. He replied we should not have the children, and that he was there to prevent their going. When I met Mrs. Rand I found he had already threatened and hustled her, and she had to warn him not to touch her again. The priests were shouting and ordering the children about in the passage-way . . . some of the women were "answering back" to the priests and reminding them [that] they had been refused bread by the Church and that now they had a chance of getting their children properly cared for; other women, worked on by the violent speeches of the priests, were wailing and calling on the saints to forgive them. . . . When we found we could do nothing more for the children we drove back to Liberty Hall through a crowd that threw mud at us and raised cries of "Throw them into the Liffey."[39]

The affronted sense of territoriality on both sides is evident even in Montefiore's openly partial narrative: the women feel the priest should not be anywhere near the room where the girls are being bathed, and the priest feels that the women should not be so intimately connected to the Catholic children. Everyone's taboos are being violated, but the parties involved operate under conflicting taxonomies. The two socialist women respond to the priests as men: they feel "threatened" and "hustled" and resent being touched. The

CLERGY PREVENT SHIPMENT OF DUBLIN CHILDREN TO ENGLAND.

4.3. The Tara Street baths. The most dramatic struggle over the "Dublin Kiddies" took place inside the Tara Street baths, where priests grabbed the children from the hands of social workers who were washing them. Montefiore's account vividly describes the "surging crowd, some with us, some against us" outside the baths. Photo credit: *Irish Independent*.

gestures tell them unmistakably that they are being bullied. The priests treat the women not as women but as English Protestant kidnappers who are endangering the children. In fact Montefiore was the nonreligious widow of an Australian Jew, and Rand was an American Catholic. But by putting their hands on the bodies of Catholic children, they were intervening in an area historically under the control of the Church.

The harassing priests were Father William Landers and Father Thomas McNevin, the curates from St. Andrew's parish, whose presbytery on Westland Row was only minutes away from the baths. According to the account in the *Freeman's Journal*, the priests first interviewed the boys, and

> almost without exception the little fellows sturdily asserted that they didn't want to go to England. Many of the lads shouted, "We won't be English children," and a few of the eldest said that they didn't want to renounce their Faith . . . [when Father Landers announced he was "strenuously opposed" to the plan, he was] accorded an ovation by the gathering.[40]

Then came the violation so distressing to Montefiore, alluded to by Larkin in a speech later that day: "One clergyman disgraced his cloth by going into a bathroom where a woman was bathing."[41] Father Landers "interviewed" the girls, some of whose mothers were present, "and when the mothers were questioned they, with one exception, not only protested against allowing the children to go, but expressed their vehement opposition to it." The mothers who confidently and rationally expressed "their vehement opposition" were, presumably, the same ones Montefiore characterizes as "worked on by the violent speeches of the priests" and "wailing and calling on the saints to forgive them." The *Freeman's Journal* noted a crowd of "200 or 250" outside the baths, who responded to Father Landers with "a very hearty cheer." To this crowd Landers read Archbishop Walsh's letter and gave a rousing speech, reminding his listeners

> that the Irish people knew what poverty was for a long time, but they were never reduced to the extremity of denying their Faith. . . . the Irish people would rather their children perish by the ditches than that they should be exposed to the risk of being perverted in their religion.[42]

Meanwhile the unrescued children, those whose mothers had "answered back" to the priests, were taken to Liberty Hall. When they were ready to leave for the 1:30 train to the Kingstown steamer, Larkin "spoke from a window of the hall to the crowd down below, and asked the men to see to it that the children reached the railway station."[43] They had need of such help, but at the station the women got separated from their escorts, and Montefiore was assaulted by one of the priests as she attempted to board the train: "A priest thrust me rudely aside and held me by the shoulder." On the train, the priests "started a systematic bullying" of the boys and "pulled off the labels and the rosettes" that had been so carefully sewn on the jerseys in the morning. As Montefiore "sat passive and contemptuous in the corner," the priests told her they "did not want any of our English charity."[44]

At the boat, more of the kiddies "saved" by the socialist women were "rescued" from them by the priests. Father McNevin said he would "see to it that the Catholic children of Dublin were not stolen from their parents." Some passengers supported the priests with cries of "Shame! Shame!" When, according to the *Freeman's Journal*, two of the lads "made a dash for the railings," the crew let them disembark, and "all the lads dashed onto the pier amid loud cheers from the four priests." Mrs. Ward, a Dublin woman who formed part of this group along with her own sons, had an altercation with one of the priests. She refused to give up the boys, saying they were her own, and Father Ryan said, "I don't believe a word of it," to which she replied, "I don't care whether you do or not." Mrs. Rand, feeling obligated to stay with all the children in her charge, disembarked with the remaining children. She was then arrested and charged at the Kingstown police station with "kidnapping a child under 14 years of age and feloniously removing it from the care of its father." The "rescued" children, in the words of the *Freeman's Journal*, were "clean and healthy-looking." But of course they were clean! They had been professionally washed only three hours earlier.[45]

Hearing of the scenes as soon as Montefiore could get back to Liberty Hall, Larkin got in the spirit of the fight, more determined to get children out. Written permissions for more children were obtained, and Grace Neal volunteered to accompany them. Once more Larkin addressed the group from the windows of Liberty Hall, telling

SAVING DUBLIN CHILDREN.

Madame Montefiore leaving the Police Court yesterday after being charged with taking away a boy, George Burke, from the custody of his father. | Father M'Nevin and Father Fleming leaving the Northern Police Court yesterday with George Burke, in respect of whom Madame Montefiore is charged.
" Irish Independent " Photos.

4.4. "Saving Dublin Children." The first picture is of "Madame Montefiore leaving the Police Court yesterday after being charged with taking away a boy, George Burke, from the custody of his father." The second shows "Father Mc-Nevin and Father Fleming leaving the Northern Police Court yesterday with George Burke, in respect of whom Madame Montefiore is charged." The contested Dublin workers' children represented an overlapping of two symbolic domains, that of the Irish Catholic Church and that of maternalist women, in this case socialists linked with the striking workers. Photo credit: *Irish Independent*.

the crowd "that he depended upon the men to see that the party got through." To the army of priests Larkin now opposed his own army: each child, as Montefiore tells it, was "carried on the shoulder of a stalwart docker," and two men were assigned to accompany Neal and her helpers on the boat.[46] This group made it to the North Wall through the crowd of "priests and Hibernians" and onto the boat. One Father Doherty had a contretemps with an official of the City of Dublin steamers, who refused to let him board without a ticket: "I told him I would take his number and report the matter," announced Father Doherty, as many a person has in similar circumstances, but another priest was able to get the clerics on board. Confronting the children, Doherty asked them "if they wanted to become English and Protestant." One lad answered "No, Father," but the male escort, wisely refusing to engage with the issues of nationality and religion, immediately led the children in a cheer of "Hurrah for Larkin." Then the siren sounded and the priests had to get off. As the steamer *Carlow* passed down the Liffey, the children "appeared on the foredeck . . . singing 'God Save Larkin,' the latter to the air of 'God Save Ireland.'"[47] Fortified by fresh milk from the cows on board, this little group of eighteen children (escorted by Grace Neal and "two Irish girls," says Montefiore) arrived in Liverpool the next morning.[48]

As the priests and the Hibernians saw it, to let a child leave the city, to let even one child out, was to lose control of the family, to let Protestant win over Catholic and English over Irish, to surrender to feminism and socialism. The flow of children had to be prevented in order to maintain the structure of society. Over the next few days—on October 23, 24, and 25—"Catholic Vigilance," as the papers called it, was at work along the quays and in the railway stations, ensuring that no child left Dublin. "Fathers and Mothers of Catholic Dublin," read a handbill. "Are you content to abandon your children to strangers, who give no guarantee to have them placed in Catholic or Irish homes? You may never see them again! Kidnappers and soupers are at their deadly work." In one "small incident" at the Laird Line office, a "woman bearing a child in her arms was accosted and questioned as to her destination." In this case, however, there was "no ground for apprehension of danger," so she was allowed to continue on her way.[49]

The *Freeman's Journal* also emphasized Montefiore's connection with suffragists by reporting in detail her talk at a meeting of the Irish Women's Franchise League, tarring both groups by the association of one with the other.[50] Of course, as the Larkinites saw it, the Church was in league with the police and the employers against the poor. Montefiore's pamphlet on the affair lists numerous instances of police brutality besides the notorious murders of James Nolan and John Byrne in the police attacks of August, at the beginning of the strike, and she quotes an account of poor people being turned away hungry from the archbishop's palace. One Mr. Drummond, a Scotsman, told those gathered outside Liberty Hall on October 23 that the Church "was taking the side of the rich instead of the poor." The trade-unionist William Partridge said that "the offer of the English workers was a standing reproach to the well-to-do Catholics of Ireland."[51]

On the next two nights, after "Catholic vigilance" in the form of large crowds of Hibernians and priests had seen to it that no children had been taken out of Dublin on the South Wall via Kingstown to

Holyhead or on the North Wall via the City of Dublin steamer to Liverpool, huge processions, led by priests, marched along the docks singing "Hail! Glorious St. Patrick" and "Faith of Our Fathers." On October 23, the crowd went from the South Wall to the North Wall, meeting up at Beresford Place with a "hostile demonstration" from an opposing crowd at Liberty Hall. A "cordon of Police" kept the two crowds apart, the Catholic group singing hymns and the strikers hissing at them. As that street theater was taking place, Dora Montefiore was arrested on kidnapping charges and bailed out by David Heuston and William Sinclair, "whose addresses," said the *Freeman's Journal,* "could not be learned, but who are believed to be of the Jewish persuasion."[52] "London Lady Arrested. Charged with Kidnapping; Bailed by Dublin Jews" screamed the headlines of the *Independent,* William Martin Murphy's paper.[53] The phrases neatly linked two despised groups. Constance Markievicz—a feminist and socialist like Montefiore, and a more radical nationalist than those who read the *Independent*—also made one of the group bailing out Montefiore. On October 24, Delia Larkin (accompanied by Montefiore) and a group of children were surrounded by Hibernians at the Amiens Street Station and prevented from boarding by the police, who blocked the trains. (Or, as the *Freeman's Journal* put it, the "timely interference of the police prevented resort to violence."[54]) Meanwhile, a crowd estimated at two thousand watched the departure of the Liverpool and Holyhead boats, ensuring that no children were aboard. Another hymn-singing procession, "six deep," walked along the quays to the Father Mathew statue on Sackville Street and then dispersed.[55]

Viewed as symbolic behavior, the movement of mobs, both Larkinite and Hibernian, appears patently territorial. The Hibernian-clerical crowds were trying to seal the boundaries of Dublin, blocking all possible points of departure. Processing along the quays and up Sackville Street after two successful days, they were recatholicizing the territory, publicizing their successful defense by their numbers, their movement, and their songs, which filled the air as their bodies filled the space. Booing and hissing from their own territory in Beresford Place, the striking workers were similarly asserting power over parts of Dublin. Philip O'Leary has written about the metaphor of the "wall around Ireland" that recurs in the writings of Irish-language revivalists in this period, a linguistic wall "against the onslaught of the enemies of our nationality and our civilisation," as Patrick Pearse put it.[56] The mobs opposing "Save the Dublin Kiddies" used their own bodies to create that wall so that the national culture could not leak out, child by child.

Fairy Abductions

Rooted in a particular historical moment and its particular dis-courses, "Save the Dublin Kiddies" also participates in the broader national discourse to be found in the abduction narratives of Irish fairy legends. Rural in origin, recorded later from traditional story-tellers speaking in the Irish language, these stories were generally known to anyone growing up in Ireland at the end of the nineteenth century: W. B. Yeats, Patrick Pearse, Father O'Hickey, Lady Gregory all knew them. They were a common narrative currency, invoked in proverbs, phrases, and allusions. The geopolitics, the gender politics, and the discourse of gestures in these stories are strongly suggestive of those in "Save the Dublin Kiddies." The stories do not distinguish among motives of protection, possession, or domination of the people—mostly women and children—who are rescued. This ambigu-ity makes it possible to read the stories as warnings about the vulner-ability of women and children, warnings that might be construed equally as threatening or as protective. As Angela Bourke has sug-gested, such stories "express aggression against women in coded form" and "carry disciplinary messages for women as well as for chil-dren, warning them about behavior considered by a patriarchal soci-ety to be unacceptable."[57]

All the Irish fairy legends make it clear: to rescue a human child from the *sí*, the fairies, you must act swiftly and decisively. Those who are successful grab, shout, interrupt the fairies, and loudly claim the child as their own. In the story "Tugaí Domhsa É!" ("Give It to Me!") told by John Henry, a man called Big Thomas, walking along the beach at evening looking for wood, knows exactly what to do when he hears a child crying and women talking:

> "Give it to me," one of them would say.
> "No," another would say, "but give it to me."[58]

Big Thomas enters the argument suddenly and definitively: " 'Not at all,' said Thomas—he spoke up—'but let me have it!' said he." They have to turn over to him the child who is the object of the argument because, as one of the fairywomen says, "Some woman with the track of holy water on her fingers has held this child . . . and there's nothing we can do about it." They give him the child because the religious mark is on him: he's a Catholic child. The message is clear; Catholicism protects the weak from unknown and unpredictable threats, but sometimes the loud voice and power of masculinity are needed to support the claim.

When, in another story, Noirín Ní Eachaidh wants to be rescued after a fairy abduction that has lasted several years, she gives a young lad explicit directions: "Every Samhain Eve twelve of us go riding on horseback and three times we go round the strand, and if you were to be there when we ride out all you have to do is pull me off the horse and I will wear a red cap and so you will know me."[59] The male posse, eight boys and a priest, who go to rescue Noirín from the fairy host, let the host ride by twice without attempting to grab her. One very determined boy, understanding the urgency of the situation, insists, "She will not go past the third time without me trying to catch her." When she rides past the third time, collective force is required: the boy "pulled her down off the horses and all the other horses tried to jump on top of her but the priest kept them back." The men take the girl home in a boat, and she is returned to her young man, whom she marries.

Gestures of repossession in these tales are always sudden, abrupt, and violent. Custodial conflicts are decided absolutely: shared custody, weekend visitations—these modern allowances for opposed claims never appear. You grab the woman or child and run for it. Then the abducted person must be ritually reappropriated and reclaimed as part of the human family with the materials of Catholicism. If you don't do this the right way, the fairies might get the person again. When Big Thomas delivers the crying child to its rightful family, the priest ratifies the child's identity, distinguishing it from the thing the fairies had left in the cradle: " 'Now,' said the priest, 'this is the right child' " (" 'Anois,' a dúirt an sagart, 'seo é an páiste ceart' "). He reads over it and then gives the family instructions: "As long as you live . . . always shake holy water on your children. And when you lay down an infant to sleep in the cradle, place an ember under the pillow and nothing can go near him."[60] John Henry also explains that Brigid's Cloak ("Brat Bhríde") must be laid over the child to protect it. In the story of Noirín, it's the priest, the one who holds the fairy horses back from trampling the abducted woman, who knows what must be done: it's he who quickly marries her to Pádraig and who orders the couple to go to America for two years before returning home.

When Noirín instructs the male posse to rescue her, the narrative may be imputing to her what is in fact a masculine wish for women to be dependent on male control. The priests in the fairy legends, themselves a patriarchy, sanctify the husbands' domination over wives and the parents' over children. Where is the line between protection and domination? The abrupt shifts of custodial authority in the stories may indicate a return to all that is good, familiar, loving, and stable, from the dangers and threats of the Other World, where the fairies live. But the violence perpetrated against woman and children may also constitute a punishment to those who stray too far from home. The sudden, definitive grabbing that gets them back home signifies an expression of power: the men own the women, the parents own the children, and the priests abet these secular authorities.

The geopolitics of most of the fairy abduction stories replicates that of the 1913 episodes. Women and children are rescued from marginal territories and conditions and returned to home, priests, and safety. Just as Archbishop Walsh and the parish priests berated the mothers for allowing their children to go with "strangers," so people in fairy legends are told that if they had only obeyed the rules, their wives or children would not have been taken away. A man whose wife is abducted while she was in labor is told, "if the husband's sleeved waistcoat . . . had been thrown over the wife's legs that night that woman would still be alive. . . . But the fairy host took her with them."[61] Why wasn't he more careful, more protective of his own? Parents shouldn't let their children go too far away: when the little girl in "Gearrchaile a Tugadh as" ("An Abducted Girl") is sent by her father to get a saucepan of cool water, she never returns. She is discovered the next day at the bottom of a cliff, as so many of the Blasket Island children were.[62] The story is a practical warning about the need for boundaries and the vulnerability of children, especially seven-year-olds, who can do simple chores but should not be allowed to go too far alone.

One story sounds more precisely like a folk version of Dublin in October 1913. In "The Battle of Glen Bolcain," the man and woman have no babysitter, so they have to leave their child alone outside while they are haying. But "along came a bold woman who caught up the child"—a bold woman, perhaps, like one of the nineteenth-century Protestant Bible ladies in Ireland, or like the aggressive Dora Montefiore. A rock face opens for her, and in she goes with the child:

> The man followed her in and found a great court, city, and castle inside full of children. He said that he must have his own child back. . . . Late in the evening an old man who was sitting by the fire saw they must yield and told his wife to give back his own child to the man as they would have no peace until he got it.[63]

As he leaves, the man rings a bell by the door and causes a battle among the fairy host "and they killed one another." The story scares parents but it also comforts them: evil may come to kidnappers. Like the terrifying rock face that opened for the bold woman carrying the couple's child, the railway stations and the docks of Dublin were the entrances to the Other World. The parish priests patrolled them so passionately to prevent the children from joining all the others who had been abducted, deported, proselytized, and otherwise alienated from family, nation, and Church. The cultural history of earlier abductions remained vestigially in the minds of the parish priests, justifying their fears even when the occasion did not warrant them.

Liverpool

Whereas the Catholic Church in Dublin was trying to estrange Liverpool, referring to the eighteen children taken there as if they had been permanently abducted to a terrain as foreign, hostile, and hopelessly remote as the fairy Other World, Jim Larkin, who had been born in Liverpool, defended it as an extension of Ireland, a home away from home:

> I know every home these children are going to. They are going to Irish Catholic homes, and where they are not, there will be no interference with their religion, and the priests will be notified of their arrival. The majority of the homes are those of Irish-born people, and they are of the same religion as ourselves.[64]

But even before the children arrived, an anonymous Liverpudlian had written Archbishop Walsh in anticipatory hysteria: "The Homes they would be invited to here," he or she claimed, "is the Homes not of Catholics but Anti-Catholics, Socialists, And various bigoted sects, who wd. do anything to rob A Catholic Child of the true Faith. . . . For God's sake," pleaded the writer at the end, "don't let A single Child leave Dublin. . . . St. Patrick pray for them."[65]

The Liverpool priests were not able to rescue the Dublin kiddies sent across the Irish Sea on the *Carlow* to the land across the waves, but it wasn't for lack of trying. Rev. J. O'Connell, Assistant Honorable Secretary of the Liverpool Catholic Children's Aid Committee, Canon Pinnington, Honorable Secretary of same, and Father Leech of Holy Cross, Great Crosshall Street, Liverpool, did their best: it might have been easier to rescue one woman on horseback in the midst of the fairy host than eighteen children among the socialists in the waiting room by the landing stage at the Liverpool docks.

"Dear Fr. Flavin," wrote Canon Pinnington to the administrator of the Pro-Cathedral in Dublin,

> I met the City of Dublin Boat this morning on its arrival in Liverpool. The Liverpool Police who have been communicated with by the Dublin Police were also in attendance. There were 18 Children—all Catholics—in the charge of a Miss Neal and two other young women also Catholics. . . . The Police at my request satisfied themselves that Miss Neal had the consent of the Parents of the children for their removal from Dublin. Consequently we could not detain them. The names and addresses from which the children came were taken and I am to be supplied with the names and addresses of the persons with whom the Children are placed and I have an undertaking from those who arranged for the children to come there that their religion will not be interfered with. As soon as they are placed out I will communicate with the Priest of the district and ask him to visit them.[66]

Pinnington hoped that some of the parents might be persuaded to "revoke their consent," in which case he would do his best "to obtain custody of the Children and return them to Dublin." But without the requisite document, "we can do nothing except keep an eye on the children."

The children were hovered over by an impressive surveillance apparatus. Long before the police, Canon Pinnington, and a number of detectives confronted the children, in fact at six in the morning the day after the kiddies had left Dublin, no doubt while they were just drinking the first of the cow's milk on board ship, Miss Walker, the "National Vigilance Visitor to the Boats," was waiting at the landing stage.[67] It was foggy, however, and the boat didn't arrive until nine. Rev. O'Connell got it from Pinnington that "the only disagreeable person was a girl of 19 who came from Dublin with the children. She was impertinent and gave vent to her feelings in regard to the way that they were treated in Dublin." Father Leech wrote with more passion: "I intend to do all I can to keep in touch with the children. . . . Certainly it was a sad sight this morning, most of the Children were crying."[68]

In the fairy abduction stories, the fairy point of view is rarely given. But the socialists recorded this event also, most notably Fred Bower (president of the Operative Stonemasons' Society) in his autobiography *Rolling Stonemason*. Bower says that he was asked to meet the children at the landing stage to escort them to their foster homes.

Detective Inspector McCoy came up to me. We knew each other. "Hello," he said. "What brings you down here so early?" "The same business as what brings you, I expect, Inspector," I replied. "I hope there will be no trouble." "There won't be any, if I can help it," he promised. The gangway was let down, and I went abord to meet Miss Neale who had charge of the bairns, pinched and ill-clad, most of them barefooted. I set off to board the ferry-boat which was to take us over the Mersey to a beautiful house in Cheshire, the occupant of which had promised to act as host for the children till they had all been fixed up in their respective destinations, when a priest stopped me. "Where are you going with the children?" he asked. I told him. "Have you their parents' permission?" "Not on me," I replied, "but it has been given." "Then I must give you in charge," he said, and called a policeman.

I explained to the officer. The detective inspector could vouch that I was known to him. Eventually we were corralled into a customs shed around a fire, and the children were regaled with cakes and hot tea. Another priest, a canon, had now appeared and began asking the scared mites what church they went to, had they attended Mass, and so on. The priest soon had the poor children crying. I said, "If you please, you might leave the children alone, they were quite comfortable before you interfered." Other things were said, but Miss Neale soothed the youngsters, and we waited.[69]

After Inspector McCoy returned with confirmation from the lord mayor of Dublin that the parents' consent had been given, Bower said to the priests, "You will have to stop annoying them, or else I shall call a policeman." The priests followed Bower on board the ferry because, as Bower told them, "I cannot stop you . . . the ferry-boat doesn't belong to me."

Although this was 1913, the phenomenon of the photo-op had already become part of the culture of human interest crises, especially those crises with pathetic-looking children. The photographer asked Bower if he would mind posing with the kiddies. " 'Not at all,' I replied. 'It may evoke sympathy with the plight of their parents, amongst the unthinking general public.' " The photo also became a site of struggle between labor and clergy: "I stood at the end of the line and just as the camera was going to click, the priest stood in the centre, and bless me, if the picture didn't cut me off, and an article stating 'our picture shows some of the strikers' children being taken to palatial foster-homes in the charge of Father Walsh of Liverpool.' "[70] The picture was printed in the *Liverpool Weekly Mercury* (as well as the *Liverpool Echo*), which indeed credited Father Leech (not Walsh, as Bower called him) with "looking after the children." Father Leech, at the far right, is definitely unsmiling. Next to him, farther right, the brim of a hat, the side of a cheek, and a shoulder, all no doubt belonging to Fred Bower, are just visible. A few of the children are smiling, looking rather pleased at all the excitement, especially a little girl in front with a striped blanket wrapped around her; and a few of the women in wide-brimmed hats are smiling also. Perhaps the girl on the far left, with her hand on her hip and an irritated expression on her face, is the nineteen-year-old Dublin girl who "gave vent to her feelings" and struck Canon Pinnington as "impertinent."

The *Mercury*'s account hints at controversy but does not make conflict explicit. The "little migrants," it says, "were well clad . . . but most of them were without overcoats or cloaks." This account also mentions the time spent in the waiting room, "where the children huddled round the gas fire" enjoying cakes and tea. Pinnington's intervention is alluded to in barely neutral understatement: "some further delay was caused by the rev. gentleman's anxiety as to the proper custodianship of the children. Police inquiries set this at rest." Miss Neal, interviewed by the reporter, was "indignant at the action of the police and priests in Dublin last night." Father Leech's involvement is treated dryly: "It was arranged that Father Rowe, Catholic rector of

DUBLIN STRIKERS' CHILDREN IN LIVERPOOL.

The children of Dublin strikers, who have arrived in Liverpool. They were taken to various houses in Wallasey. Our photograph was taken on board a ferry boat. A report of the arrival of the children will be found on this page. Father Leech, who was looking after the children, is on the right of the picture. "WEEKLY MERCURY."

4.5. The "kiddies" who were "saved." This photo of the eighteen Dublin children who were successfully "saved" by the socialists was taken on board the ferry boat after their arrival in Liverpool. On the right Father Leech, who protested against the "Kiddies" campaign, is visible. The caption erroneously says that Leech "was looking after the children." Cut off on the far right, with just the edge of his hat showing, is the socialist Fred Bower, who was sympathetic to the campaign: "Bless me, if the picture didn't cut me off," he wrote. Photo credit: Liverpool *Weekly Mercury*.

Wallasey, should visit the children, while Father Leech himself intends to call upon them daily. Being a Dublin man, he naturally feels it incumbent upon him to watch over the children's welfare while they are in this district."[71] Father Leech felt that the reports of his involvement with the children had been ambiguous to the point of inaccuracy. Complaining in a telegram sent to Dublin newspapers, he wrote,

Had the priests and people of Dublin known the atmosphere, anything but Catholic, to which the children have been taken, and in which I was forced to leave them because the parents had tied the hands of the priests here, their opposition would have been even more strenuous. I blush, as a priest and a Dublin man, to think of what I saw yesterday morning—that Irish parents could forget their sacred duty as the parents of these children have done. Where is the old spirit of the famine days?[72]

The letters to Archbishop Walsh about the abducted children in Liverpool stop at this point, but the socialists' surveillance continued. Naturally, they discovered that the children were doing beautifully: so Partridge wrote to Father O'Ryan a month later:

I have much pleasure in saying that I visited the little Dublin children in their temporary home outside Liverpool and was delighted to find them in high spirits and much improved as a result of their changed conditions. These children attend school regularly and are seen almost daily by the local priest. They are entirely in charge of a Miss Fox who went over specially from this Hall for that purpose. They go to Mass every Sunday, and the Lady of the House assured me that she would send them every day if the priest so desired.[73]

Fred Bower noted proudly, "Some three months afterwards . . . I escorted the children back. Now, bonnie and strong, and well-dressed, their own mothers hardly knew them."[74] With an ignorance of Irish anxieties perhaps as great as Montefiore's, Bower describes exactly the state of affairs that the priests had feared the most.

Eliza Doolittle

That same year, 1913, a play was published about some of these anxieties: its name was *Pygmalion.* The culture gap being negotiated in the play belonged to class, not to sect or nation, but the plot showed how traumatic cross-cultural transformation could be. The first stage of the bourgeoisifying of Eliza Doolittle was the terrifying bath forced on her by Henry Higgins's housekeeper: ablutionary domination preceded cultural domination, and both constituted aspects of total social domination. The priests knew exactly what was coming next: the bath was familiar in the popular mind as the preliminary transformative ritual when secular agents—socialists, Labour Party members, charity ladies—intervened in the lives of working-class families. The intimacy of the bath and the appropriation of the bodies of the poor by middle-class charity workers inevitably involves sexuality: it is while Eliza is being bathed, and her clothes burned, that Colonel Pickering asks Higgins if he is a "man of good character where women are concerned." The bath is an important moment in the procedure, because it signifies the transferal of ownership, or at least of responsibility for the bathed. Sexual ideas are thereafter present as a possibility, though not necessarily acted on: the bathed person is obviously sexually vulnerable but not necessarily sexually ruined. The mere presence of the possibility, however—for the 1913 children and for Eliza Doolittle—means that sexual dangers will constantly be mentioned and constantly be denied.

With Eliza as with the children, other ambiguities also loom disturbingly. For instance, who "owns" Eliza? Her father arrives at Higgins's house to find that Eliza is upstairs being bathed, and so he "sells" her to Higgins for £5.[75] The transfer of Eliza for cold cash is an ambiguous exchange: both men joke about it and take it seriously, depending on what argument they want to make. It looks bad, as if her father has sold her to be a "kept woman," but Higgins never so much as kisses her. The situation is as sexually fraught as it's possible for a situation with two heterosexual men and a young female virgin to be: but there's no sex at all until Eliza surrenders to her suitor, Freddy Eynsford Hill, after *she* has grabbed *him*. Eliza's age is as ambiguous as her sexual status: Higgins's housekeeper tells her to go home to her mother, and when her father arrives he assumes an ownership he has never assumed before. The class difference and Eliza's economic dependence on Pickering seem to perpetuate her childhood, but she began the play as an independent adult and she finishes it as one. At the end her class identity is also ambiguous, because it's not clear how much of her makeover will be permanent. All these ambiguities—sexuality, ownership, age, cultural identity—inhere in the situation of the play. And all those ambiguities inhered in the situation of the "Dublin kiddies," whose parents agreed to let them go for the sake of a better opportunity elsewhere and who turned them over to middle-class professionals. And those professionals began their intervention in the children's lives by washing them.

This parallel suggests that the anxieties kept alive by Archbishop Walsh and his priests and the Ancient Order of Hibernians were not altogether unfounded, and that they were present in the popular mind at the time. The actions involved—washing, traveling over water, being fed by strangers in a foreign country—seemed to be rituals of permanent transformation, and the intimate care of children by strangers raised other issues too. Sexual anxiety was more than a subtext in the "Save the Dublin Kiddies" campaign: it was mentioned often. One Joseph McCarroll wrote to Archbishop Walsh on October 22, "If your Grace now takes advantage of the popular indignation roused by the Deportation of our young Girls—the boys are only a blind—you will sweep Larkinism into the sea."[76] Montefiore was publicly accused of acting on behalf of the white slave trade.

To other people it was not the "kidnapping" but the situation of the slums that seemed redolent of sexuality. A Dublin woman wrote Walsh complaining that the Church had not done enough for the poor, saying: "Why don't you . . . have houses built for them and prevent them from having to put girls and boys in the one [sleeping room]—aged 14 and 16 sleeping in the same bed—now instead of building churches and schools would not my suggestion be better?"[77] Bernard Shaw, speaking at a Labour protest demonstration at the Royal Albert Hall on November 1, made sexuality an explicit issue:

> It had been said that children were a great safeguard of morality in Dublin, and there were some dwellings in Dublin that if they took the children out of them the adults would misbehave themselves. [Laughter.] Don't laugh at that, said Mr. Shaw, it is a most appalling thing, and I believe there are people who say that at the present day. I believe that within the last few days there have been people who have given that as a reason for not allowing the children to leave Dublin. Ponder over it a little and you will realize the situation.[78]

It is not clear in all these nervous suggestions where the sexual danger actually is, in the tenements or in the kidnappers, but it is pervasive. As in *Pygmalion*, the threat is in the situation, even when no sexual contact is made.

Paradigms of the Family

At the heart of "Save the Dublin Kiddies" was a radical paradigm of the family. Anxieties were inspired not only by the fear of permanent cultural transformation in the children but by the autonomy of the women organizing the campaign. Women appearing to work without male supervision were moving children about in the name of a larger socialist family. Although it was primarily women who (under various institutional auspices) fed the hungry children of Dublin, few of them appeared as independent as Dora Montefiore. Most worked in secondary and subordinate positions, or took care to appear subordinate.

The "lady mayoress," Marie Sherlock, under whose name funds were collected for those impoverished during the strike, and the "lady Hibernians" who wrote Archbishop Walsh offering their services, obviously derived their authority from the mayor and the all-male Ancient Order of Hibernians. In the many convents of the city, women religious (the Sisters of the Holy Faith, the Sisters of Charity, the Sisters of the Assumption) were feeding the children, but their authority was subordinated to that of the archbishop. The Ladies School Dinners Committee, whose members included Maud Gonne, Helen Laird, and Hanna Sheehy Skeffington, among others, managed to feed dinners daily to 450 schoolchildren in the poorer parishes of the city. They did so successfully in part because they had engaged the help of various patriarchies. As they explained to Archbishop Walsh in a letter, they worked "wholly through a parochial committee nominated by the manager" of the school.[79] Their ultimate goal was the extension to Ireland of the Schools Meals Act, which had been passed by Parliament in 1910 without any thought to the need for such legislation to cover Ireland also. To that end, they worked closely with members of the Irish Parliamentary Party, especially Stephen Gwynn. Under the auspices of the all-male Irish Transport and General Workers Union, the soup kitchen of Liberty Hall was staffed by numerous volunteers—Constance Markievicz, Hanna Sheehy Skeffington, William Orpen, and others. Even the seemingly autonomous Dora Montefiore labored with the blessing of male authority: in order to get "Save the Dublin Kiddies" off the ground, she had to pass that note to Jim Larkin to get his permission.

Yet within the patriarchal administrative structures there existed wide disparities in the amount of power assumed by the women. When the Archbishop's Children's Distress Fund, stimulated into being by "Save the Dublin Kiddies," ran into problems, men determined the way food was distributed. In the parish of Our Lady of Dolours in Dolphin's Barn, in south Dublin, there was no convent, so a local ladies committee did the actual feeding. However, Canon Cor-

4.6. The Liberty Hall soup kitchen. The artist William Orpen did this sketch of the soup kitchen in Liberty Hall, Jim Larkin's headquarters, when the starved, skeletal workers were fed. The man with the ladle is Orpen himself.

nelius Ryan, priest of that parish, "turned away the children from the tables" as they were being fed, saying he wanted to reduce the numbers. In distress, the ladies sought the advice of the curate, Father L. J. Stafford, who himself turned to Monsignor Fitzpatrick of the neighboring St. Kevin's parish. Fitzpatrick advised them not to refuse the children food. Then a further complication developed: the irate parents would not send their children back to school. Belligerently asking the children's fathers if they "belonged to Larkin's union," Canon Ryan alienated the parents of the parish. Mr. Conroy of 17 Dolphin's Barn Street said he wished he did belong to the union, because then "he wouldn't trouble Canon Ryan or his school" for food. Father

Stafford recounted these events in a letter to Archbishop Walsh, acknowledging, "it is very painful to have to write all this."[80]

An analogous decision in the Liberty Hall soup kitchen was made on the spot by the woman with the ladle in her hand, without recourse to the greater power structure. Hanna Sheehy Skeffington told this story of Constance Markievicz after "Madame's" death:

> one child that came with its bowl for the tasty stew was turned away with scorn by the other waiting ones. . . . Madame, seeing the youngster turn away, abashed, leaving the waiting queue with empty porringer, before its turn came, asked the cause and was told: "His father is a scab." Peremptorily she ordered him back into the line, filling his porringer when his turn came, saying: "No child is a scab, whatever about his father. I won't turn any child away that comes here. He'll have his canful with the rest."[81]

No organization that had room for Markievicz could require women to surrender authority. Fortunately she did not have to face Canon Ryan.

Nor did Maud Gonne surrender any authority, though she worked to some extent within the Church's structure, feeding the children at St. Audoen's and Johns Lane schools. The wisely deferential wording of the letter sent by the Ladies School Dinners Committee to Archbishop Walsh insisted with unmistakable clarity on their close collaboration with parochial authorities and on the distinctly unsocialist character of their organization. The strong feminist energies behind its labors were evident: in a speech Helen Laird referred to their work as a "domestic aspect of women's suffrage."[82] But no such wording appears in the letter to Walsh. Writing to W. B. Yeats, who contributed to the Dinners Committee, Gonne noted that she and Laird "had a most interesting & satisfactory interview with Archbishop Walsh about School Dinners."[83] Alas, no transcript exists of the meeting, but its content may be guessed at. Perhaps Gonne referred to "fat English Socialists," a phrase she used in a letter to John Quinn, or perhaps she used some similar, politer term to signal her solidarity with the Church.[84] Whatever she said, it worked. "Now that Archbishop Walsh has expressed approval of our work," she wrote to Yeats, "& will help getting the permissive act through Parliament I hope it will not be long till we get the whole thing on a municipal basis as it is in other countries."[85]

Certainly the most important thing the rich, independent, sexually unconventional Maud Gonne did was to visit the archbishop and seek his approval for a system that had in fact been functioning for three years. Of course Montefiore had sought Larkin's approval, but neither Walsh nor the Westland Row curates saw Dora Montefiore pass that note to Larkin; and Larkin was so demonized, it would have made little difference. What they did see was the efficient work of Montefiore, Lucilla Rand, and Grace Neal, aided by Delia Larkin, as they passed the children through socialist hands. Walsh knew that the treasurer of the fund was Lady Warwick and that the socialist and suffrage campaigner Emmeline Pethick-Lawrence had also helped. The involvement of so many English women in separating Irish Catholic children from their parents was threatening on all counts: where were the men to keep these women under control? "These idiot women," Stephen Gwynn called them in a letter to Walsh.[86]

With hindsight, it is possible to see larger patterns that would have unsettled Archbishop Walsh even more. For at least three of the women involved in the various charitable endeavors, feeding the Dublin kiddies was an activity so professionally important that they left their own children in the care of someone else. Lucilla Rand's infant was with her husband in London, where she had hired someone to care for it.[87] Maud Gonne had left Seagan and Iseult in France, and Constance Markievicz had long since left her daughter Medbh to be cared for at Lissadell, far from Dublin in County Sligo. The devoted nuns working so hard in the city's slums, feeding more children than all the others together, had of course sacrificed absolutely the possibility of having children, for the sake of professionally taking care of other people's children. They had sacrificed biological maternity for social motherhood. Throughout the century, women like these would be engaged professionally in social work, child welfare, and nutrition. By the century's end, they would be administering global nonprofit organizations. Montefiore's threatening autonomy was a vision of the future.

The Intelligentsia

To those undisturbed by the vision of autonomous professional women or the idea of English socialists feeding Irish Catholic children, the abuse of clerical authority brought outrage and distress. The clergy had expressed through body language their feelings about the feminist-socialist way of saving the kiddies. The great demonstration

on behalf of the Dublin strikers that took place at the Royal Albert
Hall in London on November 1 gave an opportunity for the leaders of
the left to speak. An all-star cast was seated on the platform: the cru-
sading municipal socialist and leading male feminist George Lans-
bury presided over a group that included James Connolly, Delia
Larkin, Bernard Shaw, George Russell, Dora Montefiore, the socialist
and union organizer Ben Tillet, and the suffragist Sylvia Pankhurst.
(Jim Larkin was in Mountjoy Prison, whence he had ordered the removal of the chair sent by Dora Montefiore.) The crowd, said the
Freeman's Journal, was "distinctly Socialist in character. . . . Quite a
large percentage of the audience were women, many of whom wore
Suffrage badges and sashes."[88]

So sensitive was the clerical issue that James Connolly said nothing about "Save the Dublin Kiddies" that night. He kept his focus on
the strikers: "they could not build up a free nation on the basis of
slavery. Whether there was a green flag or a red flag mattered little to
a man who had nothing in his stomach."[89] In a piece in the labor journal *Forward* published on the day of the London meeting, Connolly
said that he had "never been enthusiastic" about the scheme, but he
defended Montefiore's integrity. "Nobody wants to send the children
away . . . but neither do we wish the children to starve . . . the master
class of Dublin calmly and coldbloodedly calculate upon using the
sufferings of the children to weaken the resistance of the parents."
Connolly urged Walsh to intervene in the strike, "if your Grace is as
solicitous about the poor bodies of those children as we know you to
be about their souls."[90] But a challenge was not an insult. Months
later, at a Labour meeting in Belfast, Connolly "rose to his feet in a
white heat of indignation" when a young Dublin man appeared to
have spoken insultingly about one of the priests who had thwarted
the "Kiddies" campaign. Connolly, said a witness, began "passionately denouncing . . . the speaker for daring to speak so slightingly
and so disparagingly of a parish priest."[91]

Given his attempt, in writing, to bring the official Church over
publicly to the side of labor, and given his "white heat of indignation," Connolly must have hated Shaw's speech. It was in this company that Shaw not only mentioned "misbehavior" in the slums but,
more shockingly, purported to "apologise for the priests of Dublin."

> The honest truth about it was that those men, although they were
> pious and were doing a good deal of good work, were very ignorant and
> simple men in the affairs of the country, and especially in industrial

affairs. If by any means these words reached them he hoped they
would be obliged to him for the apology he had made for them.[92]

Shaw had raised provocation to such an art that he could disturb the
greatest number of people with the fewest words. To patronize the
Dublin priests by calling them "pious," "ignorant," and "simple,"
and then to suggest they might be "obliged" to Bernard Shaw, of all
people, for apologizing for them—only a genius at controversy could
create another one so effortlessly. The ink began flowing the day this
speech was reported. Dora Sigerson Shorter wrote in to "apologise, as
a Dublin Catholic, to the priests of Dublin for this impertinent
Protestant." Mary Maher commented that although she was not
given to "seeking a place" in any "controversial battlefield," she felt
compelled to complain about Shaw's "impertinent audacity." L. J.
McQuilland asked, "Is it not time that Mr. Shaw ceased talking non-
sense in public and reserved his apologetics . . . for his interminable
prefaces and his indeterminate plays?"[93]

The conflict between clergy and women socialists in Dublin was
replicated across the waters in another secondary controversy that developed between G. K. Chesterton and Rebecca West. In an article in
the *New Witness,* Chesterton had attacked Montefiore for her Jewish
last name and her feminism.[94] Writing in the *Clarion,* West attacked
Chesterton for his "hysterics" and his anti-Semitism; she condemned
as well the priests who were "busy getting hold of Grace Neal by the
shoulders and shaking her."[95] What had begun as a direct, physical expression of antagonisms became a series of verbal contentions published in numerous small ideological rags—*Forward,* the *New Witness,* the *Clarion,* and the *Irish Worker* (Larkin's paper, to which Yeats
had sent a letter), as well as the major newspapers of both Ireland and
England. The issue couldn't be decided, but it could be fought.

Unlike all the professional controversialists who could be depended on to make speeches, write letters, and engage in ideological
debate, Frank Sheehy Skeffington put his body on the line for this
controversy, and its essential brutality was visited on him directly.
The one man injured on behalf of "Save the Dublin Kiddies" was Ireland's most famous male feminist. On October 25 his letter to the
Irish Times complained about the treatment given Montefiore and
asked, "Why are the clerical intimidators allowed to escape? Does the
black coat put them above the law?"[96] A fearless activist, Sheehy
Skeffington wanted to confront the enemy directly.

The very day the letter appeared, openly stating his point of view, Sheehy Skeffington went to Kingsbridge railway station "as a journalist," he said later, to see if the previous days' scenes "would be repeated" and to help get two young boys, sons of a locked-out worker, out of Dublin. There he saw a crowd of AOH members and priests, who shouted "Here they are!" when he appeared with the children and the children's father. Sheehy Skeffington's "persistency roused the anger of the crowd," said the *Freeman's Journal*, and he was "forcibly ejected . . . from the station premises. There were marks on his forehead, and his hat got lost in the rush."[97] Sheehy Skeffington's own description in police court the following week was more detailed. He was "seized from behind, knocked down, and buffeted out of the station. He was bruised on the head and about the body. . . . the crowd attempted to trip witness, and there were shouts of 'Kill him.' . . . He went back for his bicycle, and the crowd again surrounded him, kicked and struck him, and gashed the tyres of his bicycle."[98] Earlier that day, when Skeffington had not turned up on time at Liberty Hall to pick up the children, Larkin had asked William Orpen to take the children to the station. Orpen had been helping out in the soup kitchen; his famous drawing shows the thin, almost skeletal bodies of the workers' families crowing around a large vat of soup. He agreed at once and was on his way out with the children when Skeffington appeared to collect them: "This is my business," he told Orpen firmly. Orpen was there later when, preceded by "great noises and loud words," Sheehy Skeffington returned. "He had nothing on except a blanket wrapped around him," wrote Orpen; "I nearly got that."[99]

"This is my business," Sheehy Skeffington had said to Orpen, because he wanted to reveal the continuing antagonism and physical brutality of the Catholic mob by drawing their hostility against himself. Frank, his son Owen Sheehy Skeffington wrote years later, liked to call himself a "crank," because "a crank is a small instrument that makes revolutions."[100] Although he did not make any revolutions in October 1913, with his typical idealism and courage Sheehy Skeffington kept the nature of mob rule before the public. He had no wish to press charges against the men who had assaulted him most directly because, as he said in court, "they are merely the dupes of more astute persons in the background," namely the secretary of the AOH and the priests who had been stirring up the mob.[101] Moreover, he had no personal animosity: what he wanted was to tell his story in court so it would be reported in the papers, as indeed it was.

Meanwhile, at the Abbey Theatre, only minutes away from the spot where John Byrne and James Nolan had died during the police baton charge back in August, absolute authority was being challenged in a safer form. Yeats's drama of political defiance *The King's Threshold* (written in 1904) echoed the struggle outside. The poet Seanchan, determined to starve rather than live without "the ancient right of the poets" to sit on the kingdom's council of state, dies on the king's threshold. A curse on the king sounded its abusive note from the stage:

> The curse of the poor be upon him,
> The curse of the widows upon him,
> The curse of the children upon him,
> The curse of the bishops upon him,
> Until he be as rotten as an old mushroom![102]

Reverberations

Like most controversies, "Save the Dublin Kiddies" was not a battle cleanly fought and definitively won. Both sides could claim victory: the plan was stopped, but the Church's image was damaged by the violence and anger displayed in so many ugly scenes. The most articulate intellectuals of the day defended Montefiore's reputation from the ludicrous charges made against her, but only eighteen out of an original three hundred children were sent to that "cleaner and more hopeful environment." Nor was it possible to divide the participants into tidy and mutually exclusive categories. Anyone who tried to would inevitably discover what a small city Dublin was and how closely connected were all the antagonists. In the angry mob that beat up Frank Sheehy Skeffington at Kingsbridge Station that Saturday was one Lizzie Farrell, who "rescued" the children Skeffington was trying to help onto the train. Farrell in turn was of course charged with kidnapping, and she was bailed out by her old friend and neighbor, James Connolly. Frank's wife, Hanna, was closely allied with Maud Gonne in her work on the Ladies School Dinners Committee. Gonne, so determined to get Walsh's approval, had been born an English Protestant; Lucilla Rand, one of the alleged "English kidnappers," was an American and a devout Catholic. As a letter to Archbishop Walsh pointed out, Rand's marriage had been performed by the papal nuncio to Portugal when her father was the American ambassador there.[103] And William Orpen, who so movingly sketched the starving strikers, painted the villainous capitalist William Martin Murphy just over a year later. In fact the portrait was commissioned as a testimonial by the Dublin Chamber of Commerce in appreciation of Murphy's services "during the recent prolonged labour troubles."[104]

After the creation of the Irish Free State in 1922, the continuing Catholic anxiety about the cultural erosion of its population became hard to distinguish from the institutional determination to control—and, when necessary, punish—female autonomy. The secretive adoption practices sanctioned by the Catholic Church in the years following independence embodied a more intimate form of control. Between the 1940s and the early 1970s, thousands of helpless unmarried Irish mothers were held as virtual prisoners in the infamous Magdalene laundries, while their babies were "rescued" and sent away for adoption.[105] The church established its own private channels for the passage of the children to ensure that they would be sent to Catholic families in the United States, not Protestant families in Northern Ireland. Few records were kept of these transactions, and although the Magdalene laundries no longer exist, the results of the adoption practices are still felt. The World Wide Web is full of sites where these children and their biological parents seek one another out.[106]

The 1957 Fethard-on-Sea boycott also provides a distant echo, with tragic consequences, of "Save the Dublin Kiddies." In that episode, a Protestant mother "rescued" her own children from the interferences of the Catholic clergy. Sean Cloney and Sheila Kelly, Catholic and Protestant, were children of friendly neighbors but had to marry in an English registry office because of the opposition of the local Catholic clergy. Although, in keeping with the "Ne Temere" decree, Mrs. Cloney had agreed to bring the children up as Catholics, she "didn't fancy being ordered," said her husband, and not long after a priest informed her that her daughter Eileen would have to attend Catholic school, she left Fethard for Northern Ireland with both her children. Catholics in Fethard began a boycott of Protestant businesses, and Mrs. Cloney's father, a cattle dealer, "was ruined," noted Mr. Cloney, and "later died of a broken heart." The boycott was ended through a joint statement issued by Mr. Kelly and the local Dáil deputy, a Catholic. Ultimately Mrs. Cloney returned with the children, who were educated at home by their parents.

Like the O'Hickey controversy, the Fethard-on-Sea controversy ended in an apology years after the fact: in 1998 the bishop of Ferns, Dr. Brendan Comiskey, apologized for the Church's role in the boycott. In 1999, the Cloneys' sorrow was made into the film *A Love Divided*. But by that time the debate over the Irish Church's control of children and their mothers had moved into territory Archbishop Walsh could never have imagined. When his successor, Dr. Connell, announced that children conceived by artificial insemination were not loved as much by their parents as children conceived non-artificially, he was greeted by protests from women and men who, like Mrs. Cloney, didn't fancy being ordered.

5

The Afterlife of Roger Casement

Memory, Folklore, Ghosts, 1916–

Bíonn dhá insint ar gach scéal, agus dhá chasadh dhéag ar gach amhrán.
There are two tellings to each tale, and twelve singings to each song.

"Pervert." The word, hissed out at the end of a sentence after long hesitation, shocked into alertness the people assembled in the magnificent high-ceilinged eighteenth-century lecture room of the Royal Irish Academy. It was the question period on the second day of the Academy's symposium on Sir Roger Casement in Irish and World History, in May 2000, and after seven hours of talk about Casement, even the most obsessive will snooze a bit, especially in the late afternoon. The squeamishness of the woman speaker, evidently reluctant to use the word *homosexual*, amused people in the audience at the same time as it made them slightly uncomfortable. Even those in agreement with her that the famous Black Diaries attributed to Sir Roger Casement had been forged were uneasy that their own point of view might be identified with someone whose *mentalité* was not the most advanced: Casement, she said, had never told his barrister "that he was a . . . pervert."

The power of Roger Casement to disturb and embarrass people, even eighty-four years after his death, was once more manifest. The heady combination of humanitarianism, nationalism, and homosexuality, topics inevitable in any debate about Casement, wrought hysteria in Free State Ireland, but that might be expected: weren't they anxious about national identity in those days, and wasn't sexuality banned from the country—or at least from public speech? "There

was, famously, no sex in Ireland between 1920 and 1960," as Derek
Mahon remarked.[1] But in the enlightened twenty-first century, seven
years after homosexual acts between consenting adults over the age of
seventeen had been decriminalized in the Republic of Ireland, surely
everyone could accept a martyr who happened to be gay, or at least air
the possibility clinically? Apparently not: the positive conclusions of
a handwriting expert who had examined the diaries, the testimony of
official British record keepers who had turned the files upside down
to look for evidence of skullduggery, even the research of a gay Northern Irish writer who had unearthed the Belfast genealogy of one of
Casement's boyfriends—all this was not enough to convert the convinced, including, most notably, the woman who would not say *homosexual*.[2]

   If a cultural genealogy were to be created for Casement, it might include those other sexually transgressive anti-imperialists Lord Byron
and Wilfrid Blunt, with T. E. Lawrence a later scion of the same family. With a histrionic sense of their own importance, and a pleasure in
shocking the more sedate members of their own class, Byron and
Blunt led colorful lives on a grand international stage. Blunt, Yeats,
and Casement, wrote Mary Colum, "were the handsomest and most
romantic-looking men I have ever seen." Meeting Casement in a
restaurant around 1914, she saw "a magnificent-looking stranger. . . .
So striking-looking was he . . . that the patrons of Pagani's stopped
eating and stared at him."[3] Casement's height, good looks, and musical voice ("with its singular intensity") can only have helped him in
his various projects over a lifetime. Casement, however, never had
money to throw around as Byron and Blunt did, and he wrote poetry
only on the side. He lacked their flamboyance and bravura display.
They, however, lacked his nobility.

   According to Martin Mansergh, who spoke as the taoiseach's representative at the Royal Irish Academy symposium, the present Irish
state takes pride in attributing the origin of the Irish international
humanitarian tradition to Casement's heroic work in the Congo and
the Putumayo region of Brazil.[4] For his labors in the Congo recording
cruelty, torture, murder, and other abuses of power in Belgian rubber
plantations, all documented and presented to Westminster in 1904,
and his later work investigating similar atrocities in the Putumayo
district of South America, Casement, who had been a British consul
in both places, was awarded a CMG (Companion of the Order of St.
Michael and St. George) in 1905 and knighted in 1911. No one else at

the time had the geographical knowledge as well as the idealism, courage, and energy to travel in such dangerous territories and photograph virtually enslaved natives whose hands or feet had been chopped off when they arrived late at work, or to interview the men who regularly flogged and murdered them.[5]

An Irish nationalist hero as well as a human rights activist, Casement later helped organize the successful Howth gunrunning in 1914, which provided arms for the Irish Volunteers, and was an active supporter of the Irish language movement. He spent the first two years of the Great War in Germany, attempting to secure the support of the Berlin government for Irish independence, to recruit Irishmen from German prisoners-of-war to fight against England in the anticipated Rising (or elsewhere—Casement's plans were unfixed), and to negotiate a German gift of arms for use in the Rising. On Good Friday morning 1916, Casement and two other men were dropped on the north Kerry coast by a German submarine. The madcap venture came to a bad end: an accompanying ship carrying guns was detected by a British cruiser and scuttled itself, and Casement was soon captured and sent to prison in London. After a trial in June 1916, he was found guilty of High Treason and was hanged on August 3.

The so-called Black Diaries, five books allegedly found in trunks in Casement's former London lodgings on Ebury Street, testify either to Casement's hidden homosexual life or to the unusual genius of a British forger, who somehow learned the names of people in the places Casement visited all over the globe. Reading the diaries at the time of the trial, John Harris of the Anti-Slavery Society found in them "suggestive episodes in Congo contexts that only he and Casement knew about."[6] For those who like their heroes pure, the diarist's interest in penis size, his romantic longings, and his detailed accounts of sexual adventures on several continents and archipelagoes confirm that he could not be Casement. Parnell's monogamous adultery looks chaste next to the diarist's infatuations, lusts, and assignations—sometimes three in one day. His coded "X" for intercourse and explicit phrases like "pulled it off on top grandly" do not, for the forgery theorists, represent actual events: these are the inventions of British Intelligence, created, as Yeats wrote, "to blacken his good name."[7] To those who accept the diaries as authentic, their entries show Casement's hearty, uncensored lust: "Biggest since Lisbon July 1904 & as big," the diarist writes in February 1910, "Perfectly huge."[8] As commentators have noted, Casement was a "size queen."[9] But whether written by the historical Roger Casement or by his British doppelgänger, the diaries express in generous detail what only an active male homosexual could have known, the hidden life of the Edwardian homosexual subculture. They offer remarkable information about cruising grounds, the cost of sexual encounters, codes, terminologies, sexual positions, and homosocial friendships.

The diaries have done much more than "blacken" Casement's name or reveal lost social histories: they have created a way of thinking about heroism, sexuality, and public life. Nor are the diaries the only problematic aspect of Casement's biography; his identity is more unstable and contested than that of the Lane paintings, where only ownership is at issue, or the Dublin kiddies, whose nationality and religion were threatened. To talk about posthumous Casement is to talk about what people have projected onto his name, and as Medbh McGuckian said in an interview, "He covers a lot of ground for a lot of people."[10] An anti-imperialist consul, a baptized Catholic and confirmed Protestant, born in Dublin of a County Antrim family, a cultural nationalist, a closeted homosexual, a butterfly collector, Casement has offered a means of thinking about much of Irish life, indeed much of human life, in the twentieth century. The "matter" of Casement continues to accumulate at an astonishing rate: poems about him have been written by Yeats, Wilfrid Blunt, Eva Gore-Booth, Alice Milligan, Maeve Cavanagh (the self-styled "poet of the Rising"), Richard Murphy, Medbh McGuckian, Bernard O'Donoghue, and numerous obscure poets; poetic sequences devoted to Casement have been written by Philip Brady (*Forged Correspondences*), Sean Hutton (*Seachrán Ruairí agus Dánte Eile*), and Medbh McGuckian, and he makes cameo appearances in poems by Louis MacNeice, Derek Mahon, Paul Durcan, and Paul Muldoon.[11] In Joyce's *Ulysses*, Casement's name comes up in the conversation in Barney Kiernan's pub:

> — . . . if they're any worse than those Belgians in the Congo Free State they must be bad. Did you read that report by a man what's this his name is?
> —Casement, says the citizen. He's an Irishman.
> —Yes, that's the man.[12]

Eimar O'Duffy, Stevie Smith, J. H. Pollock, Terence de Vere White, Neil Jordan, W. G. Sebald, Jamie O'Neill, Annabel Davis-Goff, and even Agatha Christie have also written Casement into fiction.[13] Michael Carson's 1995 novel *The Knight of the Flaming Heart* devotes itself entirely to posthumous Casement as he returns to North Kerry, a future saint and sometimes visible ghost, saving lives, helping the needy, and astonishing the local priest.[14] At least eight plays have been written about Casement, whose life was already pure drama. Sir John Lavery made at least two paintings of the trial, Sarah Purser did a handsome portrait, and there are at least five ballads about Casement, including the famous "Banna Strand."[15]

Casement is not just a curiosity for writers: he is a persistent presence in popular culture. More biographies have been written about him than about any other figure of 1916, and he has been the focus of seven radio and television documentaries. At least three monuments (at Banna Strand, Glasnevin, and Murlough Bay) are devoted to him, as well as an amazing statue that dominates the center of Ballyheigue, a town north of Banna Strand that Casement is not known to have visited. A curse on films about Casement has so far prevented five attempts from reaching completion.[16] Like any national hero, he can be found here and there in the general civic landscape: the Tralee railway station (whence he was sent as a prisoner to London on April 22, 1916) has been named after him, as has the Dublin airport (formerly Baldonnel Airfield), where his remains first touched Irish soil in February 1965. The Gaelic Athletic Association playing fields in Belfast bear his name. Opposite the Banna Strand monument, tourists may pitch their tents or park their vans at Sir Roger's Caravan and Camping Park. And quite apart from these countable manifestations of Casement, he exists in numerous jokes and anecdotes in Irish folk memory.

The newspaper controversies inspired by Casement, infinitely expandable in length and quantity, form their own subgenre of controversy. Like the characters in Luis Buñuel's *Exterminating Angel,* who for some unknowable supernatural reason cannot leave a dinner party where they are guests, the participants in Casement letter-controversies repeatedly insist on the necessity for closure but are unable to close the controversy. There is always one person (or twenty) left eager to have the last word. "The fascination of the voluminous correspondence on the moral character of Casement is only exceeded by its futility," wrote one Murroe FitzGerald to the *Irish Times* in 1956.[17] Writing to the *Irish Times* in 1973 at what seemed like the end of a Casement controversy, one Mr. Peacocke scolded, "I think the less written about the matter the better."[18] But debate about Casement has been unrelenting.

The great ambiguity that has so far existed at the heart of Casement's life—did he write the diaries? was he homosexual?—has made him especially a site for all sorts of speculations about sexuality: it was always possible to reject the authenticity of the diaries yet enjoy the titillating atmosphere they provided. One could participate in a Casement controversy from the highest celibate motives and gain thereby a kind of proximity to the diaries. Until 1959, when the pirated Peter Singleton-Gates edition of the diaries was published, most people had no idea what precisely the diaries said, but their evidently plural nature, and the general impression that they recorded something naughty and forbidden, linked them in the popular mind with a monumental expressiveness.[19] The diaries *talked;* they told things. The same Roger Casement who had died on the scaffold for Ireland had not perhaps felt the same restrictions that his fellow countrymen and women now felt: he had broken taboos, experienced forbidden things, and written about them. Because Casement was a national hero, to argue about the diaries from any point of view, even to think about them, was to take on the great subject of sexuality as it existed in a national field, where it was defined, organized, and controlled by national institutions—the state, the church, the law.

And because Casement claimed public attention for so many other, unambiguous reasons, he offered a way of thinking about difficult matters, suppressed in Ireland for most of the past century, without ever calling them by name, and without deliberately, systematically, consciously deciding to think about them. Casement's life made possible all sorts of convenient safety nets: his eloquent speech from the dock, after the guilty verdict was returned, could always be adverted to when debate about the diaries grew too hot or too hopeless; his generosity to the language movement could be invoked to counterbalance the failures of the Irish brigade and the gunrunning; and when sex and nationalism both became too fraught, there was always the Congo, where Casement achieved uncontestable success. Indeed, the thoroughness of Casement's record-keeping remains the source of his fame and his infamy, preserving for posterity the details of his amazing life. For the greater part of the twentieth century, Ireland lived vicariously through Roger Casement, using the manifold and extraordinary facts of his life to explore without risk topics otherwise unapproachable.

5.1. The Casement diaries. These ordinary-looking notebooks caused the longest-running and most passionate controversy in Irish history. Permission of National Archives Image Library (Public Record Office).

Casement's Homosexual Discourse

Casement did in fact embody precisely the kind of expressiveness about sexual matters that he came, however fortuitously and ambiguously, to symbolize. Although he never developed the public discourse of sexuality that his own life indirectly provided, he did develop various kinds of private sexual discourses. Their very privateness—diaries, unpublished poems, an unsent, coded letter— suggests how shocked Casement must have been to realize they were the subject of public scrutiny, and how astonished he would have been to discover that his posthumous reputation was forever inseparable from these private records. Even though, until 1959, few people knew what was in the notorious diaries, and even though, until the 1990s, many people assumed they had been forged, Casement was nevertheless linked with taboo sexual experiences and with the articulation of those experiences. It was as a completely

The Nameless One.

No human hand to steal to mine,
No loving Eye to answering shine,
Earth's cruel heart of dust alone
To give me breath and strength to groan.

I look beyond the stricken sky
Where Sunset paints its hopeless lie —
That way the flaming angel went
Who sought by pride Love's battlement.

I sought by love alone to go
Where God had writ an awful no :—
Pride gave a guilty God to Hell —
I have no pride — by love I fell.

Love took me by the heart at birth
And wrought from out its common Earth,
With soul at his own skill aghast
A furnace mine own breath should blast.

Why this was done I cannot tell :
The mystery lives inscrutable —
I only know I pay the cost —
With heart, and soul and honour lost.

I only know 'tis death to give
My love, — yet loveless can I live ? —
I only know I cannot die
And leave this love God made, not I.

God met this love — there let it rest :
Perchance it need my ridden breast
To heavenly Eyes the Scheme to show
My broken heart must never know.

[over]

The Nameless One

‘Lines written in Very Great Dejection at Genoa. November 15. 1900, before Sailing on "Sirio" for Barcelona.

5.2. "The Nameless One." This poem by Casement, modeled on James Clarence Mangan's poem of the same name, is thought by many readers to refer to the author's homosexuality. He writes, "I sought by love alone to go / Where God had writ an awful no. . . . Why this was done I cannot tell: / The mystery is inscrutable— / I only know I pay the cost— / With heart, and soul and honour lost." On the back of the manuscript is written the title and a comment on the poem's genesis: "Lines written in Very Great Dejection at Genoa. November 15, 1900, before Sailing on 'Sirio' for Barcelona." Printed with permission of the New York Public Library, Maloney Collection, Irish Historical Papers.

transgressive figure that Casement came to be so important to the Irish mind.

Given, then, the way so much sexual commentary came to focus on Casement, it is worth considering precisely the freedoms and the limits of his own language of homosexuality. In truth, Casement had had more experiences than most people could have imagined, and he had written more about them than they could have read. The infamous Labouchère amendment to the Criminal Law Amendment Act bill of 1885 made private male homosexual activities criminal. The only acceptable way to talk about homosexuality publicly was as sin, as crime, or as pathology—and in fact Casement, in his private writings, used all those modes. When the Scottish colonial general Sir Hector Macdonald, charged by his political enemies with homosexual practices, committed suicide in Paris in 1903 before facing a court-martial, Casement wrote in his diary: "The reasons given are pitiably sad! The most distressing case this surely of its kind and one that may awake the national mind to saner methods of curing a terrible disease than by criminal legislation."[20] This public-sounding private comment shifts the ground of wrong from criminality to disease, using the discourse of progressive journalism ("may awake the national mind to saner methods").

Even more expressive are Casement's continuing remarks on the Macdonald case; the suggestions about the "national mind" did not fully articulate what Casement felt. "Very sorry at Hector Macdonald's terrible end" he writes two days later, and eleven days after that, "Hector Mac[d]onald's death very sad."[21] On another occasion years later, sailing down the Amazon during his investigations there, Casement adopts the stern, disapproving tone of a missionary as he views an unusual scene: "The boat servants looking on practically while these three boys played with each other with laughter & jokes! A fine beastly morality for a Christian Coy at 9 a.m. with three of the domestic servants."[22] Roger Sawyer suggests that Casement "was appalled because servants, looking on while two [sic] young boys 'played with each other' found the spectacle amusing." Whatever the explanation of his response, the tone implied by his exclamation point and his conventional deprecation ("fine beastly morality") shows that he could adopt the castigatory tone expected of the occasion, that it perhaps came naturally to him.

On at least one occasion, Casement attempted to articulate and defend his homosexuality in a discourse both religious and romantic.

However tame, even bland, the poem "The Nameless One" may seem by contemporary standards, it says enough to have upset the members of the Roger Casement Foundation, whose pamphlet *The Vindication of Roger Casement* claims that the poem in question was written by John Addington Symonds and that a poem of the same title, written by Casement in 1898, was "composed on the massacre of the Armenians by the Sultan of Turkey."[23] What comfort, to transfer the title of Casement's poem about his guilty "love" to a poem of such pure and undisputed humanitarian virtue. The latter poem, printed in the pamphlet, apostrophizes "Thou murderer!" and inveighs against the man "Stupendous in the vastness of thy crime." A holograph manuscript of a poem titled "The Nameless One," signed by Casement, rests among the Maloney Irish Historical Papers of the New York Public Library with other Casement poems. Its authenticity as yet unquestioned, the page is inscribed on the back "Lines written in Very Great Dejection at Genoa. November 15, 1900, before Sailing on 'Sirio' for Barcelona":

> No human hand to steal to mine
> No loving Eye to answering shine,
> Earth's cruel heart of dust alone
> To give me breath and strength to groan.
>
> I look beyond the stricken sky
> Where Sunset paints its hopeless lie—
> That way the flaming Angel went
> Who sought by pride Love's battlement.
>
> I sought by love alone to go
> Where God had writ an awful no:—
> Pride gave a guilty God to Hell—
> I have no pride—by love I fell.
>
> Love took me by the heart at birth
> And wrought from out its common Earth,
> With soul at his own skill aghast
> A furnace my own breath should blast.
>
> Why this was done I cannot tell:
> The mystery lives inscrutable—
> I only know I pay the cost—
> With heart, and soul and honour lost.

I only know 'tis Death to give
My love,—yet loveless can I live?
I only know I cannot die
And leave this love God made, not I.

God made this love—there let it rest:
Perchance it needs a riven breast
To heavenly Eyes the scheme to show
A broken heart must never know.[24]

Casement's poem bears some similarity to James Clarence Mangan's famous poem, also called "The Nameless One" (1849). The person of Mangan's title suffers from alcoholism, and the poem traces his life from the "griefs and gloom" of boyhood through the "groans and tears" of his adult life. Like Casement's poem, Mangan's uses a religious discourse primarily for its rhetorical traditions and moral framework, a "God" to whom complaints may be addressed and a Hell where human beings are punished.

Tell how this Nameless, condemned for years long
    To herd with demons from Hell beneath,
Saw things that made him, with groans and tears, long
        For even Death.

Go on, to tell how, with genius wasted,
    Betrayed in Friendship, befooled in Love,
With spirit shipwrecked, and young hopes blasted,
        He still, still strove—

. . . .

Him grant a grave to, ye pitying Noble,
    Deep in your bosoms! There let him dwell!
He, too, had tears for all souls in trouble,
        Here and in Hell.[25]

The first line of Casement's final stanza echoes Mangan's ending: "God made this love—there let it rest."

In an age before support groups and telephone help-lines, an age before newspapers daily published articles about all sorts of addictions and sexualities, Casement evidently turned to Mangan for help. It would be natural for Casement—like Yeats in "To Ireland in the Coming Times"—to consider one of the most famous Young Ireland poets as a literary and political precursor. This poem, especially, would have appealed to Casement, because Mangan discusses how the "Nameless One" of his title "pawned his soul for the Devil's dismal / Stock of returns" without once explicitly naming his problem: that, too, is "nameless." The poem provides a perfect model for "the love that dare not speak its name." Mangan mentions (William) Maginn and (Robert) Burns, both alcoholics, but he never refers to drink. Like Mangan, Casement doesn't wallow in his alienation from conventional bourgeois life but regrets it, and he insists on keeping his miseries within a religious framework. Using Mangan's title, invoking "God," "hell," and the familiar Christian framework of sin, punishment, and redemption, adapting the poem of complaint to his own private and otherwise unspeakable misery, Casement articulates his helplessness before the "mystery" of his transgressive love. Casement iterates, however, that "God made this love," and he never considers giving it up; instead, he relies on "heavenly eyes the scheme to show." As Brian Inglis observed of this poem, "When he met his Creator, Casement did not propose to accept that the fault lay all on one side."[26]

Mangan offered Casement a way to talk about the source of his personal misery without naming it, and Mangan's fame as a Young Irelander offered the sanction of a link with nationalist politics, however unrelated the poem's theme. In stark contrast, the sexual discourse of the diaries never invokes religion. With no apparent guilt, Casement as diarist writes down every bit of pleasure: "Gabriel Ramos—X. *Deep to hilt*" says the very first entry of the 1910 Black Diary.[27] Every fleeting lust is remembered:

> Also on Barca [boat] the young caboclo (thin) dark gentleman of Icarsby. Eyed constantly & wanted—would have gone but Gabriel querido [darling] waiting at Barca gate! Palpito—in *very* deep thrusts.[28]

The breakthrough into another kind of discourse, beyond guilt and lust, occurs in a passage that has been much cited:

> Left for Warrenpoint with *Millar.* Boated & *Huge* Enjoyment. Both Enjoyed. He came to lunch at G Central Hotel. Turned in together at 10:30 to 11 after watching billiards. Not a word said till—"Wait—I'll

untie it" & then "Grand" X Told many tales & pulled it off on top
grandly. First time—after so many years & so deep mutual longing.
Rode gloriously—splendid steed. Huge—told of many—*"Grand."*[29]

When the *Irish Times* was publishing excerpts from the diaries in the
spring of 1994, just after the Public Records Office in London had
opened the files, the sentence ending "so deep mutual longing" was
printed in boldface in a box in the midst of the complete text of the encounter.[30] Forgery theorists would be hard put to explain the level of detail ("after watching billiards") and the intensity of emotion in this passage. It is gratifying to know that the thirty-six-year-old Casement, who
ten years earlier had lamented, "No human hand to steal to mine, / No
loving eye to answering shine," had the satisfaction of a relationship
with "so deep mutual longing." When, this time, he recorded the precise details of sexual positioning and the sensual joy, he was not concerned about going "where God had writ an awful no." The factual details Casement was driven to record so completely, the information
about time, place, and position, acquire here an emotional coloration.

One example of Casement's sexual discourse has never been discussed, no doubt because it has never been read as sexual discourse. Biographers treat as only a factual record of Casement's October 1914 voyage to Norway and arrival in Germany an amazing forty-four-page
handwritten letter (now in the National Library of Ireland) in which
Casement cross-writes as an American girl. This unmailed letter, addressed "Dear Sister," functions as a record of events and does not seem
ever to have been intended for Casement's sister Nina Newman. The
letter indulges in at least four codes: its authorial persona is female; she
is American; the planned Irish Rising is termed a change in the "Book
of Common Prayer"; and what is clearly a diary is disguised as a letter.[31]

Outside the letter, Casement was also not himself, traveling incog-
nito. Within a few short weeks in October 1914, eluding detection as he
slipped into enemy territory (Germany) by way of New York and Norway, Casement became, in quick succession, Mr. R. Smythe of London
(in New York); James E. Landy of New Jersey (on board the ship); and
Mr. Hammond of New York (in Berlin). A life between accents, nation-
alities, allegiances, and genders, hybrid and subversive, was given local
habitation in these aliases. No wonder fellow travelers assumed he was
a spy. Casement had boarded the *Oskar II* in his own person, but as a
disguised, effeminized Sir Roger, having shaved off the famous beard
and washed his face in buttermilk to lighten his complexion. As the

ship sailed out of New York harbor, he turned into James Landy (whose passport he carried) and openly joined his lover Adler Christensen, a Norwegian sailor who accompanied him, traveling as his servant.

In the "letter" Casement creates a simpering, camp persona, one that sounds like MacNeice's "Hetty to Nancy" in *Letters from Iceland.* These artificial girlish utterances occur at moments when gender comes into play. When the *Oskar II* was stopped by the British ship *Hibernia,* whose sailors may have been searching for Sir Roger himself, Casement had to shave quickly and get rid of the razors: "that dear Norwegian girl helped and stowed all the old Hairpins away smarter than I ever saw done before. By the time I'd got through with my hair and things and felt I was looking my best . . . ," the British sailors boarded the *Oskar II,* "and do you know, dear Sister, the name of that ship was 'H.M.S. Hibernia.' Now, when I saw that on the caps of the men I nearly kissed them—but it took my breath fair away." Sir Roger obviously enjoyed allusions to Miss Casement's personal appearance as well as coy references to his own: the letter's author liked "the dear, kind captain, such a nice Dane with a beard just like cousin Roger's." Patently comprehensible like all the codes Casement attempted, this one was intended to record his journey but to deceive British agents, should they ever come across it. But at the same time as the letter hid treason (masking it as religious revisionism), its style suggested its author's sexual preference—or might have, to an alert reader.

From Gossip to Controversy

All these private sexual discourses—the poetic, the pornographic, the romantic, the camp—have now become publicly available, historical evidence of the way one Edwardian homosexual thought about himself. When Casement was brought to Scotland Yard after his arrest, the Metropolitan Police searched the trunk in his Ebury Street flat and found the diaries: political transgression made his life as well as his few material possessions public property. But Sir Edward Grey in the Foreign Office and the professionals in MI6 had long been aware of Casement's sexuality. The "dear Norwegian girl" was not, it turned out, dear at all: she was Casement's Bosie. Adler Christensen tried to sell Casement to the British minister to Norway, Mansfeldt Findlay, informing his office of Casement's intended treason and handing over copies of documents Casement had left with Christiansen for safekeeping. "It was well I trusted her," Casement naively wrote in his "letter," believing the lie Christiansen told, that Findlay had come to him with a bribe, offering Christiansen money for killing Casement. According to Findlay, Christiansen "implied that their relations were of an unnatural nature and that consequently he had great power over this man who trusted him absolutely."[32]

Transformed suddenly into political documents, Casement's private diaries became weapons to use against him during the trial and the appeal of his conviction. The official British "outing" of Casement was every bit as equivocal as Casement's coded letter. When Sir Ernley Blackwell, legal adviser to the Home Office, recommended that Casement's private diaries be circulated, he was (although the term did not then exist) outing Casement: "I see not the slightest objection to hanging Casement and afterwards giving as much publicity to the contents of his diary as decency permits, so that at any rate the public in America and elsewhere may know what sort of man they are inclined to make a martyr of."[33] Neither the Foreign Office nor the Home Office nor the attorney general wanted to be known publicly to be giving the diaries publicity, so the publicity had to be private publicity, sub rosa but not red-handed. Like dirty books in a primary school, typed transcripts and photographed copies of pages were surreptitiously—but systematically—shown to members of the press, to important supporters of Casement, to diplomats, and to politicians. The private publicity was sanctioned by officials of state: "Excellent," Asquith observed to the U.S. ambassador at dinner the day before Casement's execution, learning that he had seen the diaries, "and you need not be particular about keeping it to yourself."[34] Once leaked, the private records became international smut.

During the trial, the diaries were hinted at and condemned in print but never quoted or discussed directly. An openly public "scandal," such as the romance between Parnell and Mrs. O'Shea, or Oscar Wilde's trial, is recorded, debated, and judged in newspapers. But the *Times* (London) and the *Irish Times,* covering the Casement trial in detail, never mentioned the diaries.[35] Lesser papers did: the *Weekly Dispatch* was nasty but cryptic. Of Sir John Lavery's grand painting *Casement on Trial,* which Yeats was later to mention in "The Municipal Gallery Revisited," the paper wrote,

> Mr Lavery ought not to paint his picture without knowing the contents of the two diaries found on Casement. . . . the forthcoming pic-

ture is sure to attract immense attention, but scarcely the kind of notice that so popular an artist is seeking.[36]

In a similar oblique attack, the same paper cast slurs on other people
who supported Casement, carefully naming them as if to make them
guilty by association:

> Roger Casement's diary is being greatly discussed at the present
> time, . . . and people are wondering whether Mr. Clement Shorter,
> who is raising an appeal for the reprieve of Casement, has perused
> that remarkable document, and also whether Sir Arthur Conan Doyle
> is aware of its contents.[37]

According to Casement's biographer René MacColl, after the death
sentence was handed down, "the headlines" (paper unnamed) announced, "Death for Sir Roger Casement. The Diaries of a Degenerate." In what MacColl says was "the first allusion in print to Casement's perversions," an article read: "It is common knowledge that
Sir Roger Casement is a man with no sense of honour or decency. His
written diaries are the monuments of a foul private life. He is a moral
degenerate."[38]

The phrase "common knowledge" alluded to the general awareness
that had been created by the selective exhibition of the diaries. It
would be impossible to reconstruct all the channels through which
the information moved, but reading private accounts makes it possible at least to imagine a "field of gossip," an unmapped area in
which information has circulated.[39] In a 1927 letter to T. E.
Lawrence, Charlotte Shaw described the circulation of the stories
from the receiving end: "you could go nowhere in London at that
time without hearing this scandal whispered. It was put about in in-
fluential people's houses: discussed in low tones in drawing-rooms:
shouted in Clubs: there were tiny, obscure little paragraphs in society
papers."[40] William Allen Hay, a man who had known Casement
when he was consul in Portuguese West Africa, wrote to George
Gavan Duffy, Casement's solicitor, distressed by what a Glasgow
newspaper had printed about his kind old friend. The paper (unnamed) had talked about the diaries in tabloid language: "nothing so
filthy, so pornographic, so infinitely disgusting as what Casement set
down in black and white can be imagined." Duffy wrote back, "Pay
no attention to that kind of rubbish."[41] When Charlotte Shaw was

5.3. *Casement on Trial.* This famous painting by Sir John Lavery is mentioned in Yeats's late poem "The Municipal Gallery Revisited." The *Weekly Dispatch* said, "Mr Lavery ought not to paint his picture without knowing the contents of the two diaries found on Casement. . . . the forthcoming picture is sure to attract immense attention, but scarcely the kind of notice that so popular an artist is seeking." Permission of the Hugh Lane Municipal Gallery of Modern Art, Dublin.

first told about the diaries, their contents were not specified: there were only "dark hints . . . impossible to describe— —could not be mentioned before a lady—most unfortunate—!" She was part of a small group discussing ways to help Casement, and on behalf of these sympathizers the radical journalist Henry Massingham "went to Scotland Yard & demanded, as a prominent journalist, to be told the truth of this matter." To everyone's surprise he was indeed shown the diaries, "& he told us they were as bad as it was possible to conceive, & they undoubtedly appeared to be in Casement's handwriting." And so, she writes, "it was a crushing blow" to the "little committee" and "entirely killed any English sympathy there might have been for Casement."[42] Charlotte Shaw's account occurs in letters written to

T. E. Lawrence in 1927: he wanted to write a biography of Casement—
in many ways a fellow traveler—but was forbidden access to the diaries.

The briefest but richest private exchange about the diaries took
place in Casement's cell in Brixton Prison, when his close friend
Richard Morten visited him:

> "What about the other thing, Roddie?"
> "Dick, you've upset me."[43]

Implicit in these two suggestive lines is the presence of a large but
vaguely defined "field of gossip." Morten somehow heard about a
"thing" "other" than the treason, something so terrible that he cannot specify it. And Casement also, somehow, has heard that this
"other thing" has gotten about, but he cannot name it either. Morten
does not say he believes the gossip, but the mere fact that he feels he
needs to ask about it upsets Casement. Gertrude Bannister, Casement's cousin, determined to accompany his friend (later her husband) Sidney Parry on his visit to the cell, "for then he cannot make
any faux pas in that direction."[44] Bannister's role seems to have involved damage control: to Charlotte Shaw she said, "*If* he had written
such things . . . he must have been mad at the time."[45]

What began as carefully constructed gossip became controversy.
The very mode by which the stories were circulated created doubts,
anxieties, and uncertainty around them, and out of such feelings the
controversy was later to emerge. Posthumous Casement, like living
Casement, endured in a blur of gossip, romance, and innuendo, public pronouncements and private confusion. Even the impeccably nationalist Denis Gwynn, author (in 1930) of one of the first biographies
of Casement, presented the diaries in a cagey and ambiguous way,
managing to imply that the British had slandered Casement but never
precisely saying that the diaries had been forged. In fact Gwynn believed they were authentic: to a friend he wrote, "I find it hard to believe in face of what I have discovered, that the diary was something
he had copied out . . . as evidence against some blackguard he was exposing on the Putumayo," a favorite theory of why such terrible
things were written in Casement's own handwriting.[46] Gwynn had
Lady Gregory fooled: she read his book and believed the diaries were
evidence used against Putumayo criminals.[47]

To the unnameable matters in the diary, matters almost beyond
public discourse at the time, another distressing issue was added.

Casement was subjected to continuing, unambiguous humiliation because successive British governments refused to return his body to Ireland until 1965. His own words on the subject were well known: when Gertrude Bannister visited him in Pentonville Prison just before his execution, Casement had said, "Go back to Ireland, and don't let me lie here in this dreadful place. Take my body back with you and let it lie in the old churchyard in Murlough Bay."[48] But Casement's body, like that of every other criminal who had been executed at Pentonville, was put into quicklime in the prison grounds, and all requests for the remains were rejected until 1965. As Eva Gore-Booth wrote,

> No cairn-shaped mound on a high windy hill
> With Irish earth the hero's heart enfolds
> But a burning grave at Pentonville
> The broken heart of Ireland holds.[49]

Casement had not been keened, waked, or buried: he was one of the unquiet dead. Lady Gregory noted in her journal, "I never hear or notice his name among those of others to whom that Rising of 1916 brought death."[50] At the twentieth anniversary of the Rising, its leaders were honored in a state ceremony with a salute fired over their mass grave at Arbour Hill and wreaths placed on it. At the same time, thousands of people at a demonstration in London heard Hanna Sheehy Skeffington and other speakers demand the return of the remains to Ireland.[51] In the heat of a 1937 Casement controversy, a member of the government's Executive Council said that the Irish people "loved Roger Casement and await always, hoping for the bringing home of his remains, even of his dust."[52]

So long as this unfinished ritual business loomed, anxieties focused on a national father figure who could not quite be mourned and could not quite be venerated. When British Prime Minister Stanley Baldwin refused de Valera's 1935 request for the return of the remains, Baldwin wrote that the ensuing "publicity . . . would be bound to lead to a recrudescense of controversy."[53] And when in 1953 Winston Churchill turned down the same request from de Valera, Churchill, in the typically evasive language of the powerful, insisted that the "law on the subject is specific and binding" and that "we should avoid the risk of reviving old controversies and reawakening the bitter memories of old differences."[54] But these "old controversies" remained fully alive and awake. Victim, hero, and martyr, evoked in the pious political discourse of post-Treaty Ireland, Casement appeared regularly as the subject of interminable letter controversies, whose participants attempted obsessively to stabilize and purify him.

The First Great Casement Controversy

"A polluting person," wrote the anthropologist Mary Douglas, "is always in the wrong. He has developed some wrong condition or simply crossed some line which should not have been crossed and this displacement unleashes danger for someone."[55] Casement certainly unleashed danger for the young Alfred Noyes. The author of "The Highwayman" was working in the News Department of the Foreign Office in the spring of 1916 when the librarian handed him typed transcripts of the notorious diaries. Several months later, while Noyes was lecturing in America, a Philadelphia newspaper asked him his opinion of what he had seen: "I cannot print his own written confessions about himself," Noyes said of Casement, "for they are filthy beyond all description. But I have seen and read them and they touch the lowest depths that human degradation has ever touched. Page after page of his diary would be an insult to a pig's trough to let the foul record touch it."[56]

But Casement had his Antigone in the person of Nina Casement Newman, desperate to save her brother's life and, after the execution, just as desperate to defend his honor. In the autumn of 1916, as Noyes stood to deliver a lecture in Philadelphia, Mrs. Newman—"a lady of distinguished bearing," Noyes calls her in his memoir—

rose in the audience and asked if she might say a few words. I at once made way for her, and, to my horror and that of the audience, she announced that she had come for the express purpose of exposing the speaker of the evening as a "blackguardly scoundrel." . . . "Your countrymen" she cried, "hanged my brother, Sir Roger Casement." Then, her tall spare figure quivering and her face white with anger, she poured out a torrent of invective against England. . . . Overwrought and distraught as she was, there was a strange irrational nobility shining through all her wild charges and accusations.[57]

To Nina Newman's mind, Alfred Noyes was a "polluting person," and her public denunciation of him performed the kind of ritual that sprang up everywhere in the years between Casement's execution and reinterment. What Mary Douglas calls "rites of reversing pollution," rites, that is, of "untying, washing, erasing, and fumigating," serve to "expunge" a pollution that has threatened the life of a particular culture by transgressing the "internal lines of its system."[58] The kinds of pollution Douglas talks about include things like cooking food improperly, or touching an untouchable person, or committing incest, cases in which social and moral issues are linked with a material form of pollution.

Certainly Noyes's image of the "pig's trough" besmirched by the diaries' "foul record" conveys a vivid sense of the material; a material pollution is vestigially present in Newman's phrase, as Noyes quotes it, "blackguardly scoundrel," because blackguards originally were scullions who cleaned pots and pans. (The diaries came, of course, to be known as the Black Diaries.) The feeling that, in Douglas's terms, "danger" had been "unleashed," and important boundaries violated, explains much of the passion, intensity, and hysteria of the purifying rituals that sprang into being around Casement at odd moments and occasions, in poems, orations, letter controversies, and even christenings: the sculptor Herbert Ward, a friend of Casement's from Congo days, unnamed his third son Roger Casement Ward when he learned about the treason and the diaries. The young man (by petition of Parliament) became "Rodney," so he could keep his nickname Roddy, without the contamination of the original Roger.[59] However, de Valera named his next-born son Ruairí, after Casement, so the name was also considered to carry the sanctity of martyrdom.

These issues were aired in de Valera's Ireland in one of the most memorable appearances of the Casement controversy, a passionate correspondence in the *Irish Press* in February 1937. Its chief hero was Yeats, who seemed to speak as a Free State poet laureate, although the state's idea of pollution was hardly his. Yeats actually liked the transgressive sexual activities of public figures and had been gathering expertise on the subject most of his life. In 1925 he had written about the "three monuments" of Lord Nelson, Daniel O'Connell, and Parnell, three dirty old men on their Dublin pedestals who laughed aloud at the notion that "purity built up the state, / And after kept it from decay."[60] In August 1936 he had been visited by the aging Parnellite Henry Harrison, who had written a book to restore Parnell's honor.[61] Duly and passionately responding to this vindication, Yeats had written "Come gather round me, Parnellites." In the lines "And Parnell loved his country, / And Parnell loved a lass," the syntactic parallel makes the two activities of equal value and deprives the hearty, ballad-like love for a "lass" of its adulterous pollution.

Purity, however, had been legislated into existence with the 1925 bill prohibiting divorce legislation, the 1929 Censorship of Publications Act, the 1935 Public Dance Halls Act, and the prohibition of the sale of contraceptives in the same year (section 17 of the Criminal Law Amendment Act). In a sense this legislation also constituted a large-scale "rite of reversing pollution," the social influence of English mores. The pollution of Casement's name had that same colonial origin, and there was individual and collective effort to reverse it. Parnell had Harrison as apologist, and Casement had (among others) William J. Maloney, a New York doctor, who had written a very long book. *The Forged Casement Diaries* (1936) argues that the British had interpolated into Casement's innocent consular diaries those of one of the Peruvian criminals he had been investigating in 1910. All the homosexual acts, then, were those of Armando Normand, a rubber agent of the Peruvian Amazon Company, and the true villains were the forgers in the War Office and their allies in the Home and Foreign offices, Scotland Yard, and the British embassy in Washington.[62]

Maloney's research, published chapter by chapter in the *Irish Press* throughout the winter of 1936–37, reversed the pollution, but it was Yeats's poem, also published in the *Irish Press*, that provided the mnemonic device that made this idea stick in the popular mind. And stick it did, because it has been cited in every subsequent Casement controversy. Written in Yeats's faux-Catholic ballad stanza, it was eminently quotable:

I say that Roger Casement
Did what he had to do,
He died upon the gallows
But that is nothing new.[63]

The poem had instant and sundry ramifications. Yeats himself, excited by reading aloud his own poem, had to drink a glass of port to calm down. On the day the poem appeared in the newspaper (February 2), Mrs. Yeats (not knowing of the publication) was surprised to find herself treated with unusual deference by shopkeepers all over

Dublin; the people had been longing, it seems, for the restoration of their hero's purity. Acknowledging this national service, the government thanked Yeats. As he wrote to Dorothy Wellesley, "I was publicly thanked by the vice-president of the Executive Counsil [sic], by De Valera's political secretary, by our chief antiquarian & an old revolutionist, Count Plunket, who calls my poem 'a ballad the people much needed'. De Valera's newspaper gave me a long leader saying that for generations to come my poem will pour scorn on the forgers & their backers."[64]

Inadvertently, Yeats had formulated the official state position. Outraged by apparent forgery ("They turned a trick by forgery / And blackened his good name"), he had seemed to speak out for purity; he appeared to be doing the work of Free State hagiography. In fact his opinion of Casement was not high; Casement was "not a very able man," Yeats wrote to Ethel Mannin, though he was "gallant and unselfish."[65] But Yeats's hidden opinion, hidden that is from the Fianna Fáil press, was more shocking: he wanted the diaries to be authentic. "Public opinion is excited," he wrote Wellesley, "& there is a demand for a production of the documents & their submission to some impartial tribunal. It would be a great relief to me if they were so submitted & proved genuine. If Casement were homo-sexual what matter! But if the British Government can with impunity forge evidence to prove him so no unpopular man with a cause will ever be safe."[66] The man praised by patriots and thanked by the government for defending Casement from the charge of homosexuality was in fact involved in a complicated romantic affair with the lesbian Wellesley and would have been quite happy, himself, with a homosexual martyr.

There may have been an even more surprising element in the controversy, the possibility that de Valera believed Casement to have been homosexual. On February 17 de Valera, whose newspaper had published Maloney, Yeats, and all the ensuing correspondence, was questioned in the Dáil about whether he would ask the British government to "submit the alleged Casement Diary" to examination by that "impartial tribunal." He must have surprised his supporters when he answered, "No, Sir. Roger Casement's reputation is safe in the affections of the Irish people, the only people whose opinions mattered to him."[67] The situation at that very moment—commotion over Maloney's "revelations," a Nobel Prize–winning poet supporting the purity of a martyred founding father, general outrage at England's treatment of Casement—was absolutely perfect. Why ruin it by look-

ing at the "alleged diary" and perhaps re-polluting Casement and purifying the English? Perhaps de Valera knew that Michael Collins,
shown the diaries during the 1921 Treaty negotiations, had judged
them to be authentic; or perhaps he had spoken with Tom Casement,
Roger's brother, who commented ambiguously, "I won't be happy
until the thing is burned."[68]

Both governments' refusals to have anything to do with this issue
meant that it remained interstitial; the responsibility devolved on
two poets to settle the thing, as if on behalf of their respective countries. Maloney's book had linked Noyes with the circulation of the diaries—the innocent thirty-six-year-old Alfred Noyes, quietly working
in his News Department office and handed something "filthy beyond
description." Yeats (who had praised Noyes's first volume of poetry)
had named names and called on Noyes directly:

> Come Alfred Noyes and all the troup
> That cried it far and wide,
> Come from the forger and his desk,
> Desert the perjurer's side;
>
> Come speak your bit in public
> That some amends be made
> To this most gallant gentleman
> That is in quicklime laid.

The *Irish Press* created a layout that dramatized national antagonisms visually: "Irish Poet's Striking Challenge" shouted their huge
boldface headline, under which photographs of the poets, like two
boxers, took up opposite sides of the page, Yeats on the left, Noyes on
the right, each identified by a brief resumé.[69]

To Yeats's surprise Noyes did speak his bit in public. The *Irish
Press* had called Yeats's poem a "challenge to a brother poet," and in
his letter to the paper Noyes responded fraternally, quoting "The
Lake Isle of Innisfree," alluding to *Hamlet*, and even praising Casement's speech from the dock. Noyes called for an official reexamina-
tion of the diaries, and Yeats (in his letter responding to Noyes's letter
responding to his poem) agreed. Pleased to be speaking as if from the
lofty plane of Culture, to be sounding "noble" and magnanimous, yet
uneasy about judging handwriting they had never seen, the poets happily deferred to some other, future, "impartial" judgment.[70] Yeats
also revised the poem, reversing the pollution of Noyes's name, and

Irish Poet's Striking Challenge

ROGER CASEMENT

(After reading "The Forged Casement Diaries," by Dr. Maloney).

I say that Roger Casement
Did what he had to do,
He died upon the gallows,
But that is nothing new.

Afraid they might be beaten
Before the bench of Time,
They turned a trick by forgery
And blackened his good name;

A perjurer stood ready
To prove their forgery true;
They gave it out to all the world—
And that is something new.

For Spring-Rice had to whisper it,
Being their Ambassador,
And then the speakers got it,
And writers by the score.

Come Alfred Noyes and all the troup
That cried it far and wide,
Come from the forger and his desk,
Desert the perjurer's side;

Come speak your bit in public
That some amends be made
To this most gallant gentleman
That is in the quick-lime laid.

W. B. YEATS.

(Tune: The Glen of Aherlow).

WILLIAM BUTLER YEATS

Born in Dublin, 1865, son of an Irish artist. Educated at the High School, Dublin, and then studied art for three years. His first book of verse, "Mosada," appeared in 1886. Lived for many years in London, where he was the friend of William Morris, Lionel Johnson, Arthur Symons, and other poets and artists of the 'nineties. Came back to Ireland and in co-operation with Lady Gregory, George Russell and Edward Martyn, established the Irish Literary Theatre, which later became the Abbey Theatre. Since 1904 has been a director of the Abbey, where his plays, including "Cathleen ni Houlihan," "The Countess Cathleen," "The Pot of Broth," etc., have been first produced and frequently revived. Was a Free State Senator from 1922 to 1928, and was awarded the Nobel Prize for Literature in 1923. Published an autobiography last year entitled "Dramatis Personæ" and has recently edited The Oxford Book of Modern Verse. Is regarded by reputable critics as the greatest living poet.

LAND AND WATER.

ALFRED NOYES

An Englishman and a convert to the Catholic Church. Born in Staffordshire in 1880. Educated at Oxford and immediately made poetry his profession. His first book of verse, "The Loom of Years," was published in 1902. Visited the United States to deliver the Lowell lectures in 1913. Was Professor of English Literature at Princeton University, U.S.A., 1914-23. During the war years was attached to the British Foreign Office and was prominent in circulating the Casement slanders. Wrote of Casement in the Philadelphia Public Ledger (August 31, 1916):

"... the chief leader of these rebels—I cannot print his own written confessions about himself, for they are filthy beyond all description. But I have seen and read them and they touch the lowest depth of human degradation ever reached. Page after page of his diary would be an insult to a pig's trough to let the foul record touch it."

Was made Commander of the Order of the British Empire in 1918. Is, in addition to being a poet, a novelist, a dramatist and a biographer. His recent Life of Voltaire has been the subject of much controversy.

THIS HAPPENED TO-DAY

THE "MACARONI PARSON"

THERE was no preacher in London who could attract so fashionable an audience as the Rev. William Dodd. When he delivered his charity sermon at his chapel in Pimlico, the edifice was filled to overflowing, and princes and fine ladies came to listen. "The lost sheep," says Horace Walpole, "wept."

But there were many who stayed away. They did not like the pastor's flashy style of dress, nor his gilded coach, and they thought it unbecoming in a clergyman to publish a volume of verse containing epistles to dainty ladies. They nicknamed him the macaroni parson. Nevertheless, when the news was ...

HERONS

5.4. The first great Casement controversy. The layout in the *Irish Press* on the day Yeats's ballad was published pitted Yeats and Noyes against one another, though Noyes wrote a polite letter in response to Yeats's accusation that he had spread gossip about Casement's diary. Yeats then rewrote the poem, which was published in revised form without Noyes's name. In fact, Yeats wrote privately, "what matter if Casement were homosexual," and in the long run Noyes came to believe that the diaries had been forged.

the newspaper printed it. As revised, the relevant lines after "And then the speakers got it, / And writers by the score" now read, "No matter what the names they wear!"

Flexible and not obsessively honest, like all good controversialists, Yeats had many private opinions about Casement, not one of them matching exactly his published opinion. Writing to the Fenian Patrick McCartan, who had just organized a testimonial gift to Yeats of one thousand pounds, Yeats explained away his polite response to the Sasanach Noyes: the revision was a "verse full of Christian Charity," he wrote mockingly, "which was entirely the result of influenza."[71] Writing to Dorothy Wellesley, who was lesbian and English, Yeats expressed the hope that Casement had been gay and the English not forgers.[72] Writing the politically active Ethel Mannin, to whom Yeats had once refused his signature on a petition, he insisted that his Casement poems had nothing to do with politics: "In them I defend a noble-natured man, I do the old work of the poets but I will defend no cause."[73]

Simpler in all respects than Yeats, and not the slightest bit intellectually playful, Noyes was overwhelmed by the political issues entailed in the controversy. The new intrusion of Casement into his life changed his entire notion of what, had he known the discourse, he might have called the relation of culture to imperialism. Twenty-one years earlier, as a young man, he had been happy to do the cultural work of his government. He had, as requested, written an article on "the Irish troubles" of 1916, an article issued through the government press bureau to American newspapers. That autumn, as England waited to see if America would enter the war, Noyes had been lecturing all over America on "the case for English civilisation." After Nina Casement Newman's interruption, Noyes says he "made no reply or comment on what she had said, but continued my address on the great English poetry of the past," as if under the circumstances that was not a reply.[74]

Not altogether innocently, Noyes was giving the cultural Anglophiles a soft-sell approach to the war. But after two visitations from the accusing ghost of Roger Casement, once as Nina C. and once as WBY, Noyes performed his own final rite-of-reversing-pollution in his book *The Accusing Ghost or Justice for Roger Casement* (1957). He demanded "that the body of this wronged man . . . be returned to his native country" and condemned the "stupid and bull-headed bureaucracy" of his own country.[75] By this time Noyes (a

Catholic convert) had learned that Casement had died a Catholic death, and he had discovered what a tall, good-looking family the Casements were. In his letter to the *Irish Press* Noyes had written, "I had known nothing of Casement personally, and the appearance of his sister was a tragic revelation to me of the distinguished race from which he sprang, and the blood that ran in his veins."[76] The oddity of a judgment of character based on stature is matched by a line in *The Accusing Ghost* about Casement on trial, a person "whose princely bearing more than confirmed his manhood." This distinguished race had also been blessed in an earlier generation, because Casement's father had helped to save the Hungarian patriot Louis Kossuth (1802–94), to whom tributes were "paid . . . by two great English poets, Landor and Swinburne."[77] Noyes took seriously the Yeatsian notion of "the old work of the poets," and in that "princely bearing" the "gallant gentleman" is visible. Had Casement been short, ugly, and stooped, his posthumous fate might have been that of Richard III.

The danger of not acknowledging that there was pollution to reverse became clear when Shaw joined the controversy. His letter explicitly denied all the articles of faith subscribed to by the readers of the *Irish Press*. Maloney's book, he said, was adding to the "bad blood" between England and Ireland—but of course it was! That was the point of it! Shaw said that there was "no villainy" because F. E. Smith (who as attorney general presided over Casement's trial) could not have known that the "documents" were "memoranda of Putumayan cases" rather than Casement's own records. With typically Shavian provocation, he insisted that Smith was "irresistibly likeable" and had acted with "good faith and good nature." Only Shaw, at that time and in that paper, could have treated the diaries nonchalantly: "The trial occurred at a time when the writings of Sigmund Freud had made psychopathy grotesquely fashionable. Everybody was supposed to have a secret history unfit for publication. . . . We associated no general depravity with psychopathic eccentricities." Having treated colonial rule and homosexuality with flippancy, having said in print the kind of thing Yeats only said in letters to his lovers, and having violated the taboos of most *Irish Press* readers, Shaw finally acknowledged that "Casement's high reputation is still befouled by a slander" and suggested that the British government "clear up" the "misunderstanding."[78]

Naturally the response was hysteria. This was more pollution, a reversal of the reversal, and in a tone as offensive as the content. It had to be expunged. Yeats, of course, did not take it too seriously; to Dorothy Wellesley he called it a "long, rambling, sexless, vegetarian letter."[79] But two days later the paper published a long, rambling sexless letter from Francis Stuart criticizing Shaw for being a "good-natured busybody" and disassociating himself from Shaw's position. Stuart wanted to reestablish the moral clarity of the status quo, in which there *were* villains. He concluded his letter,

> If any apology is needed for what I have written about a famous dramatist who did me the honour to invite me to become a member of the Irish Academy of Letters, founded by himself and Mr. Yeats, let me say this: It is only because he has in the past been considered the spokesman of what I may call the Irish Intelligentsia that as a writer I repudiate any association with the views expressed in Mr. Shaw's letter. On the other hand, Mr. Yeats's poem, as a tribute from a great poet to "a gallant Irish gentleman", has set a fine precedent.[80]

Shaw had now taken the place of Alfred Noyes as the bearer of British pollution, and alliance with Yeats, against Shaw, on the part of a member of the younger generation, would serve to reaffirm Casement's and Ireland's purity.

But then on February 16, 1937, the paper published a letter from Diarmuid Murphy accusing Francis Stuart of not having a sense of humor. The hysteria had now become intertextual. The heading over the letter says "The Casement Diaries," but Casement's name does not occur anywhere in it, nor does any issue connected with him. Murphy wrote, "Let me quote but Mr. Stuart's quotation from Mr. Shaw." Mr. Murphy, too, wanted to keep the national identity pure, but his taboos were different. "Mr. George Bernard Shaw," he claimed, "has now every reason to excommunicate us from all kinship of the Irish nation, for we have, through the mouth of a 'novelist,' shown ourselves more lacking in humour than the dullest Saxon."[81] So Mr. Murphy, like Francis Stuart before him, was purifying the controversy of the previous letter.

Writing for that same purpose several days later, in order to reestablish the Maloney-Yeats point of view and to condemn Shaw, Maud Gonne complained about the "monumental impudence of such a man offering to write Casement's last speech for him."[82] She was wrong about that: Shaw had advised Casement not to waste money on lawyers but to defend himself with a speech *such as* the one Shaw enclosed as a sample. So, to undo the pollution of Shaw's reputation, on February 24 the *Irish Press* reprinted a letter Shaw had written to an English newspaper in 1916, urging the British government not to execute Casement. Adding to the intertextual hysteria on the same day as Maud Gonne's letter (February 22), a letter from Hanna Sheehy Skeffington alluded to the "recent controversy over Noyes, Yeats, Shaw, and Casement" and then went on to quote her own 1918 pamphlet about British anti-Irish propaganda in America during the Great War.[83]

There was so much anxiety and so little to go on. In the absence of that "impartial tribunal" Noyes and Yeats had called for, in the absence of any reliable truth, texts, all kinds of texts—poems, biographies, memoirs, government records, pamphlets, old newspapers, current newspapers, the "alleged diaries" themselves—offered bewildering and incompatible forms of evidence. Textual analysis, interpretive, editorial, and even factual disputes about texts, gave a focus for all the anxieties stirred up by the indeterminate moral status of Casement. And the voices heard in these debates—nervous, witty, pompous, hysterical, posturing and performing to a small audience they knew and a larger audience they imagined—remained ineffective. They could not soothe the uneasy, condemn or forgive the guilty, or redeem the wronged—or terminate the conflict. Hence the perpetual need for just one more letter, poem, or document to provide the definitive, absolute ending. Newspapers and publishers provided arenas for the conflict, and the traditions of print controversies provided the rules of the game.

The Continuing Tradition

In the years before the reinterment, every review of every biography of Casement set off a new controversy, and letters to the editor hastened to contradict the book, or the reviewer, or some previous letter, or all the above. A 1956 *Irish Times* controversy inspired by a review of the René MacColl biography shows a typical dynamic, generating spin-off controversies about who wrote what when and what it might mean. The MacColl book required an instant and assured response, because it was unpleasant in tone (MacColl didn't like Casement) and because it claimed that the diaries were genuine. The *Irish Times* reviewer, Thomas Hogan, began the reversal of pollution by saying it was a pity the book perpetuated an injury to "this most gallant gentleman / That is in quicklime laid."[84] (The one stable point in Casement's posthumous life has always been Yeats's ballad.) MacColl had seen the diaries, but according to the strictures of the Official Secrets Act he was not allowed to mention that fact, so his belief in their authenticity had no apparent foundation. MacColl's description of the diaries quickly became one of the disputed texts, as historians such as Owen Dudley Edwards wondered how he could characterize by number, size, and color documents whose existence no one could confirm. Two members of the Irish Bar focused on MacColl's interview with Sergeant A. M. Sullivan, who had defended Casement and (forty years after the trial) had betrayed lawyer–client confidentiality by revealing (if what he said could be trusted) that Casement had discussed homosexuality with him.[85] (Hence, forty-four years later, the comment made in the Royal Irish Academy's Casement symposium, that Casement never told Sullivan that he was a "pervert.")

Because the MacColl book restored the sexual taint, some of the secondary controversies had to confront the issue of sexuality, which they did with less evasion than the 1937 controversy had. The sexual taboo seemed to have lifted slightly, and there appeared, in print, a savoring of salacious details. But this commentary also remained focused on texts. In one of these, the sexual pollution was displaced onto Sir Basil Thomson, the Scotland Yard official who had found the diaries. The matter in question involved a 1925 episode in Hyde Park: had Sir Basil been found in flagrante delicto with a *man* or a *woman*? Or, as the letter writers put it, was Thomson a "pervert" engaged in a "form of bestiality," or was he enjoying himself with a female prostitute whose name, according to some records, was Thelma de Lava? And did he or did he not say to the arresting policemen that if they would ignore the crime he would make them "independent for life"? And did he die a suicide on the Continent, or of natural causes at home in Teddington?[86]

In another secondary controversy, one reader audaciously suggested that Ireland's homophobia, not Casement's sexuality, was at fault. Monk Gibbon (Yeats's second cousin) found proof of homosexuality in Casement's poem "The Streets of Catania," which was duly sent in to the *Irish Times* by another reader. Catania is a city in Sicily, and, Gibbon wrote, "to those who know the reputation of Sicily in this respect" the author's sexuality was clear. "I suppose," he added, "that I am starting another argument now which can be carried on till doomsday. . . . A man is a great patriot; at all costs it must not transpire that he was also a homosexual! Ireland, presumably, would not still want his bones if he were?"[87] Less diplomatic than his cousin Yeats, and writing nineteen years later, Gibbon confronted the taboo directly and impatiently.

Gibbon was at least thirty-seven years ahead of his time in one respect: homosexual acts were not decriminalized in Ireland until 1993. But his letter, as well as some of the less daring ones, shows that Casement controversies had become a site for Irish thinking about sexual behavior and, more generally, about all the behavioral boundaries through which the Irish state defined itself. The controversies allowed letter writers to linger near areas of taboo without any danger of violating the taboos. Nor did the genre of the newspaper controversy require closure of any sort. Editors seemed willing to let the letters inspired by a single book review go on for months. In the adversarial but ludic mode of controversy, almost anything could be said, and at odd moments new ideas (such as Monk Gibbon's) could be snuck in without attracting censure. Like the unscripted sequence of the audience's ideas on *The Late Late Show*, the letters to the editor in a controversy revealed what was on the national mind; and because Casement was the alleged subject, the most forbidden issues were on people's minds from the beginning.[88]

The Reinterment

During the forty-eight-and-a-half years following Casement's execution, layers of identity evolved in the Casement of Irish memory, each subverting the selves above it. Whichever Casement you liked, he was a man with many secrets, and he was bad at keeping them: the charm of fiasco on the grand scale was not the least of his charms. Beneath the knighted Protestant consul-traitor lay the classic martyr, the Catholic Irish-speaking gunrunning rebel; such was the Casement of Yeats's poems, the hero of the 1937 *Irish Press* controversy. But Casement Martyr was obviously as official, as much a figment of state ideology, as Casement Traitor, and beneath the perfect martyr another rebel Casement had been evolving, a rebel against the dominant pieties of the high de Valeran period. So long as the state involved was Britain, an Irish Casement was a folk hero. But once the Irish state had him, another folk Casement emerged.

The return of the remains released the silent dissidents from the need to maintain a sober patriotic attitude to Casement, or rather, from the need to maintain it exclusively. It was possible to maintain many concurrent ideas about Casement, and the newspaper controversies continued in wearyingly familiar form. But almost as soon as the plane carrying what was said to be Casement's calcified remains touched down on Irish soil, a new "people's" Casement, a troublemaker, appeared on the scene, interrupting the pious with the scatological. In late February 1965, as soon as it was known that the remains were to be returned—even before the plane landed—an entirely new Casement made his entrance. Playful, irreverent, homosexual, camp, an odd mixture of bones and beard, a humorous dissident, a troublesome subversive—was this the man Ireland had waited forty-nine years for? The burial in Glasnevin marked a major turning point in Casement's posthumous life, and quite apart from the grand, theatrical state ritual, the rituals of popular memory changed dramatically once the remains had been reburied in Irish soil. The dug-up, reinterred, post-posthumous Casement was ready for the rapidly secularizing Ireland of the 1960s, eventually to become the Ireland of Mary Robinson and Sinéad O'Connor.

If jokes and gossip tell anything at all about the collective national mind, they tell us in this instance that Ireland, north and south, was obsessed with what precisely of Casement was coming back. That mind was fixated on the physical remains of the man, as well it might be, considering that he had been buried in quicklime for almost half a century. Eilis Pearce, who worked as senior assistant for broadcasting in Ireland's Government Information Bureau, says it was "commonly accepted that it was unlikely there were any bones" in the coffin.[89] The *Irish Times* reported an "Ingenious Theory" explaining why the "Irish authorities" had no trouble identifying Casement's body. The body "is almost wholly preserved—teeth, hair and flesh, even his beard. . . . the quicklime—possibly because it had an impure substance which mixed with the damp ground—formed a kind of plaster cast around the body and preserved it extremely well." In dry, formal tones, the *Irish Times* commented, "It is an ingenious theory, but one understands it is incorrect."[90]

Two days later the *Irish Times* printed a less whimsical account of the exhumation, one that accords with Sean Ronan's official account, offering verification by the governor of the prison and clerical sanction by an attendant priest. The prison records were consulted be-

5.5. The return of the remains. The return of Casement's remains in 1965 released new feelings about Casement: journalists joked about his bones, and poets began to write about his sexuality.

cause "Details, identifying each grave, were kept by the prison governor and these were examined before the exhumation work began." And, as "prison staff" started digging "while British and Irish officials looked on," Father Thomas Keane, the "Cork-born Catholic chaplain of the prison," stood by the graveside. All the "principal members of the skeleton were uncovered," and the "skeleton corresponded to Casement's known physical measurements."[91]

This was the moment, the visiting of the tomb, around which stories clustered. David Rudkin's radio play *Cries from Casement as His Bones Are Brought to Dublin* added its own version:

LYNCH: Officer Mahoney, how shall we be sure we dig up all the one man?
MAHONEY: How do yous mean?
LYNCH: Not minus something, or plus parts of another?

MAHONEY: You know the official line on that: impossible.

LYNCH: But Officer Mahoney, I see what I can see. And what I see is, 'tis anybody's guess what's goin in this box.

MAHONEY: It's the thought that counts. Here. These bones'll do. (*Brief formalized tearing of bones*)[92]

The rumor that bits of the murderer Crippen got mixed in with bits of Casement is elaborated in Rudkin's script, while inside that coffin, so respectfully greeted by de Valera at Baldonnel Airfield, Casement and Crippen have a cozy chat about national identity.

The same folk Casement appeared in the North. According to a headline in the *Belfast Newsletter*, "Casement Ghost Seen in Belfast."

> The tall, dark man pushed the door of the bar open and undid the buttons of his overcoat. Outside the heavy rain continued . . . the new arrival was bearded and boasted a head of dark, curly hair, thinning at the temples. His dark grey overcoat was perfectly dry, and his very narrow, rather old-fashioned trousers were creased. "I wonder if I could trouble you for a meat pie with all the trimmings," he inquired.[93]

The manager of the Golden Jubilee public house in Cromac Street was puzzled because "there was something peculiar about the man." Then, twenty minutes later, the customer "walked to the oldest toilet in the pub—a toilet so situated that only long-standing customers knew its whereabouts." More curious behavior followed: the customer never ate the meat pie, ordered a Guinness but didn't drink that either. As he explained, "He had come a long way, he was tired, and . . . he didn't really drink." When the pub manager read the next day about the return of the remains of Sir Roger Casement, the mystery cleared up. "It's certainly very strange. I'll swear the man was Roger Casement. The whole thing is really quite unbelievable."[94]

The anxiety that the return be well staged was inseparable from an impulse to think of unholy issues such as the identity of the remains or the digestive systems of ghosts. The general feeling about Casement at the time of the reinterment, that he was "a noble character," especially because of his humanitarian work in Africa and South America, coexisted with jokes speculating about why de Valera did not walk closer to the coffin.[95] And the great concern with the reinterment as a public spectacle and media event arose, according to Eilis Pearce, because "it was generally recognized that this was a dress rehearsal for de Valera's funeral," an opportunity for Ireland on the international stage. Telefís Éireann was just four years old, and this was its chance to compete in the great age of televised state funerals such as Kennedy's and Churchill's.[96]

The entire affair took place on a huge scale. Care was taken that every moment between the arrival of the remains at Baldonnel Airfield at 5:00 p.m. on February 23, 1965, and the funeral on March 1, with burial in Glasnevin, be dignified, ritualized, and recorded for posterity. Casement's closest surviving relatives, the daughters of his brother Charles, were flown in from Australia by the Irish government; Casement cousins had special seats at the funeral. Civil servants were given the day off, and many schools and businesses were closed. So many representatives of different religious faiths, Irish cities, and political parties were present as the coffin was wheeled to the graveside that, said the *Irish Times*, "All Ireland was there."[97]

The grand, impressive, magnificent funeral enacted a literal stabilization, and de Valera's eloquent graveside oration, in Irish and English, put the official mark of sanctity on Saint Roger:

> This grave, like the graves of the other patriots who lie in this cemetery, like the graves in Arbour Hill . . . will become a place of pilgrimage. . . . If there had been no 1916 and there had been no European war of 1914, the man whose bones lie here would deserve to be honoured and revered for the noble part he played in exposing the atrocities in the Congo . . . [and in] Putamayo [sic].[98]

But as the newly interred man was being sacralized, writers were at their subversive work, making something different of the scene. That moment reimagined by David Rudkin sounds a bit different: Casement is explicitly antagonistic to the "sacred relic" he has become. Outraged to discover he's being buried in Glasnevin, not Murlough Bay, he insists *"I will not lie here"* but is silenced by the captain attending the coffin:

> CAPTAIN: Whisht Casement, the President is making a moving speech, your biographers have come, there's not a dry eye in the graveyard.
> CASEMENT: Why not in Antrim, to my specific dying wish?

CARDINAL: Balls to your specific dying wish, we've got you now. . . . Be
a good hero, shut your mouth.[99]

Thus Casement enters a Casement controversy. In fact a burial plot
in Murlough Bay is still being saved for him by the Casement Repatriation Committee. His sister Nina had selected the plot in Glasnevin, so until 1965 Casement actually had three burial sites, in Pentonville, Glasnevin, and Murlough Bay.

Richard Murphy, watching the ceremonies on "the small screen,"
was reimagining them and meditating on all the changes in Ireland
since 1916. His poem "Casement's Funeral" says everything that
couldn't be said at the big ceremonial moments; he speaks the officially unspeakable.

> After the noose, and the black diary deeds
> Gossiped, his fame roots in prison lime:
> The hanged bones burn, a revolution seeds.
> Now Casement's skeleton is flying home.
>
> A gun salutes, the troops slow-march, our new
> Nation atones for her shawled motherland
> Whose welcome gaoled him when a U-boat threw
> This rebel quixote soaked on Banna Strand.
>
> Soldiers in green guard the draped catafalque
> With chalk remains of once ambiguous bone
> Which fathered nothing till the traitor's dock
> Hurt him to tower in legend like Wolfe Tone.
>
> From gaol yard to the Liberator's Tomb
> Pillared in frost, they carry the freed ash,
> Transmuted relic of a death-cell flame
> Which purged for martyrdom the diarist's flesh.
>
> On the small screen I watch the packed cortège
> Pace from High Mass. Rebels in silk hats now
> Exploit the grave with an old comrade's speech:
> White hair tossed, a black cape flecked with snow.[100]

Murphy could not have known in 1965 what a turning point that
decade would prove to be in Ireland's twentieth-century history, but
the mild impieties of the poem reveal the barely emergent secular

point of view. Murphy expresses all the thoughts no one was supposed to have during Casement's funeral: the funny line about the flying skeleton picks up on the popular fixation on the material nature of the remains, the curiosity about what precisely had been flown back and what was in the coffin. He suggests that martyrdom transformed Casement's sexuality: his "once ambiguous bone . . . fathered nothing" until he was hanged for treason. And the calcification of Casement's body in quicklime burned away his sexuality: it "purged for martyrdom the diarist's flesh," so now, as Monk Gibbon had suggested back in 1956, Ireland can take the bones. The diarist, then, must be this man, this Irish martyr: subtly, casually, Murphy outs Casement.

The poem also confronts the unpleasant fact of Irish complicity in Casement's fate: it was, after all, members of the Royal Irish Constabulary who arrested him in Kerry, and ordinary Kerry people, happening to be in the wrong place at the wrong time, who were subpoenaed as witnesses in his trial. To Murphy, the extravaganza of the funeral is atonement for that betrayal: "our new / Nation atones for her shawled motherland / Whose welcome gaoled him." Rudkin, too, examines this unpleasant issue. In *Cries from Casement* all the Kerry witnesses visit the coffin as it lies in state and ask forgiveness. Each announces himself—"John MacCarthy, farmer," "Mary Gorman, farmgirl," "Martin Collins, with the pony and trap"—and then says, "I'm sorry." At the time of the lying in state, an article in the *Irish Times* titled "Betrayal of Casement through Ignorance" said resonantly of the witnesses, "They knew not what they did."

But the issue was more complicated than Murphy, Rudkin, and the *Irish Times* implied: the witnesses had nothing to apologize for. In 1966, at the occasion of the fiftieth anniversary of the Rising, the *Kerryman* honored them with a large, boldface, page-one headline ("Ardfert Is Defended") and minutely detailed accounts of the traumas suffered by the Kerry people who, as the article said, "got innocently involved in this chain of misfortune that was forged in Banna's lonely Beach on that Good Friday morning 50 years ago."[101] But "all Ireland" did not read the *Kerryman*, and the popular belief persists that "the local people betrayed him." One resident of Tralee claims to have heard a local balladeer sing a song about Casement so insulting to the people of Kerry that it could never be written down or even quoted. For all these contradictory reasons, Casement looms as more of a presence in Kerry than in any other part of the Republic of Ireland.

The Tralee office of Bord Fáilte is the only place in Ireland where a postcard of Casement (printed in Herefordshire) may be bought. Scoil Mhic Easmainn (Roger Casement School), also in Tralee, boasts possession of the plate from which Casement ate during the appeal of his conviction at the Court of Criminal Appeals. The North Kerry Museum in the Rattoo Heritage Centre contains the boat in which Casement and his two companions set off from the German submarine on Good Friday morning 1916, and a statue of Casement rejected by Dun Laoghaire has found a site in Ballyheigue.[102]

Gay Casement

The new Casement of the writers' imaginings—dissident, gay, outrageous—tapped the secular energies suppressed but never eradicated in the first decades of independence. There is little print evidence for the non-official Casement of the years before decriminalization, though he can be found in Yeats's letter to Dorothy Wellesley ("If Casement were homosexual, what matter") and in Monk Gibbon's daring suggestion that "The Streets of Catania" is about a homosexual encounter. Here and there in exchanges unrecorded in the papers, a hidden Ireland persisted, tolerant of sexual preferences. In a 1973 *Irish Times* Casement controversy, Mrs. Ita Kelly of Ballsbridge wrote in to "concur" with a previous letter writer, Mrs. Irving, who had claimed that homosexuality was "just another kind of loving." To this opinion Mrs. Kelly added an anecdote from her school days "many moons ago" under the tutelage of Mother Scholastica. Reading "The Ballad of Reading Gaol" to her students, Mother S. explained that Wilde had been imprisoned "just for loving another man." Mrs. Kelly called this a "splendid reply to a class of girls of seventeen years old" and wished Mother Scholastica were alive to participate in the present correspondence: "Her opinions certainly would be very valuable." The obscure but radical Mother Scholastica was, said her student, a "brilliant intellectual" whose authority the girls never questioned.[103]

Ireland must have had many unrecorded Mother Scholasticas forming the minds of people who wrote to the *Irish Times* in 1973 saying things like "It does not matter a damn whether Roger Casement was a homosexual or not" and "I am quite certain that the younger generation of Irish don't give one damn if the 'supposed diaries' were black,

SÍR ROGER CASEMENT

Philanthropist and Patriot   1864 - 1916

5.6. Casement as heritage. This postcard of Casement (designed in Wales and printed in Herefordshire) was sold in the Bord Fáilte office in Tralee, County Kerry, near where Casement landed in April 1916. Permission of RM Graphic Design, Llangunllo, Powys. Printed by Centre Print, Leominster, Herefordshire.

red, pink, or blue."[104] Kieran Rose notes how difficult it is to find evidence of lesbian and gay lives in Ireland except in legislation intended to control that behavior.[105] Although it might be even harder to find evidence of toleration of homosexuality, the letters from *Irish Times* readers—especially women—indicate that it did exist in forms other than embarrassment.

Even as Ireland secularized, Casement retained the power to make people feel uncomfortable. When Casement's cousin, Professor A. J. Otway-Ruthven of Trinity College Dublin, was asked sometime in the 1960s for her comments on Casement, she responded, "In our family we don't discuss the failures."[106] Casement's aura was still powerful enough in 1988 for Oxford University Press to prevent Medbh McGuckian from using an epigraph by Casement for her volume *On Ballycastle Beach* and from mentioning him by name in the title poem.[107] When the musical McPeake family was performing in Sligo in 1993, the patriarch of the family noted that the pipes on stage had been played at a *feis* in the presence of Roger Casement. He then leaned forward to the audience and said, "It's not true what they say about him."[108] As recently as 1998, a volume containing an essay on Casement became one focus of a small Irish-American controversy. The book, which also included an essay on the "masculinities" of George Moore, Edward Martyn, and Yeats, and another on "homosocial" friendships in Irish drama, was said to have "glorified paedophiles."[109]

Mischievous, impious Casement has been, par excellence, sexual Casement, but as the atmosphere around sex changed in the 1990s, in Ireland and in the West generally, public discourse about sexuality evolved a new kind of piety, and Casement lost much of his naughty aura. It has, on occasion, seemed wrong *not* to talk about sex, wrong to suppress, hide, or lie about it. The unspeakable (homosexuality, child abuse, clerical sexuality) is now spoken on a regular basis. Casement has been repoliticized and claimed as a homosexual ancestor. In *Swoon*, an independent, low-budget cult film about the Leopold and Loeb murder case, the guests at a transvestite party leaf through a book of famous gay people as the camera zooms in on photographs and the voiceover says, "Oscar Wilde . . . Sir Roger Casement . . . Marcel Proust."[110]

For lesbian and gay Irish people, Casement is a precursor in a more particularized history, and Irish groups have claimed him often and audibly, in recent works such as Kieran Rose's *Diverse Communities*

and Eibhear Walshe's "Oscar's Mirror."[111] When the members of
ILGO (the Irish Lesbian and Gay Organization) march on St. Patrick's
Day in New York, protesting their exclusion from the parade, they
often carry posters with pictures of Irish homosexuals (Frances Power
Cobbe, Somerville and Ross, Wilde, Casement, Eva Gore-Booth), establishing a genealogy of people who never conceptualized such a genealogy themselves, at least not on paper. Paul Muldoon emphasized
this ancestry in a poem printed on the editorial page of the *New York
Times* in 1992, the first year that the Ancient Order of Hibernians refused to let ILGO march:

> As for the "Hibs" standing in the way
> Of Irish Lesbians and Gays,
> would they have stopped Casement when he tried to land
> a boatload of guns on Banna Strand?[112]

Emerging from the politicized sexual discourse of the 1990s, Jeffrey
Dudgeon's biography, *Roger Casement: The Black Diaries, with a
Study of His Background, Sexuality, and Irish Political Life* (2002), is
the first to treat Casement's sexual life as serious social history.[113]
Commenting on Casement's cruising, the fee scale he recorded for
sexual favors, and the many photographs of young men among his papers, Dudgeon's biography contextualizes the practical and material
aspects of Casement's sex life.

It was in the liberalizing atmosphere of spring 1993, after the de-
criminalizing in Ireland of homosexual acts between consenting
adults over the age of seventeen, that Roisin McAuley and Nigel
Acheson of the BBC decided to devote the September 24 weekly radio
broadcast *Document* to the diaries.[114] For the first time the diaries
were forensically examined and declared genuine. The permission
thus granted to the BBC led the Home Office to make the diaries
available to the general public the following year. On the day after the
new accessibility, the *Irish Times* printed generous excerpts from the
diaries, and the timing was such that these passages (the most explicitly pornographic, of course) were published during Holy Week 1994
(March 29).[115]

Although the ensuing debate evolved along predictable lines, there
emerged a totally outed Casement with almost nothing left to hide:
folk Casement, the active homosexual hidden beneath the Republi-
can martyr, was now a public persona. With details of his intercourse

with Joseph Millar Gordon on May 28 in a hotel in Warrenpoint printed unexpurgated on page 6 under the heading "Home News," he was no longer part of "hidden Ireland." No one in Ireland could miss the most private of Casement's notations: "First Time after So Many Years and So Deep Mutual Longing."[116] The *Irish Times* editor wanted to emphasize the love, not the sin or the criminality. No longer naughty, no longer the all-purpose subversive, Casement became an object lesson in the many forms of patriotism for the new, revisionist Ireland. As Emer O'Kelly wrote in the *Sunday Independent*, "the well-meaning custodians of Casement's political history and reputation are wrong when they suggest that his sexuality and sexual practices should now be put to rest.... They must be kept alive, not because they show Casement in all his human unhappiness and loneliness (although they do), but because we have to learn to de-mythologize our history."[117] Thus remoralized, Casement was now an emblem of the united Ireland that Yeats, Monk Gibbon, and maybe even Mother Scholastica had envisioned, in which patriotic reverence and homosexual love were acknowledged to coexist.

It seems to be Casement's fate always to be remoralized, and for those "well-meaning custodians" to assert themselves in new ways. In the postnational, postcolonial twenty-first century, it is global Casement, not Irish Casement, whose heroism must be purified of his sexuality. The Irish government's official representative to the 2000 Royal Irish Academy symposium, Martin Mansergh, one of those whose efforts led to the 1998 Good Friday Agreement, argued that the author of the diaries—not Roger Casement, he hoped—was "predatory" and had "absolutely no conscience in regard to his own sexual life." It was the good, celibate Casement whom Mansergh wished to "co-opt . . . as a forerunner of Ireland's independent foreign policy."[118] Although the lusty and promiscuous diarist did nothing that would have been illegal in post-1993 Ireland, even in the first year of the new century, homosexuality, in some circles, retained a degree of pollution. Sir Ernley Blackwell, encouraging the exhibition of the diaries back in 1916 to preclude martyrdom, never dreamed that the Irish would keep their martyr and invent another diarist.

The Casementistas

Are they the Casementistas or the Casementalists? Whatever the nomenclature, the term refers to contemporary Casement controversialists, people active and visible enough to have been designated as a category and given two names.[119] Since the mid-1990s, the Casementistas have been busily producing Casementia: biographies, editions of Casement's writings, radio programs, television documentaries, reviews (of the biographies, editions, and audio-visual materials), academic conferences, handwriting analyses, polemical essays, dissertations, and gossip about one another.[120] Whenever any two Casementistas meet, they are sure to be talking about the others.

Although these activities occasionally inspire letters to the editor, the old passion—that is, the popular emotions exacerbated by and expressed through Casement controversies—no longer exists. In the ancient days of the mid-twentieth century, Casement offered one of the few sanctioned ways of airing ideas of sexuality in a public arena. Now there are many such opportunities; the scandal of clerical sex abuse, among others, attracts the anger and the volume of letters that Casement used to. Disagreements about the authenticity of the diaries have come to interest only those with a professional stake in the issue. Now it is the Casementistas who have become talking heads in the latest miniseries: soon, in the darkened space of a university lecture hall, students will take notes or doze while the videotape plays, offering in sound bites the urgent matters the entire country used to fight about.

⊞ Epilogue

Controversy as "Heritage"

Beagán, is é a rá go maith.
A little, and to say it well.

"Magna sed inutilis controversia" (a large but useless contro-versy): the sigh is audible in Fr. Anthony Bruodine's disapproving phrase. He was describing the famous argument carried on in *The Contention of the Bards* (*Iomarbhágh na bhFileadh*) a half century earlier, at the beginning of the seventeenth century.[1]

It is conventional to deplore controversies, to condemn them as mere anger or a waste of time or both, squabbles that could be re-solved if only all sides would be polite and listen patiently to one an-other. They are "intemperate speech," in Yeats's phrase; hatred "maimed us at the start." Yet however Irish controversies may have maimed their participants, wasted their time, or shortened their lives, forces within the culture tend to treat these fights as significant and valuable, a type of *dúchas* or heritage worthy of preservation and display. Lip service says controversies are tiresome, but history shows they are considered national cultural capital.

Irish language traditions privilege controversies in both manuscript and oral versions. *The Contention of the Bards* survives in many manuscripts, and modern scholarly attention to it suggests that this complex series of bardic disputes is not any more *inutilis* than any other work of art.[2] The *agallamh beirte* (argument between two people) remains a competitive performance genre at annual meetings of the *Oireachtas na Gaeilge* (Irish cultural gathering) in contemporary Ireland. A miniature controversy, the *agallamh beirte* constructs disagreement between two people as a witty, hilarious dramatic tour de force: "two characters sing their comic lines back and forth blending the most modern (and most outrageous) issues with the traditional lore."[3]

Not only in the Gaeltacht but in the middle of Dublin 2, controversy is exhibited as a worthy form of Irish culture. The Royal Irish Academy's 2000 symposium "Sir Roger Casement in Irish and World History" staged the Casement controversy, deliberately pitting against one another speakers known to have opposed views. The editors of the *Field Day Anthology*'s fourth and fifth volumes put controversy on display in another way, anthologizing documents from recent controversies ("Magdalen Asylums, 1765–1992"; "Infanticide in Nineteenth-Century Ireland"; "Contesting Ireland: The Erosion of Heterosexual Consensus, 1940–2001"). The section "The Republic of Ireland: The Politics of Sexuality, 1965–2000" focused on another small site in which large forces came into conflict during the 1980s and 1990s, the Irish womb. Essays, interviews, memoirs, and editorials record a series of controversies involving Irish women and pregnancy: the death of Ann Lovett, the Kerry Babies, the X-Case, the continuing debate about abortion, and the story of former bishop Eamon Casey's paternity.[4] Selections from Veronica Guerin's interview with Casey look, on the page, like an *agallamh beirte:*

Q. Have sexual relationships been a feature of your life?
A. This is an improper and rude question to ask anybody. . . .

. . . .

Q. Did you have sex with her often?
A. This is an improper and rude question.
Q. There has been controversy over sex in your car at the gravel pit.
A. As I told you, I am not going into any of the intimacies of my life.[5]

This dialogue sounds like the opposite of one performed at the 1994 Oireachtas, an exchange between a priest and a woman that begins

Beannaigh mé, a Athair,
    Má's peacach mé
Ach sílim fhéin, nach ea!

Bless me Father, for I have sinned,
　　Although I myself don't think so![6]

(translation: Eileen Moore Quinn)

As high, low, or middle culture, in Irish or English, argument is enjoyed without apology and endowed with cultural value.

Yeats called attention in print to the "three public controversies" that "stirred [my] imagination" in *Responsibilities*, and controversies continue to provide inspiration for poetry.[7] The audiences who heard Seamus Heaney read in 1993 from *The Midnight Verdict*, his translation of Brian Merriman's *Cúirt an Mheán Oíche*, recognized in its passion a response to the controversy over the original *Field Day Anthology of Irish Writing* (1992).

Maeve and Sive and Sheila! Maureen!
Knot the rope till it tears the skin.
Let Mr. Brian take what we give,
Let him have it. Flay him alive
And don't draw back when you're drawing blood.
Test all of your whips against his manhood.
Cut deep. No mercy. Make him squeal.
Leave him in strips from head to heel
Until every single mother's son
In the land of Ireland learns the lesson.[8]

Heaney's listeners could not help but call to mind the real-life equivalents of "Maeve," "Sheila," and the rest, the women who had been most vocal in their attacks on the male-edited anthology. And if they missed it in *The Midnight Verdict*, they could not fail to hear it in the translation Heaney paired with it, Ovid's version of the death of Orpheus:

. . . a band of crazed Ciconian women,
A maenad band dressed up in wild beasts' skins,
Spied him from a hilltop with his lyre.
As he tuned his voice to it and cocked his ear,
One of them whose hair streamed in the breeze
Began to shout, "Look, look, it's Orpheus,
Orpheus the misogynist. . . ."[9]

As Heaney said, working on the Ovid translation while preparing a lecture on Merriman, he "gradually came to think of the Merriman poem as another aspect of the story of Orpheus's death."[10] A stylish intervention in the *Field Day* controversy, Heaney's book transformed the popular culture of controversy into the high culture of poetic translation.

In more recondite fashion, the short film *Aqua* uses controversy as cultural capital.[11] The film's hidden genesis suggests the way many artistic expressions may be seen not as originary gestures but as responses in a continuing argument never directly alluded to. In this fable, two poor Irish students sell audiotapes with the sounds of Irish rivers as "relaxation" aids to Irish-Americans. The students' success makes them rich, but they ignore a mysterious voice in the water chanting "aaaaquaaaa" and warning in Hiberno-Latin that the world will be destroyed by water. In the final sequence, as the students sleep contentedly in their new designer bed, water drips with increasing power through their ceiling, and the frame slowly fills with water. The holy landscape, desecrated by the couple, commodified, sold for filthy lucre, takes its revenge. And thus also (the film implies) to all who package the Irish landscape and profit from it: the film makes a subtle and witty intervention in the continuing series of battles in the 1990s over heritage centers in Mullaghmore, County Clare, Luggalo, County Wicklow, and the Boyne Valley (Brú na Bóinne, including Newgrange and Knowth). These controversies involved the conflicting and overlapping interests of environmentalists, Dúchas (the government department concerned with architecture, monuments, and landscape), archaeologists, and local entrepreneurs.[12] Although *Aqua* never mentions a specific heritage center, the narrative constitutes a comment on contemporary Irish tourism, and the film's origin in a time of landscape controversy gives force to the expression of anger in the magic voice.

Controversy in Ireland is not just a feature of high cultural nationalism; it is a type of unscripted public debate that continues to come into being, expressing and registering, though not resolving, the conflicts of a particular moment. In the twentieth century as in earlier ones, controversies flourished during the gaps between wars. Introducing his 1918 edition of *The Contention of the Bards*, Fr. McKenna speculated that "the reason why the controversy created so much excitement among the bards, and throughout the country, was that in the beginning of the seventeenth century there was established over Ireland a state of peace." That peace, he continued, "forced the nation back on her own thoughts."[13] Had McKenna looked back on the ten previous years, he might have noticed that the "peaceful" years be-fore the Easter Rising had also seen the emergence of a great number of controversies. After the period of greatest violence in modern Irish history, 1916–23, during the uneasy peace that followed the end of the Civil War, the Lane and Casement controversies reemerged, and new controversies (the Tailor and Ansty in 1942, the Liberal Ethic in 1950, the Fethard-on-Sea boycott in 1957, the Language Freedom Movement in 1966) were born. The quietest years for modern Irish controversies were the worst years of the Northern Ireland troubles, the 1970s and the first half of the 1980s. From the mid-1980s through the end of the 1990s, however, controversies were as plentiful as in the years before the Rising.[14]

Controversies in their abundance emerge when the cessation of wars releases their energies. And when the wars return, the contro-versies recede once more. As they flare and rage, inspiring angry re-torts, media frenzies, and works of art, controversies do not follow a "commodius vicus of recirculation"; they are not *plus ça change*. Their tracks form spirals, not circles; the same battles are not fought again, at least not in identical terms. Sites and participants alter be-cause cultural controversies happen at the edge of social change. Nasty to some, entertaining to others, controversies are morally neu-tral, turning hatred into sport, theater, and poetry.

◲ Chronologies of the Controversies

A Chronology of the Controversy over Hugh Lane and the Thirty-Nine Paintings

1875
November 9   Hugh Percy Lane born in Douglas, a suburb of Cork; son of
Frances Adelaide Persse and the Rev. James William Lane.

1880s   HPL does not attend school because of poor health; is tutored at
home (various locations in England and Europe) by his mother.

1893   Starts work at Bond Street Gallery in London, run by Martin
Colnaghi (position gotten for him by his aunt, Lady Gregory);
attends sales at Christie's.

1896   Starts work at Marlborough Galleries, London.

1897   Sets up independently as a "gentleman dealer."

1901   Visits Lady Gregory at Coole; visits exhibition of contemporary painting in Dublin, with work by Nathaniel Hone and
J. B. Yeats.

1902   Organizes an exhibition of Old Masters paintings (from private collections in Irish houses) for the RHA, Dublin.

1904
Spring   Organizes exhibition of Irish art for the Guildhall, London.

Summer   Travels to Paris and Madrid with Irish painter William Orpen.
At Durand-Ruel art dealers, purchases works by Manet (*Eva
Gonzalez*), Pissarro, Monet, and others, with Orpen's guid-
ance.

November   Exhibition at the RHA of works promised to the new Dublin
Gallery of Modern Art (whenever it might open). Works in-
clude nineteenth-century French paintings by Corot,
Courbet, Fantin-Latour, and Degas; exhibition also includes

	works by Irish painters (N. Hone, Walter Osborne, George Russell, JBY, et al.).
1905	Dublin Corporation supports allocation of funds for "maintenance of a Municipal Gallery of Modern Art."
1907	
September	Libraries Committee of Dublin Corporation recommends acquisition of No. 17 Harcourt St. as temporary gallery.
Winter	Lane "chucks out" certain members of audience during *Playboy* riots.
December	Private opening of Municipal Gallery with Lane as director.
1908	
January 20	Public opening of Municipal Gallery.
February	Lane becomes an "Honorary Freeman of the City of Dublin."
Autumn	Named member of the board of governors of the new National University.
1909	Knighted for his services to art.
1912	
November 5	Lane writes letter to the clerk of Dublin Corporation (1) handing over certain paintings "on the condition that they are always on view free to the public," and (2) stating that other paintings (the thirty-nine) will be removed at end of January 1913 if permanent gallery not decided by then.
November 18	Lorcan Sherlock, lord mayor of Dublin, calls meeting to elect committee to find a site (Citizens Provisional Committee); Frank Craig suggests bridge gallery.
1913	
August	Lane removes paintings from Harcourt Street to Mansion House (Dawson Street).
September 8	Dublin Corporation rejects bridge site.
September 27	Lane removes paintings from Mansion House, they go on loan to Belfast, then on loan to National Gallery, London; writes will in which the thirty-nine paintings are left to the National Gallery in London on assumption that they will be exhibited as a group.
1914	
January	Board of Trustees of London National Gallery "reverses decision" to show all thirty-nine in one room. Lane irritated; did not want trustees to make "artistic" decisions.
February 26	Appointed director of the National Gallery of Ireland.
1915	
February 3	Writes codicil to will, leaving thirty-nine paintings to the city of Dublin "if a suitable building is provided within 5 years of my death."
March–April	Travels to New York for Lloyds of London "to give expert opinion on damage caused to paintings aboard a burning ship in New York" (Dawson).

May	Returns to Ireland on board the *Lusitania*; dies along with 1,200 others when it is torpedoed by German U-boat on the west coast of Cork, May 7. According to survivors' accounts, Lane was last seen helping women and children board lifeboats; he said, "This is a sad end for us all," and left to see if he could help a Mrs. Pearson (whose body, like Hugh Lane's, was never found).
Summer	Codicil found in Lane's desk at NGI, leaving the thirty-nine paintings to the city of Dublin.
1918 and following years	Lady Gregory in touch with Michael Collins, Edward Carson, de Valera, and many other politicians about getting the thirty-nine back.
1924	Committee appointed by British government finds that Lane believed codicil was legal but that if he had seen the new Tate Gallery, "he would have destroyed the codicil." Sarah Purser founds Friends of the National Collections of Ireland, which devotes itself to getting the thirty-nine paintings back.
1928 *June*	Public meeting held at Theatre Royal "to give the younger generation" an account of the controversy. Lady Gregory speaks; letter of support from de Valera and Sean O'Casey.
1929	Irish government adopts Sarah Purser's idea to use Charlemont House as the municipal gallery.
1933 *June 19*	President Eamon de Valera opens new gallery at Charlemont House, Parnell Square.
1956 *April 12*	Berthe Morisot's *Jour d'été* stolen from Tate by Irish students.
April 16	Painting returned.
1959	Agreement: thirty-nine paintings divided into two groups, which alternated between the National Gallery, London, and the Dublin Municipal Gallery, for a five-year period over twenty years.
1979	Fourteen-year agreement: thirty paintings in Dublin; eight in London; one, Renoir's *Les parapluies*, alternates.
1993	Twelve-year agreement: twenty-seven paintings in Dublin for twelve years; remaining eight "alternate in two groups of 4 each for 6 years."

A Chronology of the O'Hickey Controversy

1908

November 27 Inaugural meeting of the Gaelic Society of the Catholic University College.

December 7 Gaelic League meeting at the Rotunda, where Douglas Hyde reads O'Hickey's letter aloud.

December 13 O'Hickey addresses students of the Columban League (the Gaelic literary society), St. Patrick's College, Maynooth, on the "University Question."

December 19 O'Hickey's lecture published in *Sinn Féin*.

1909

January 19 Standing Committee of the Bishops issues statement calling the essential Irish issue "a question for fair argument" but adds "it is quite possible that in existing circumstances compulsion instead of being a help would be a hindrance to the language movement."

January 29 O'Hickey receives letter saying that the "Bishops take exception to the language" of his letters in the newspapers.

Spring Publication of O'Hickey's pamphlets *An Irish University, or Else* and *The Irish Bishops and an Irish University*.

June 22 Trustees of St. Patrick's College, Maynooth, pass resolution calling on O'Hickey "to resign his position as professor of Irish."

July 29 O'Hickey, having refused to resign, is dismissed from his position.

August 3 Testimonial meeting for O'Hickey held at Gresham Hotel; MacNeill in chair.

September 19 In Dublin, 500,000 people march in support of essential Irish.

1910–16

O'Hickey in Rome putting case before papal Rota: complex, exhausting, and ultimately futile expenditure of time, money, and energy.

1910

June 23 Senators of the new university approve "essential Irish," with the requirement to begin in 1913.

1916

Summer O'Hickey returns home to his brother Martin's house in Portlaw, County Waterford, and awaits word of a new mission from his bishop.

November 19 Death of Dr. O'Hickey.

1988

July 24 Cardinal Tomás Ó Fiaich unveils Cliodna Cussen statue of O'Hickey in Carrickbeg.

A Chronology of the *Blanco Posnet* Controversy

1909
February 16–
March 8   Shaw writes *The Shewing-up of Blanco Posnet.*
May 13   *Blanco* (already in rehearsal with Herbert Beerbohm Tree in
lead) refused license by British censor (Examiner of Plays)
George Redford because of its alleged blasphemy.
June   GBS and his wife, Charlotte Shaw, attend the Abbey's London
performance of *Kathleen ni Houlihan.* Soon after, Lady Gre-
gory invites GBS to become one of the Abbey directors; he re-
fuses, but offers her *Blanco* for the Abbey.
July 30 and
August 5   GBS testifies at hearings of the parliamentary Joint Select
Committee on Stage Plays (Censorship).
August 6   Note from the Dublin Metropolitan Police Office to Under-
secretary Sir James Dougherty at Dublin Castle, pointing out
that the Abbey has been advertising the performance of a play
censored in England.
August 12   Lady Gregory meets with the undersecretary at Dublin Castle.
August 13   Gregory's solicitor tells her that the crown solicitor at the
Castle has said that the Lord Lieutenant (viceroy) "would use
every power the law gave him" to stop the play.
August 13
and 14   Gregory and Yeats talk to undersecretary.
August 14
and following
days   Correspondence between Gregory and GBS about possible
changes in the script.
August 17   Letter from Lord Lieutenant to Gregory requesting interview.
August 20   Gregory meets with Lord Lieutenant in viceregal lodge and is
joined by Yeats; then Gregory and Yeats meet with undersecretary.
August 21   *Sinn Féin* asks its readers not to riot, that is, not to "play the
Castle game"; Lord Lieutenant issues a "precautionary notice"
saying that if the first performance of *Blanco Posnet* leads to a
riot, the Abbey Theatre's patent will be rescinded; Thomas
LeFanu, chief clerk of the Irish Office, testifies at the Select
Committee's hearings in London that the lord lieutenant does
not have the power to prevent production of the play; Abbey
Theatre issues press release saying, "If our patent is in danger it
is because the English Censorship is being extended to Ireland."
August 25   Opening night of *Blanco* ends in "thunderous applause."

A Chronology of the "Save the Dublin Kiddies" Controversy

1913

August 21   William Martin Murphy, editor of the *Irish Independent* (II)
             and owner of the Dublin Tramway Company (TC) and other
             businesses, dismisses workers from II and TC when he learns
             they are members of Jim Larkin's Irish Transport and General
             Workers Union.

August 26   Irish Transport and General Workers Union strike begins in
             Dublin.

August 30   During clashes between strikers and Dublin Metropolitan Po-
             lice in Burgh Quay and Eden Quay, James Nolan is killed;
             John Byrne dies several days later from wounds received in
             clash.

August 31   "Bloody Sunday": after Larkin appears on balcony of the Im-
             perial Hotel (owned by Murphy) on O'Connell Street to ad-
             dress the strikers, Dublin Metropolitan Police charge work-
             ers' demonstration.

End of
September   From 20,000 to 25,000 workers on strike or dismissed for
             membership in Larkin's union.

September 27 Arrival in Dublin of British ship *Hare,* carrying food sent by
             the British Trades Union Congress.

October 19   Articles about "Save the Dublin Kiddies" begin appearing in
             Dublin newspapers.

October 20   Publication in Dublin newspapers of Archbishop Walsh's let-
             ter urging "Catholic mothers" not to take part in plan "to
             send away their little children to be cared for in a strange
             land, without security of any kind that those to whom the
             poor children are to be handed over are Catholics, or indeed
             are persons of any faith at all."

October 22   At Tara Street Baths in central Dublin, parish priests inter-
             rupt washing of fifty children about to be sent to temporary
             homes in England as part of Dora Montefiore's "Save the
             Dublin Kiddies" scheme; eighteen children finally leave for
             Liverpool; Montefiore's helper Lucilla Rand arrested at
             Kingstown police station and charged with kidnapping.

October 23   Dora Montefiore arrested on kidnapping charges; bailed out.

October 24   Delia Larkin et al. stopped from putting children on trains at
             Amiens Street Station by mob.

October 25   Frank Sheehy Skeffington beaten by mob at Kingsbridge
             Station.

October 27   Archbishop Walsh establishes Dublin Children's Distress
             Fund.

November 1   Protest meeting on behalf of Dublin strikers held at Albert
Memorial Hall in London; Shaw, Connolly, "AE," and others
speak.

November 19 Formation of the Irish Citizen Army to protect the workers
from the police.

November 25 Formation of the Irish Volunteers.

1914
January 18
and following
weeks   Gradual return to work by strikers.

March   Women workers in Jacob's Biscuit Factory, "the first to be
locked out on a large scale," are the "last to return" to work.

A Chronology of the Casement Controversy

1916
April 21   Roger Casement captured soon after a German submarine
leaves him and two companions on the Kerry coast.

June 26–29   Casement on trial in London for High Treason.

August 3   Casement executed; buried on grounds of Pentonville Prison.

1936   *Irish Press* publishes William Maloney's *The Forged Casement
Diaries* in installments.

1937
February   Yeats publishes the ballad "Roger Casement" in *Irish Press*,
causing first long-running Casement newspaper controversy.

1956   Publication of René MacColl's biography *Roger Casement: A
New Judgment; Irish Times* review of the book is followed by
long controversy.

1957   Publication of *The Accusing Ghost, or, Justice for Roger
Casement* by poet Alfred Noyes.

1959
February   Publication of *The Black Diaries of Roger Casement* edited
by Peter Singleton-Gates and Maurice Girodias.

August   British government begins policy of allowing scholars access
to the Casement diaries.

1965
January   British government agrees to return Casement's remains to
Dublin.

February   Casement's remains exhumed from Pentonville Prison and
flown to Dublin; coffin carrying remains lies in state in
chapel at Arbour Hill.

March 1   Casement's funeral.

1966   Banna Strand monument erected.

1984	Statue of Casement at Ballyheigue (North Kerry) unveiled by Tánaiste Dick Spring.
1994	Diaries made accessible to all readers; excerpts published in British and Irish newspapers.
1997	Roger Sawyer and Angus Mitchell both publish editions of Casement's 1910 diaries: Sawyer's considers the Black Diary material for 1910 authentic; Mitchell's declares it forged.
2000 *May*	Royal Irish Academy symposium "Roger Casement in Irish and World History"
2002 *March*	Giles Report makes case for authenticity of the diaries.

⊞ Notes

Introduction

1. W. B. Yeats, "Notes," in *The Variorum Edition of the Poems*, ed. Peter Allt and Russell K. Alspach (New York: Macmillan, 1975), 818. The word *controversy* as it has been used in litigation, in the titles of pamphlets and books, in newspapers and other media, may apply to a case at law, an issue of international politics, an irresolvable philosophical question, or a particular cultural debate. Whatever it is, the matter of a controversy is adversarial, and there are at least two points of view. It may be literary and ludic, as in John Lydgate's "Controversy between a Lover and a Jay," or immediate and practical, as in "The Controversy over a New Canal Treaty between the United States and Canada." It may be narrow and specific, as in "The controversy on article sixteenth of the lease of the Pittsburgh, Fort Wayne & Chicago railway to the Pennsylvania railroad company," or general and cosmic, as in "The Controversy between True and Pretended Christianity." Occasionally the word is used for a deliberate rhetorical exercise, as in "A controversy between the four elements, viz. fire, water, earth and air.: Wherein each of them claims superiority, and extol their own goodness and worth to mankind.: With their various arguments why they ought to be deemed superior." Most often in the past hundred years, the word *controversy* has been used for the kind of debate that doesn't get resolved easily, if at all: "Controversy: The Birth Control Debate, 1958–1968," or "Controversy: Catastrophism and Evolution: The Ongoing Debate," or "Controversy between Rev. Messrs. Hughes and Breckenridge: On the Subject 'Is the Protestant Religion the Religion of Christ?'" All these titles may be found in the Harvard On-Line Library Information Services.

2. As the epigraphs to this introduction indicate, Irish people consider themselves more verbally combative than other peoples. As Seamus Brennan said in 1949, "there is nothing the average Irishman loves more than a real live argument or discussion" (quoted in Luke Gibbons, *Transformations in Irish Culture* [Cork: Cork University Press, 1996], 77). Controversies exist in many societies,

but they may be more prevalent in Irish society for a number of reasons. According to the Celtic scholar Nerys Patterson, in Ireland the "internal and autochthonous development of political culture got aborted by the Tudor conquest, which imposed judge-made foreign law in place of native institutions for the arbitration of conflict. This imposed law never had full legitimacy amongst the Irish population. . . . There are no descriptions of the process whereby incipient feuds were headed off through negotiations, but judging from a welter of details, I would say that there was much posturing and display of wealth, power, aggressiveness etc., also much testing of nerve through verbal repartee to see who could best the other at sarcasm, and much dickering back and forth as different parties to the conflict probed the attitudes of other parties. In other words, while there was hierarchy there was no strong authority" (private communication to author). See Nerys Thomas Patterson, *Cattle Lords and Clansmen: The Social Structure of Early Ireland* (South Bend, IN: Notre Dame University Press, 1994).

The seventeenth-century series of poems in Irish, *Iomarbhágh na bhFileadh* (The contention of the bards), has many of the characteristics of controversy: it is an undecidable argument about cultural power, composed severally by bards seeking to stabilize and define the nature of bardic poetry, and hence the nature of political power in Ireland, because "for these poets there was no split whatsoever between the realms of artistry and public pronouncement" (Joep Leerssen, private communication to author). See Joep Leerssen's fine commentary *The Contention of the Bards (Iomarbhágh na bhFileadh) and Its Place in Irish Political and Literary History* (London: Irish Texts Society, 1994). As poem 10 says, "Spare not your speech, Ó Lughaidh. Give free rein to your wrath. Though your spitefulness is uncalled for, give full course to your tongue" (Rev. L. McKenna, S.J., trans. and ed., *Iomarbhágh na bhFileadh: The Contention of the Bards* [London: Irish Texts Society, 1918], 109). Joseph O'Rourke's work on eighteenth-century Irish legal argument shows it to be lengthier and more flamboyant than English legal argument of the same period. Of her play *The Workhouse Ward*, which consists entirely of two elderly men arguing with one another, Lady Gregory wrote, "I sometimes think the two scolding paupers are a symbol of ourselves in Ireland—'it is better to be quarrelling than to be lonesome'" (Augusta Gregory, *Lady Gregory: Selected Writings*, ed. Lucy McDiarmid and Maureen Waters [London: Penguin, 1995]). Eileen Moore Quinn's analysis of the genre *agallamh beirte* (argument between two people) as performed at the 1994 Oireachtas (Irish-language gathering) in Waterford reveals many similarities to the controversies discussed in this book. The genre is a minidebate "in which two characters, sometimes in appropriate costume, express contradictory points of view." Because the form is "primarily entertainment-oriented, it allows for the creation of a platform by which hegemonic frictions between church and penitent, male and female, parent and child, government and tax payer, Irish speaker and English speaker, are allowed to articulate with the jocular." In other words, it is a licensed form (Eileen Moore Quinn, "Anthropological Poetics and Ireland: *An tOireachtas*, 1994," paper delivered at the 1995 meeting of the American Conference for Irish Studies at Queen's University, Belfast; see also Gearóid Denvir, *An Ghaeilge, an Ghaeltacht agus 1992* [Baile Átha Cliath: Glór na nGael, 1991]). In spite of all these sources, I carefully use the word *may* in the first sentence of this note be-cause American cultural controversies in the 1990s, such as the debate over New York's funding of the "Sensation" exhibit at the Brooklyn Museum of Art, or the Ebonics controversy in California, resemble in many respects the Irish controversies discussed here. On verbal battles (of which controversy is one type) generally, see John McDowell, "Verbal Dueling," in *Discourse and Dialogue*, vol. 3 of *Handbook of Discourse Analysis*, ed. Teun A. Van Dijk (Orlando, FL: Harcourt, 1985), 203–12; and Ward Parks, *Verbal Dueling in Heroic Narrative: The Homeric and Old English Traditions* (Princeton: Princeton University Press, 1990).

3. Seamus Deane, "What Is Field Day," insert in the program for the first production of Brian Friel's translation of Chekhov's *Three Sisters* (Derry: Field Day Theatre Company, 1981), n.p.

4. Michael O'Hickey, ALS to R. A. Sheehan, bishop of Waterford and Lismore, January 31, 1909, O'Hickey file 7/4 (4), 11. Russell Library, St. Patrick's College, Maynooth.

5. All page references to poems by Yeats will be to the *Variorum* edition.

6. For a sense of the nationalist public culture from which the cultural nationalism of the Irish Revival evolved, see Mary Helen Thuente, *The Harp Restrung: The United Irishmen and the Rise of Irish Literary Nationalism* (Syracuse, NY: Syracuse University Press, 1994); Joep Leerssen, *Remembrance and Imagination: Patterns in the Historical and Literary Representation of Ireland in the Nineteenth Century* (South Bend, IN: Notre Dame University Press; Cork: Cork University Press, 1997); and Gary Owens, "Popular Mobilisation and the Rising of 1848: The Clubs of the Irish Confederation," in *Rebellion and Remembrance in Modern Ireland*, ed. Laurence Geary (Dublin: Four Courts, 2001), 51–63.

7. Lady Gregory, *Seventy Years: 1852–1922* (New York: Macmillan, 1976), 13.

8. Michael O'Hickey, *The True National Idea* (Dublin: Gaelic League, 1898), 6.

9. See Andrée Sheehy Skeffington's comments on "The Liberal Ethic" controversy of 1950–51: some of the participants "deplored the 'conspiracy of silence' among the rest. The main value of the controversy lay in the breaking of this silence. It allowed 'so many things to be said which otherwise either could not or would not be mentioned,' Owen wrote" (Sheehy Skeffington, *Skeff: A Life of Owen Sheehy Skeffington, 1909–1970* [Dublin: Lilliput, 1991], 42).

10. Carol Coulter, "Archbishop Criticises Child-as-Product View," *Irish Times*, March 3, 1999, 1.

Chapter 1. Hugh Lane and the Decoration of Dublin, 1908–

1. All photos mentioned in the opening paragraph may be found in the archives of the Hugh Lane Municipal Gallery of Modern Art. "The End of a Controversy," *Irish Times*, January 20, 1961, 6; "Home at Last," *Daily Mail*, January 20, 1961, n.p.

2. The idea of objects being "culturally redefined" is taken from Igor Kopy-

toff, "The Cultural Biography of Things: Commodity as Process," in *The Social Life of Things: Commodities in Cultural Perspective*, ed. Arjun Appadurai (Cambridge: Cambridge University Press, 1986), 67.

3. Sources of information for the history of the Lane paintings include Barbara Dawson, "Hugh Lane and the Origins of the Collection," in *Images and Insights* (Dublin: Hugh Lane Municipal Gallery of Modern Art, 1993); Lady Gregory, *Hugh Lane's Life and Achievement* (London: John Murray, 1921); and Thomas Bodkin, *Hugh Lane and His Pictures* (Dublin: Browne and Nolan, 1934). The thirty-nine contested paintings are Antoine Louis Barye, *The Forest of Fontainebleau*; François Bonvin, *Still Life with Book, Papers, and Inkwell*; Eugène Boudin, *The Beach at Tourgéville-les-Sablons*; John Lewis Brown, *The Mountebank* (*The Performing Dog*); Jean-Baptiste-Camille Corot, *Avignon from the West, Summer Morning*, and *A Peasant Woman*; Jean-Désiré-Gustave Courbet, *The Diligence in the Snow*, *The Pool*, *In the Forest*, and *Self-Portrait* (*L'homme à la ceinture le cuir*); Charles Daubigny, *Honoré Daumier*; Honoré Daumier, *Don Quixote and Sancho Panza*; Hilaire-Germain-Edgar Degas, *Beach Scene* (*Bains de mer: Petite fille peignée par sa bonne*); Narcisse Virgile Diaz, *Venus and Two Cupids* (*The Offspring of Love*); Ignace Henri Théodore Fantin-Latour, *Still Life with Glass Jug, Fruit, and Flowers*; Jean-Louis Forain, *L'assistance judiciare* (*Legal Assistance*); French School, nineteenth century, *Negress*; Jean-Léon Gérôme, *A Student of the École Polytechnique*; Jean Ingres, *Le duc d'Orléans*; Johan Jongkind, *Skating in Holland*; Raimundo de Madrazo, *Portrait of a Lady*; Antonio Mancini, *The Customs* (*La douane*), *The Marquis del Grillo*, *En voyage* (*On a Journey*), and *Aurelia*; Édouard Manet, *Le concert aux Tuileries*, *Eva Gonzales*; Jacob Maris, *A Girl Feeding a Bird in a Cage*; Claude Monet, *Lavacourt under Snow*; Adolphe Monticelli, *The Hayfield*; Berthe Morisot, *Jour d'été*; Camille Pissarro, *Printemps, vue de Louveciennes*; Pierre-Cécile Puvis de Chavannes, *The Beheading of St. John the Baptist*, *A Maid Combing a Woman's Hair* (*La toilette*); Pierre-Auguste Renoir, *Les parapluies* (*The Umbrellas*); Theodore Rousseau, *Moonlight: The Bathers*; Alfred Stevens, *The Present*; and Edouard Vuillard, *The Mantelpiece* (*La chiminée*).

4. John Kelly, " 'Friendship is the only house I have,' " in *Lady Gregory, Fifty Years After*, ed. Ann Saddlemyer and Colin Smythe (Gerrards Cross, Bucks.: Colin Smythe, 1987), 247.

5. This point is made with particular force by Lane's friend Alec Martin in an RTÉ interview, "Talk on Hugh Lane by Sir Alec Martin," IDLPROC OOOO4, RTÉ Radio Archives, produced July 12, 1955.

6. Gregory, *Hugh Lane's Life*, 69.

7. Ibid., 177–78.

8. Grant Richards, *Caviare* (New York: Houghton Mifflin, 1912), 178.

9. Gregory, *Hugh Lane's Life*, 261.

10. William Orpen, *Stories of Old Ireland and Myself* (London: Williams and Norgate, 1924), 54.

11. Gregory, *Hugh Lane's Life*, 254.

12. Ibid., 37.

13. Bodkin, *Hugh Lane and His Pictures*, 44.

14. Elizabeth, Countess of Fingall, as told to Pamela Hinkson, *Seventy Years Young* (Dublin: Lilliput, 1991), 264.

15. Gregory, *Hugh Lane's Life*, 246.

16. Bodkin, *Hugh Lane and His Pictures*, 78. Bodkin's story was used earlier by Gregory in *Hugh Lane's Life*, 262.

17. Orpen, *Stories of Old Ireland*, 55, 56.

18. *Augusta Gregory, Lady Gregory's Diaries, 1892–1902*, ed. James Pethica (Gerrards Cross: Colin Smythe, 1996), 34.

19. Gregory, *Hugh Lane's Life*, 31.

20. ALS Hugh Lane to Lady Gregory, September 27, 1913, folder 10, Berg Collection, NYPL.

21. Untitled editorial, *Irish Times*, December 9, 1904, 4.

22. Adrian Frazier, *George Moore, 1852–1933* (New Haven: Yale University Press, 2000), 339.

23. Gregory, *Hugh Lane's Life*, 195.

24. Ibid., 200.

25. *Tribute to Sir Hugh Lane* (Cork: Cork University Press, 1961), 35.

26. Ibid., 34.

27. Ibid., 35–47.

28. J. M. Synge, "Good Pictures in Dublin" (January 24, 1908), in *Collected Works*, ed. Robin Skelton (London: Oxford University Press, 1962–1968), 2:391.

29. *Tribute to Lane*, 32.

30. *Report of the Committee of Inquiry into the Work Carried on by the Royal Hibernian Academy and the Metropolitan School of Art, Dublin*, Parliamentary Papers 31, Cd. 3256 (1906), 837.

31. For an excellent analysis of galleries and their patrons, see Carol Duncan, *Civilizing Rituals: Inside Public Art Museums* (London: Routledge, 1995), 72–101.

32. Rupert Hart-Davis, ed., *A Catalogue of the Caricatures of Max Beerbohm* (London: Macmillan, 1972), 228.

33. Gregory, *Hugh Lane's Life*, vii, ix.

34. *Report of the Committee of Inquiry*, 835.

35. Duncan, *Civilizing Rituals*, 26.

36. Gregory, *Hugh Lane's Life*, 106.

37. Bodkin, *Hugh Lane and His Pictures*, 33.

38. Subscription form with heading ("Threatened Loss of Valuable Works of Art to the Municipal Art Gallery") and list of names, HLG Archives. Dan H. Laurence and Nicholas Grene, eds., *Shaw, Lady Gregory, and the Abbey: A Correspondence and a Record* (Gerrards Cross: Colin Smythe, 1993), 82–83.

39. The title was changed later to "To a Wealthy Man who promised a Second Subscription to the Dublin Municipal Gallery if it were proved the People wanted Pictures."

40. ALS Lady Gregory to Hugh Lane, "Saturday" [1913], folder 15; ALS Hugh Lane to Lady Gregory, August 27, 1912, folder 4, Berg Collection, NYPL.

41. *Irish Times*, September 8, 1913, 6.

42. *Sinn Féin*, November 30, 1912, 1.

43. Bodkin, *Hugh Lane and His Pictures*, 32.

44. From *Irish Life*, February 28, 1913, 321, HLG Archives.

45. From *Saturday Herald*, April 12, 1913, HLG Archives.

46. Robert O'Byrne, *Hugh Lane, 1875–1915* (Dublin: Lilliput, 2000), 178.

47. *Sinn Féin*, August 9, 1913, 5.

48. ALS Lady Gregory to Hugh Lane, August 14 [1913], folder 12, Berg Collection, NYPL.

49. *Sinn Féin*, August 9, 1913, 5.

50. Lady Gregory to Hugh Lane, August 14 [1913].

51. The issue of Lutyens's nationality was first raised in the *Irish Builder* and then taken up by the *Irish Architect*. See Sean Rothery, *Ireland and the New Architecture, 1900–1940* (Dublin: Lilliput, 1991), 49–50. I am grateful to Howard J. Keeley for the reference.

52. Lady Gregory, Letter, *Irish Times*, September 8, 1913, 7.

53. *Irish Times*, August 12, 1913, 5.

54. Ibid.

55. Ibid., 4.

56. Thomas Morrissey, S.J., *William Martin Murphy* (Dundalk: Dundalgan Press, 1997), 58.

57. *Irish Times*, August 13, 1913, 7.

58. *Irish Times*, August 12, 1913, 5.

59. W. M. Murphy, Letter, *Irish Times*, August 11, 1913, 6.

60. Ibid.

61. Morrissey, *William Martin Murphy*, 37.

62. *Sinn Féin*, September 20, 1913, 3.

63. *Irish Independent*, January 17, 1913.

64. W. B. Yeats, *Letters*, ed. Allan Wade (London: Rupert Hart-Davis, 1954), 579.

65. Donal Nevin, "AE and the Dublin Lock-out," in *James Larkin: Lion of the Fold*, ed. D. Nevin (Dublin: Gill and Macmillan, in association with RTÉ and SIPTU, 1998), 214.

66. ALS Hugh Lane to Thomas Bodkin, September [27?] and November 20, 1913, Bodkin Papers, Trinity College Dublin.

67. *Irish Citizen*, September 27, 1913, 1.

68. Theresa Moriarty, "Larkin and the Women's Movement," in Nevin, *James Larkin*, 93.

69. Anne Haverty, *Constance Markiewicz: An Independent Life* (London: Pandora, 1988), 107.

70. "Minutes of a Special Meeting of the Municipal Council of the City of Dublin," Monday, September 8, 1913, 458.

71. *Irish Times*, September 9, 1913, 6.

72. ALS Lady Gregory to Hugh Lane, September 16, 1913, folder 12, Berg Collection, NYPL.

73. *Irish Times*, September 9, 1913, 6.

74. Ibid.

75. ALS Hugh Lane to Lady Gregory, July 31 [1913], folder 8, Berg Collection, NYPL.

76. O'Byrne, *Hugh Lane*, 231.

77. Gregory, *Hugh Lane's Life*, 46, 231–33.

78. Ibid., 235.

79. John J. Reynolds, *Statement of the Claim for the Return to Dublin of the 39 Lane Bequest Pictures Now at the Tate Gallery, London* (Dublin: Educational Company of Ireland Ltd., 1932), 31.

80. Bodkin, *Hugh Lane and His Pictures*, 53.

81. Ibid., 56.

82. Reynolds, *Statement of the Claim*, 41.

83. Ibid., 236; also Nicola Gordon Bowe, "The Friends of the National Collections of Ireland," in *Art Is My Life: A Tribute to James White*, ed. Brian P. Kennedy (Dublin: National Gallery, 1991), 15.

84. Bodkin, *Hugh Lane and His Pictures*, vi.

85. See *Irish Times* and *Times* (London), April 13, 1956, et seq.; also Elizabeth Coxhead, *Lady Gregory: A Literary Portrait* (London: Secker and Warburg, 1961), 206–7. The three tellings of this tale are William P. Fogarty, "Coup de Tate," *Pegasus: Magazine of the Veterinary Students' Union* (1956), 13–18; interview with Fogarty, titled "Theft of the Lane Collection Picture 1956," RTÉ Radio Archives IDLPROC, L 127/77, produced August 18, 1976 (never aired); and P. O'Driscoll, producer, RTÉ television documentary, (also called) "Coup de Tate," shown December 19, 2002.

86. Fogarty, "Coup de Tate," 10, 12.

87. Ibid., 15.

88. Fogarty interview, RTÉ radio tape.

89. Fogarty, "Coup de Tate," 14.

90. Fogarty interview, RTÉ radio tape.

91. "Tate Picture Taken," *Times*, April 13, 1956, 10.

92. Fogarty interview, RTÉ radio tape.

93. Ibid.

94. O'Driscoll, RTÉ television documentary.

95. Fogarty interview, RTÉ radio tape.

96. Hector Hughes, "Exquisite Critic," in "Speech of the Right Honourable the Lord Mayor of Dublin, Councillor Maurice E. Dockrell," typescript, in envelope titled "Lane Pictures: Correspondence and Press Clippings, 1961," HLG Archives.

97. "Modern Art: The New Gallery in Dublin," *Irish Independent*, January 21, 1908, 5–6.

98. "Dublin's Municipal Gallery of Modern Art," special supplement to *Irish Decorators' and Builders' Review*, July 1933, 2.

99. "The End of a Controversy," *Irish Times*, January 20, 1961, 6; "Home at Last," *Daily Mail*, January 20, 1961, n.p.

100. *Dublin Opinion*, December 1959, 309. The return of the Lane paintings to Dublin provided a rich source of cartoons for *Dublin Opinion*. See figure 1.10.

101. Handwritten instructions, no signature, in envelope titled "Lane Pictures: Correspondence and Press Clippings, 1961," HLG Archives.

102. Typescript of press release, 1961, HLG Archives.

103. "Not Admitted to Gallery Reception," *Irish Times*, February 17, 1961, unpaged clipping in HLG Archives.

104. TLS Lord Moyne to Thomas Bodkin, February 4, 1949; ALS Lord Moyne to Thomas Bodkin, February 11, 1949; TLS Lord Moyne to Thomas Bodkin, January 5, 1951; TLS Lord Moyne to Thomas Bodkin, August 23, 1956. File 6968/53–90, Bodkin Papers, Trinity College.

105. Letter from Barbara Dawson, Director, Hugh Lane Municipal Gallery of Modern Art, to author, October 10, 1992.

106. Interview with Barbara Dawson, August 1993.

107. Although I never met Bill Fogarty, I did have the pleasure of a telephone conversation with him in 1999. I thought I was going to ask him about the theft of the Morisot painting, but instead he quizzed me about hospitals in Pittsburgh, a subject about which I was unable to enlighten him.

Chapter 2. The Man Who Died for the Language

1. Michael Coady, "The Rehabilitation of Michael O'Hickey," *Nationalist and Munster Advertiser* (centenary supplement), December 1990, 1997. Translation by M. Coady. The speech was delivered on July 24, 1988.

2. *Nationalist and Munster Advertiser*, Saturday, July 30, 1988, 1.

3. Louis MacNeice, "Autumn Journal XVI," in *Collected Poems of Louis MacNeice* (Boston: Faber and Faber, 1966), 133.

4. Richard Ellmann, *Oscar Wilde* (London: Penguin Books, 1988), 553.

5. For biographical material on O'Hickey, see Msgr. Pádraig Mac Fhinn, *An tAthair Mícheál Ó hIceadha* (Baile Átha Cliath: Sairseal agus Dill, 1974); a few paragraphs (in English) by O'Hickey himself in "Statement concerning the Dismissal of Dr. O'Hickey from the Irish Chair of St. Patrick's College," at the beginning of the appendix of Mac Fhinn, *An tAthair Mícheál Ó hIceadha*; Pádraig Ó Fiannachta, "An tAthair Mícheál Ó hIci," in *Léachtaí Cholm Cille* (Maigh Nuad: An Sagart, 1986), 16:140–74; and entry in Diarmuid Breathnach and Máire Ni Mhurchú, "Additions and Corrections to Volumes I and II," in *1882–1982 Beathaisnéis a Trí*, Leabhair Thaighde 72 (Dublin: Clochomar, 1992), 165. Biographical information may also be found in the essay by O'Hickey's great-nephew, Mícheál Briody, "From Carrickbeg to Rome—The Story of Fr Michael O'Hickey," *Decies: Journal of the Waterford Archaelogical and Historical Society* 57 (2001): 143–66.

6. "Irish in the National University. Decision of the Senate," *Irish Times*, June 24, 1910, 7. An incorrect date is given in Tomás Ó Fiaich, "The Great Controversy," in *The Gaelic League Idea*, ed. Seán Ó Tuama (Cork: Mercier Press, 1972), 73.

7. See, for instance, "In Dublin," *Irish Nation*, March 13, 1909, 8. Also Thomas J. Morrissey, S.J., *Towards a National University: William Delany S.J. (1835–1924)* (Dublin: Wolfhound Press, 1983).

8. Walter McDonald, *Reminiscences of a Maynooth Professor* (London: Jonathan Cape Ltd., 1925).

9. Sean O'Casey, *Drums under the Window*, in *Autobiographies* (1939; reprint, New York: Carroll and Graff, 1984), 1:403.

10. Stephen Greenblatt, "Culture," in *Critical Terms for Literary Study*, ed.

Frank Lentricchia and Thomas McLaughlin (Chicago: University of Chicago Press, 1990), 231.

11. Michael O'Hickey, *An Irish University, or Else* (Dublin and Waterford: M. H. Gill and Sons, Ltd., 1909).

12. Minutes of the Meeting of the Visitors, June 18, 1909 (copy 1922), O'Hickey file 100/7/4 (2), 1. O'Hickey File, Russell Library, St. Patrick's College, Maynooth. The copy of the minutes is dated June 18, but the meeting actually took place June 20.

13. *An Claidheamh Soluis,* November 30, 1907, 7.

14. *An Claidheamh Soluis,* June 26, 1909, 12.

15. See O'Donovan's fictional account *Father Ralph* (Dingle, County Kerry: Brandon, 1993), originally published 1913. For an account of the conflict between O'Donovan's cultural nationalism and the conservatism of the church, see John Ryan, "Gerald O'Donovan: Priest, Novelist, and Irish Revivalist," *Journal of the Galway Archaeological and Historical Society* 48 (1996): 1–47. As a Maynooth student, O'Donovan was chastised for reading books "of a 'somewhat unbecoming kind' " (4). At a meeting in May 1900 of the first Representative Congress of the Gaelic League, O'Hickey seconded O'Donovan's motion, "calling on the Members of Parliament to pressurise the Government to make education in schools in Irish-speaking districts bilingual" (22). In the Gaelic League's annual report for 1901, "telling indictments" (of "the place of Irish in the new Intermediate regulations") were said to have been made by O'Hickey, MacNeill, and O'Donovan at the meeting of that year's Representative Congress (22–23).

16. J. J. Lee, *The Modernisation of Irish Society* (Dublin: Gill and Macmillan Ltd., 1973), 43.

17. James Joyce, *A Portrait of the Artist as a Young Man* (reprint, New York: Viking Press, 1966), 33.

18. W. P. Ryan, *The Pope's Green Island* (Boston: Small, Maynard, 1912), 23, 26. O'Hickey file 100/7/4 (2), 1.

19. ALS Michael, Cardinal Logue, to Archbishop Walsh, July 10, 1909, Dublin Diocesan Archives 375/7.

20. O'Casey's *The Drums of Father Ned* (New York: St. Martin's Press, 1960) is dedicated to four maverick priests, three of them friends of O'Hickey: his Maynooth colleague Dr. Walter McDonald, prefect of the Dunboyne Establishment; Fr. Peter Yorke, a language activist; and Fr. Michael O'Flanagan, O'Hickey's former student and famous for his social activism. "The Memory be Green of Dr. Walter McDonald, courageous theologian in Maynooth for forty years; of Doctor Morgan Sheedy, his lifelong friend, banished for venturing to defend a Parish Priest against a Bishop . . . ; of Fr. Yorke of San Francisco, who warned Irish Ireland of fond delusions many years ago . . . ; of Canon Hayes, Founder of Muintir na Tire . . . ; and of Fr. O'Flanagan, who, when his poor flock were shivering through a black winter, bade them go to a private-owned bog, and take from it all the turf they needed . . . and was, consequently, banished from his Parish . . . by his Bishop. Each in his time was a Drummer for Fr. Ned, and the echoes of their drumming sound in Ireland still" (v).

21. See Briody, "From Carrickbeg to Rome," 148.

22. O'Hickey, *The Irish Language Movement: Its Genesis, Growth, and Progress*, Gaelic League Pamphlets, no. 29 (n.d.), 7.

23. Ibid., 8, 9.

24. Ibid., 6, 12.

25. Patrick J. Corish, *Maynooth College, 1795–1995* (Dublin: Gill and Macmillan, 1995), 290.

26. ALS O'Hickey to Col. Maurice Moore, June 15, 1909, NLI ms. 10, 567. For the controversy surrounding Mannix himself, years later, when he became a passionate nationalist, see Colm Kiernan, *Daniel Mannix and Ireland* (Dublin: Gill and Macmillan, 1984; Morwell, Victoria: Alella Books, 1984).

27. "Dublin University Gaelic Society. A Plea for Irish Studies," *Irish Times*, November 18, 1908, 7.

28. Ibid.

29. Morrissey, *Towards a National University*, 322–23.

30. "Irish in the New University," *Freeman's Journal*, November 28, 1909, 8–9.

31. Morrissey, *Towards a National University*, 324–26; and "Irish in the New University."

32. Patrick Pearse, "Friends and Foes," in *A Significant Irish Educationalist: The Educational Writings of P. H. Pearse*, ed. Séamus Ó Buachalla (Dublin and Cork: Mercier Press, 1980), 208.

33. Morrissey, *Towards a National University*, 237. The writer of this letter sounds like Simon Dedalus in the Christmas dinner scene: "Didn't the bishops of Ireland betray us in the time of the union when bishop Lanigan presented an address of loyalty to the Marquess Cornwallis? Didn't the bishops and priests sell the aspirations of their country in 1829 in return for catholic emancipation? Didn't they denounce the fenian movement from the pulpit and in the confessionbox? And didn't they dishonour the ashes of Terence Bellew MacManus?" (*Portrait of the Artist as a Young Man*, 38).

34. See, for example, *Irish Nation*, February 20, 1909, 5.

35. *Irish Times*, December 8, 1908, 7.

36. O'Hickey, *An Irish University*, 158

37. First published in *The Nation*, April 22, 1843. When no one else could track this quotation, it was Maura Cronin, Fr. O'Hickey's great-niece, who found it.

38. O'Hickey, *An Irish University*, 132.

39. Ibid., 132, 137.

40. Ibid., 141.

41. Ibid., 146.

42. For the complete text, see Seamus Deane, Andrew Carpenter, and Jonathan Williams, eds., *The Field Day Anthology of Irish Writing* (Derry: Field Day Publications, 1991), 2:107.

43. O'Hickey, *An Irish University*, 136, 147.

44. *Irish Nation and Peasant*, February 6, 1909, 6.

45. O'Hickey, "Statement concerning the Dismissal," 215.

46. Ibid., 181.

47. *Freeman's Journal*, December 8, 1908, 8.

48. O'Hickey, "Statement concerning the Dismissal," 213.

49. ALS Michael O'Hickey to Liam Bulfin, July 8, 1909, NLI 13, 820.

50. Ibid.

51. McDonald, *Reminiscences*, 251.

52. Ibid., 247–48.

53. Letter dated June 28, 1909, in Deirdre McMahon, *The Moynihan Brothers in Peace and War, 1908–1918: Their New Ireland* (Dublin: Irish Academic Press, 2004), 18.

54. Quotations from the following: R. A. Sheehan, bishop of Waterford &c., to Dr. O'Hickey, January 29, 1909; O'Hickey to Sheehan, January 31, 1909. O'Hickey file 100/7/4(4), 9 and 11.

55. Minutes of the Meeting of the Standing Committee of the Bishops, January 20, 1909, Maynooth College Archives 100/7/4/ (2). The complete text of the bishops' statement follows: "The framing of the curriculum is the business of the Senate and with all our concern for the young life of the New University we should not allude to the course of studies or the programme of examinations did we not notice with deep pain that the Senate is receiving in the columns of the Public Press treatment which is neither creditable nor serviceable to the nation. Whether it be good for the Irish language movement, and good for the new University to make Irish compulsory is a question for fair argument. For our part we look forward to the day when Irish will again be spoken throughout the country and will in consequence become largely the medium of instruction in the Constituent Colleges. But to reach that stage we consider that by far the best means is to set up in the Colleges bright centres of Gaelic study, that will by their light and by their rewards attract young Irishmen within the sphere of their Irish influence. The progress of Irish in our Seminaries and in numbers of the Intermediate schools of the country so far from being an argument for compulsion shows what the voluntary system under our constant encouragement has hitherto done and what no doubt it will do still more successfully in the Colleges of the new University. It is quite possible that in existing circumstances compulsion instead of being a help would be a hindrance to the language movement. It certainly would drive away from the University not a few students who if once brought under the influence of the Gaelic School of a Constituent College would grow up good Irishmen. Entertaining those views and deeply concerned alike for the revival of our National Language and for the success of the National University we deem it right to put them on record for the information of our people."

56. Briody, "From Carrickbeg to Rome," 160.

57. *Irish Nation and Peasant*, March 6, 1909, 5.

58. Corish, *Maynooth College*, 291.

59. Ibid.

60. Ibid., 292.

61. *Irish Nation and Peasant*, February 13, 1909, 6, 4.

62. *Irish Nation and Peasant*, February 20, 1909, 5.

63. "The Suppression of the Rev. Dr. O'Hickey," editorial, *Irish Nation and Peasant*, February 13, 1909, 4.

64. Lawrence Taylor, *Occasions of Faith: An Anthropology of Irish Catholicism* (Philadelphia: University of Pennsylvania Press, 1995), 159–60.

65. Letter dated March 14, 1909, in Deirdre McMahon, *The Moynihan Broth-*

ers in Peace and War, 1908–1918: Their New Ireland, 6–7. Letter dated June 30, 1909, ibid., 18–19.

66. ALS Roger Casement to Bulmer Hobson, September 7, 1909, NLI ms. 13158 (6). Courtesy of Séamas Ó Síocháin.

67. Michael O'Hickey, *The Irish Bishops and an Irish University* (Dublin: Sealy, Bryers, and Walker, 1909), 3–4. Published anonymously "by an Irish Priest." After he was "silenced," O'Hickey published three pamphlets: *An Irish University, or Else, The Irish Bishops and an Irish University,* and *Wanted—An Irish University.* This third pamphlet (introduction dated June 3, 1909) contains some of the material in the previous two pamphlets as well as other letters to newspapers. In the same year (month unknown), O'Hickey also edited another pamphlet, *A Plea for an Irish University: Essays. Collected and Edited by an Irish Priest.* Both pamphlets were published by Sealy, Bryers, and Walker in Dublin. I am grateful to Mícheál Briody for this information.

68. O'Hickey, *Irish Bishops and an Irish University,* 8.

69. O'Hickey, *An Irish University,* 148.

70. O'Hickey, "Statement concerning the Dismissal," 181, 183.

71. Ibid., 184.

72. See Corish, *Maynooth College,* 150–54; and Lee, *Modernisation of Irish Society,* 44.

73. O'Hickey, "Statement concerning the Dismissal," 188 (my emphasis).

74. See, for instance, *Sinn Féin,* August 14, 1909, 4, and August 21, 1909, 4.

75. "Professorship of Irish in Maynooth. Dismissal of Dr. O'Hickey. Proposed Testimonial," *Irish Times,* August 4, 1909, 5.

76. Pearse, *Significant Irish Educationalist,* 233.

77. O'Hickey's attempts to seek legal redress of the papal courts in Rome came to nothing. When the case was finally scheduled to be heard by the Rota, in June 1912, O'Hickey's advocate had not gotten the required documents to the court, and the Rota "judged O'Hickey to have abandoned the case." The appeals court, the Signatura, turned down his appeal. In May 1914 the pope "sent the case back to the Rota, to preclude an appeal to the civil courts, it was surmised, but withdrew it again shortly afterwards, the Rota being apparently unwilling to take it up" (Corish, *Maynooth College,* 295–96). See also Briody, "From Carrickbeg to Rome"; and McDonald, *Reminiscences.*

78. Séamus Ó Maoleóin, *B'fhiú an Braon Fola,* 2nd ed. (Dublin: Sairseal and Dill, 1972), 11. Thanks to Deirdre McMahon for this source.

79. I owe thanks to Michael Coady for the story. Mícheál Briody informs me that there were two other copies of the "Statement . . ." a typed copy now in the possession of the Glynn family and an original borrowed from Maurice Hickey by Fr. Michael O'Flanagan but never returned. The copy that surfaced in Carrick was in O'Hickey's handwriting and therefore probably the original manuscript.

80. O'Hickey, "Statement concerning the Dismissal," 221.

81. Ibid., 233.

82. Information courtesy of Maura Cronin, daughter of Mary Murphy. Mrs. Murphy was the daughter of Martin and Johanna Hickey, in whose house in Portlaw Dr. O'Hickey died. Only four years old when her uncle returned to Ire-

land, Mrs. Murphy (who died in November 2002) must have been one of the last people to remember Dr. O'Hickey. Although on many occasions she was eager to distance her own point of view from O'Hickey's perceived point of view, she was also proud of the connection, and it was mentioned by the priest who concelebrated her funeral mass. Mrs. Murphy told her daughter that on a hot day in August 1916, just after Dr. O'Hickey had returned from Rome and had come to live at their house, she poured out a large jug of lemonade into several glasses and then announced, "I'm going to drink them all myself!"—to which Dr. O'Hickey responded, "Then you would be a very selfish little girl." In an interview in June 2001, Mrs. Murphy told me that after O'Hickey died, it was she who then slept in the bed that had been his. Later in her life, priests who learned that she was O'Hickey's niece were always interested in and sympathetic to him.

83. According to Walter McDonald's account, O'Hickey delayed going to see his new bishop, Dr. Hackett, until he was able to buy a new suit: "The wife of his brother Maurice, with whom he spent a good deal of time at Carrick-on-Suir, told me after his death that every Monday morning, when episcopal letters making arrangements for priests are usually received, he watched the post, and that week after week he seemed disappointed and depressed when there were no letters for him" (McDonald, *Reminiscences*, 368–69). And from Mícheál Briody comes this bit of folklore: "My mother told me that on the day of the Dúchas held in Carrick in May 1985, the then Bishop of Waterford was conferring children in the town and sent word across the river to inform those gathered to commemorate O'Hickey that on the morning of O'Hickey's death a letter was posted to him with news of an appointment. My mother says that the family had no knowledge of this. . . . Maybe this was a piece of folklore passed down from bishop to bishop or circulated among senior clerics of the diocese, or maybe it was a piece of episcopal imagination or fabrication concocted on the spot to get his office off the hook" (private correspondence, March 1999).

84. English translation of address courtesy of Michael Coady.

85. O'Casey got all of his information about the funeral from Walter McDonald's description. Somewhere between McDonald and O'Casey, the numbers changed and the weather got added; what O'Casey drew on primarily was McDonald's tone. "His friends believed—and who can blame them?—that he died of a broken heart. We buried him at Carrick-beg, with his fathers, in the graveyard attached to the Friary. The Bishop came to the funeral, as also a fair number of the diocesan clergy. There were two or three of us from the College, and two or three personal friends from among the members of the Gaelic League in Dublin. The clerical members of the League throughout the country were notable for their absence. . . . The Gaelic League, I thought, did not shine at his death, nor is it creditable to the members of that body that there is no monument to . . . the memory of a man who was not only its champion but its martyr." In the last sentence of this chapter, "The Death of Dr. O'Hickey," McDonald refers to "Dr. O'Hickey's lonely grave" (*Reminiscences*, 370, 378).

86. O'Casey, "Lost Leader," in *Drums under the Windows*, 530–31.

87. O'Hickey, *The True National Idea* (Dublin: Gaelic League, 1898), 6.

88. "Death of the Very Rev. Dr. O'Hickey. A Great Irish Scholar," *Waterford*

News, November 24, 1916. Agnes O'Farrelly also gave the most generous contribution of anyone to the testimonial fund organized by Eoin MacNeill. O'Hickey stayed at the O'Farrelly house on Upper Leeson Street in Dublin during parts of July and August 1909.

89. English translation of address delivered in Irish, May 26, 1985, courtesy of Michael Coady.

90. Coady, "Rehabilitation of Michael O'Hickey," 97.

91. Ibid.

92. During a 1966 meeting called "Freedom of Speech," organized by the Language Freedom Movement, Fr. Tomás Ó Fiaich was particularly noticeable. The LFM challenged "the policy of compulsory Irish in schools and its requirement in some areas of employment," and Ó Fiaich was part of "an organized campaign" to disturb the meeting: "He was accused of heckling the speakers, standing up and waving his arms, in the din created by his supporters. He finally made a speech. The meeting came abruptly to an end when an attempt was made to set fire to the platform." Andrée Sheehy Skeffington, *Skeff: The Life of Owen Sheehy Skeffington, 1909–1970* (Dublin: Lilliput Press, 1991), 224. In one of a series of RTÉ lectures given in honor of the seventy-fifth anniversary of the founding of the Gaelic League, Ó Fiaich focused on the 1909 controversy. See Ó Fiaich, "Great Controversy."

93. Corish, *Maynooth College,* 296. The unsympathetic article by Ó Broin is "The Gaelic League and the Chair of Irish at Maynooth," *Studies* 52 (1963): 348–62. The most complete and sympathetic account of the controversy is Ó Fiannachta's "An tAthair Mícheál O hIci."

94. Jeremiah Newman, *St. Patrick's College Maynooth,* Irish Heritage Series, no. 47 (no pagination).

95. Interview with Maura Cronin, December 1998.

96. An informal beginning to such a history may be found in Denis Carroll, *Unusual Suspects: Twelve Radical Clergy* (Dublin: Columba Press, 1998). See also the writings of Fr. Pat Buckley, such as *Faith and Fatherland* (Belfast: Belfast Historical and Educational Society, 1991), of which chapter 5 is titled "The O'Hickey Crisis."

97. Story from Mícheál Briody.

98. Frank O'Connor, "The Future of Irish Literature," *Horizon* 5, 25 (January 1942): 56–57.

99. Sean O'Faolain, *The Irish: A Character Study* (London: Penguin, 1947), 123.

100. Nuala Ní Dhomhnaill, *Pharaoh's Daughter* (Oldcastle, County Meath: Gallery Press, 1990), 154–55. Translation of "Ceist na Teangan" by Paul Muldoon.

Chapter 3. The Shewing-up of Dublin Castle

1. Marquess of Aberdeen and Temair, K.T., *Tell Me Another* (London: Edward Arnold and Co., 1926), 107–8.

2. Lady Gregory, *Journals,* 2:174–75.

3. AG to GBS, July 6, 1909, in Dan H. Laurence and Nicholas Grene, eds., *Shaw, Lady Gregory and the Abbey: A Correspondence and a Record* (Gerrards Cross: Colin Smythe, 1993), 4–5. ALS Michael O'Hickey to Liam Bulfin, July 14, 1909, NLI 13, 820.

4. *Irish Times*, August 5, 1909.

5. Lady Gregory, *Seventy Years* (New York: Macmillan, 1976), 13.

6. Ibid., 14.

7. Michael O'Hickey, *The True National Idea* (Dublin: Gaelic League, 1898), 6.

8. ALS O'Hickey to Bulfin, July 8, 1909, NLI 13, 820. Gregory, *Seventy Years*, 3.

9. Lady Gregory, "The Felons of Our Land," in *Lady Gregory: Selected Writings*, ed. Lucy McDiarmid and Maureen Waters, 254–69 (London: Penguin, 1995).

10. Seamus Deane, "What Is Field Day?" insert in the theater program for the first production of Brian Friel's translation of Chekhov's *Three Sisters* (Derry: Field Day Theatre Company, 1981), n.p.

11. AG to GBS, August 9, 1909; GBS to AG, August 12, 1909; both in Laurence and Grene, *Shaw, Gregory*, 13, 18.

12. Bernard Shaw, *Collected Letters, 1874–1897*, ed. Dan H. Laurence (New York: Dodd, Mead, 1965), 757–58.

13. John Johnston, *The Lord Chamberlain's Blue Pencil* (London: Hodder, 1990), 26–27. Great Britain. Parliament. Commons. Select Committee on Theatres and Places of Entertainment. *Report from the Select Committee on Theatres and Places of Entertainment Together with the Proceedings. . . .* (London: HMSO, 1892), 232–39.

14. Samuel Hynes, *The Edwardian Turn of Mind* (Princeton: Princeton University Press, 1968), 232.

15. Bernard Shaw, *The Shewing-up of Blanco Posnet*, in *Complete Plays with Prefaces* (New York: Dodd, Mead, 1962), 5:254.

16. Ibid., 263.

17. Ibid., 275.

18. Shaw, letter, *Times*, June 26, 1909, 10.

19. Great Britain. Parliament. Lords and Commons. Joint Select Committee of the House of Lords and the House of Commons on the Stage Plays (Censorship). *Report from the Joint Select Committee of the House of Lords and the House of Commons on the Stage Plays (Censorship) Together with the Proceedings. . . .* (London: HMSO, 1909), 14.

20. Ibid., 24.

21. Ibid., 21–22.

22. Ibid., 48.

23. Ibid., 47.

24. Lady Gregory, *Our Irish Theatre* (1913; reprint, New York: Oxford University Press, 1972), 23.

25. Review from the *Freeman's Journal*, quoted in Robert Hogan and James Kilroy, eds., *The Abbey Theatre: The Years of Synge, 1905–1909* (Atlantic Highlands, NJ: Humanities Press, 1978), 125. For a lively discussion of this episode,

see Ben Levitas, "The Loy in Irish Politics," in *The Theatre of Nation: Irish Drama and Cultural Nationalism, 1890–1916* (Oxford: Clarendon Press, 2002).

26. Nicholas Grene, *The Politics of Irish Drama* (Cambridge: Cambridge University Press, 1999), 86.

27. Ibid., 104.

28. Adrian Frazier, *Behind the Scenes: Yeats, Horniman, and the Struggle for the Abbey Theatre* (Berkeley: University of California Press, 1990), 102.

29. See Gregory, *Journals*, 1:115.

30. See AG to GBS, August 24, 1909, in Laurence and Grene, *Shaw, Gregory,* 46.

31. Ibid., ix.

32. Bernard Shaw, preface to *John Bull's Other Island*, in *Complete Plays with Prefaces* (New York: Dodd, Mead, 1963), 443.

33. Ibid., 471.

34. Laurence and Grene, *Shaw, Gregory,* xiii.

35. Gregory, *Seventy Years,* 447.

36. As also in the case of *Playboy,* with *Blanco* Lady Gregory was fighting on behalf of a play she did not like very much. See R. F. Foster, *The Apprentice Mage: 1865–1914,* vol. 1 of *W. B. Yeats: A Life* (Oxford: Oxford University Press, 1997), 409.

37. AG journal, August 12, 1909, in Laurence and Grene, *Shaw, Gregory,* 15.

38. AG to GBS, August 9, 1909, ibid., 12–13.

39. GBS to AG, August 12, 1909, ibid., 18–19.

40. GBS to AG, August 19, 1909, ibid., 36.

41. Great Britain, *Report from the Joint Select Committee,* 359.

42. GBS to AG, August 12, 1909, in Laurence and Grene, *Shaw, Gregory,* 19.

43. AG journal, August 12, 1909, ibid., 16.

44. AG journal, August 20, 1909, ibid., 34. WBY does not appear to have kept a detailed record of events in the *Blanco* controversy. Because Gregory was directing the play and was in regular correspondence with Shaw, Yeats may have considered it primarily their episode. The Civil Affairs Entry Book of this period in the National Archives contains no record of any of the meetings.

45. AG journal, August 13 and 14, 1909, ibid., 20, 24.

46. Aberdeen to AG, August 17, 1909, ibid., 30.

47. The extent to which Gregory and Shaw shared the same social space as their opponents in this controversy is worth noting. Lady Gregory's husband, Sir William Gregory, was born in the undersecretary's lodge in Phoenix Park, Dublin, during the period (1813–32) when his grandfather William Gregory served as undersecretary for Ireland. In the summer of 1909 Shaw stayed in Bantry House, County Kerry, as did the Lord Chamberlain himself, Sir Douglas Dawson. I am grateful to Nicholas Grene for telling me about the passage in which Nora Robertson, who was also staying at Bantry House then, recounts the sequence of visits:

Recently [Sir Douglas] had prohibited the public performance of "The Shewing-up of Blanco Posnet." . . . He had hardly arrived before he told us how Shaw wrote this, and he wrote that, up to the final Shaw letter. He looked every inch the Lord Chamberlain when he declared: "I did not bother to answer the fella." When Bernard and Charlotte arrived they "just missed" Dawson, but they were still as much excited by the prohibition as he had been. Again we were told how I wrote this, he wrote that, until the author's last letter was recited. After repeating it Shaw gave a gusty laugh: "Of course the man had not another word he could say!"

(Nora Robertson, Crowned Harp: Memories of the Last Years of the Crown in Ireland [Dublin: Figgis, 1960], 93–94.)

48. Gregory, Our Irish Theatre, 92–93.

49. Anne Haverty, Constance Markiewicz: An Independent Life (London: Pandora, 1988), 96; F. S. L. Lyons, Ireland since the Famine (Bungay: Collins, 1973), 565–66.

50. AG journal, August 20, 1909, in Laurence and Grene, Shaw, Gregory, 33. Lord Aberdeen's Tell Me Another confirms him as a supporter of the drama, and the chapter titled "Memoirs Dramatic" tells the story of his experience as Irving's pallbearer (181–82).

51. Laurence and Grene, Shaw, Gregory, 32. Sinn Féin was concerned that the directors of the Abbey, "by their blundering," had given the Castle an opportunity to spread the English censorship to Ireland that otherwise would not have existed. See "The Castle and the Theatre," Sinn Féin, August 21, 1909, 2. Some interesting teamwork was used to "permeate" Sinn Féin. Yeats asked AE to talk to Arthur Griffith, and Griffith complied. As AE wrote Lady Gregory, Griffith "sets his face against any row in the theatre & that is what Yeats told me he wanted" (Foster, Apprentice Mage, 605).

52. Great Britain, Report from the Joint Select Committee, 189. In his memoirs Lord Newton records at length his response to the committee hearings. He notes, "the intellectuals were inclined to make a tremendous grievance over trivialities, but I could sympathise with their view that it was ridiculous to sanction immorality and indecency in farce and stamp relentlessly upon any such tendency in high comedy and tragedy" (Lord Newton, Retrospection [London: Murray, 1941], 172). A few years later Lord Newton recorded his own ability to stamp relentlessly on immorality. On February 2, 1914, he "went to the Hippodrome with some of my family, and was so disgusted with the vulgarity and offensiveness of one of the turns, which exposed certain members of the audience to ridicule, that I wrote and expostulated with the management." When the Hippodrome responded that the manager was not then available to answer the complaint, Newton threatened to "go to the Lord Chamberlain unless the turn was immediately withdrawn. They then capitulated at once. This little incident shows that objectionable exhibitions can be stopped by private individuals if they take the trouble to act" (203).

53. AG journal, August 14, 1909, in Laurence and Grene, Shaw, Gregory, 23 (Lady Gregory's account; my lineation).

54. JD to AG, August 20, 1909, ibid., 40–41.

55. "Mr. Shaw's Play in Dublin. Lord Aberdeen Takes Action. A Precautionary Notice," Irish Times, August 21, 1909, 7.

56. Laurence and Grene, Shaw, Gregory, 42; Gregory, Our Irish Theatre, 218.

57. As Lionel Pilkington writes, the ideological importance of the Abbey "lay

in its ability as a national institution to lay claim to the cultural and symbolic apparatus of an envisaged Irish state" (Pilkington, *Theatre and the State in Twentieth-Century Ireland* [New York: Routledge, 2001], 61).

58. Gregory, *Our Irish Theatre*, 94.

59. AG to JD, August 20, 1909, in Laurence and Grene, *Shaw, Gregory*, 41. At Lady Gregory's suggestion, not Lord Aberdeen's, Shaw also changed a passage in which Blanco discusses the origin of "the croup." See plates between pages 26 and 27 in *Shaw, Gregory*.

60. AG journal, August 20, 1909, ibid., 33–34.

61. Bernard Shaw, *Collected Letters, 1898–1910*, ed. Dan H. Laurence (New York: Viking, 1985), 860–61.

62. "The Shewing-up of Blanco Posnet. The Reported Interview with the Lord Lieutenant," *Irish Times*, August 25, 1909, 7.

63. AG journal, August 20, 1909, in Laurence and Grene, *Shaw, Gregory*, 33.

64. AG journal, August 12, 1909, ibid., 16.

65. GBS to AG, August [19?], 1909, ibid., 37.

66. Shaw, *Letters 1898–1910*, 865.

67. Ibid., 885.

68. Holloway, journal entry, August 25, 1909, in Laurence and Grene, *Shaw, Gregory*, 47–48.

69. ALS Lily Yeats to John Butler Yeats, August 26, 1909, NLI 031.112 (2).

70. Ibid.

71. Gregory, *Our Irish Theatre*, 96.

72. AG and WBY to GBS, August 25, 1909, in Laurence and Grene, *Shaw, Gregory*, 48.

73. AG to GBS, August 25–26, 1909, ibid., 49.

74. "T.C.D," letter, *Irish Times*, May 17, 1915, 8.

75. Letter, *Irish Times*, May 18, 1915, 8.

76. "Viceregal Court," *Irish Times*, August 28, 1909, 6. And Sir James Dougherty's wife and daughter attended an at-home that Lady Gregory gave a year later (Foster, *Apprentice Mage*, 411).

77. "Abbey Theatre and the Castle," *Dublin Evening Mail*, August 26, 1909, 5.

78. J.R.A Moore, letter, *Irish Times* (August 29, 1909), 8.

79. Gregory, *Our Irish Theatre*, 96.

80. *Irish Times*, August 26, 1909, 6.

81. James Joyce, review of *The Shewing-up of Blanco Posnet*, as published in *Il Piccolo della Sera*, in *Shaw: The Critical Heritage*, ed. T. F. Evans (London: Routledge, 1976), 199.

82. "Abbey Theatre. The Shewing-up of Blanco Posnet," *Irish Times*, August 26, 1909, 7.

83. Holloway, journal entry, August 25, 1909, in Laurence and Grene, *Shaw, Gregory*, 48.

84. W. B. Yeats, *Letters*, ed. Allan Wade (London: Rupert Hart-Davis, 1954), 535.

85. Ibid., 541.

86. Hogan and Kilroy, *Abbey Theatre*, 294.

87. Anna MacBride White and A. Norman Jeffares, eds., *The Gonne–Yeats Letters, 1893–1938: Always Your Friend* (London: Hutchinson, 1992), 280.

88. T. S. Eliot, "Tradition and the Individual Talent," in *Selected Essays* (1932; reprint, London: Faber and Faber, 1953).

89. GBS to AG, September 14, 1915, in Laurence and Grene, *Shaw, Gregory,* 95.

90. GBS to WBY, October 12, 1915, ibid., 104.

91. GBS to WBY, November 15, 1915, ibid., 110.

92. WBY to AG, [November] 1915, ibid., 106.

93. MN to GBS, November 16, 1915, ibid., 112.

94. Christopher Murray, "The Last Battle: *The Drums of Father Ned* and O'Casey's Final Myth," manuscript, courtesy of author. Later published in revised form as "O'Casey's *The Drums of Father Ned* in Context," in *A Century of Irish Drama: Widening the Stage,* ed. Stephen Watt, Eileen Morgan, and Shakir Mustafa (Bloomington: Indiana University Press, 2000), 117–29.

95. Christopher Morash, *A History of Irish Theatre, 1601–2000* (Cambridge: Cambridge University Press, 2002), 219.

96. Padraic O'Farrell, "The Rose Tattoo Affair," in *Tales for the Telling: True Life Stories of Irish Scandals* (Cork: Collins Press, n.d.), 168. Thanks to Skip Thompson for giving me this book.

97. Ibid., 175.

98. For the complete painful, funny, terrible story, see Gerard Whelan with Carolyn Swift, *Spiked: Church–State Intrigue and the Rose Tattoo* (Dublin: New Island, 2002).

Chapter 4. Hunger and Hysteria

1. "Alleged Kidnapping," *Freeman's Journal,* October 28, 1913, 9.

2. "Kidnapping Stopped," *Freeman's Journal,* October 30, 1913, 10.

3. Isabella Richardson, letter, *Irish Times,* October 29, 1913, 6.

4. "Archbishop's Letter," *Freeman's Journal,* October 21, 1913, 7.

5. Curriculum Development Unit, *Dublin 1913: A Divided City* (1978; reprint, Dublin: O'Brien Press, 1982), 96.

6. Joseph O'Brien, *"Dear, Dirty Dublin": A City in Distress, 1899–1916* (Berkeley: University of California Press), 236–37. See also W. P. Ryan, "The Struggle of 1913: An Overview," in *James Larkin: Lion of the Fold,* ed. D. Nevin (Dublin: Gill and Macmillan, in association with RTÉ and SIPTU, 1998), 173.

7. Dora Montefiore, *From a Victorian to a Modern* (London: E. Archer, 1927), 156.

8. See Barbara Winslow, *Sylvia Pankhurst: Sexual Politics and Political Activism* (London: UCL Press, 1996), 63.

9. "Archbishop's Letter," 7.

10. Archbishop William Walsh, *The Dublin Children's Distress Fund, the Society of St. Vincent de Paul: The Archbishop's Statement* (n.p.: October 27, 1913), 1. DDA, AB6, Laity, 385/1.

11. Archbishop Walsh to Mrs. Montefiore, October 22, 1913, typescript, corrected carbon copy, DDA, 385/1.

12. Montefiore, *Victorian to Modern,* 166.

13. Eily Esmonde, letter, *Freeman's Journal*, November 8, 1913, 8.

14. Anna Davin, "Imperialism and Motherhood," *History Workshop Journal*, 5 (Spring 1978): 9, 10.

15. Seth Koven and Sonya Michel, "Introduction," in *Mothers of a New World: Maternalist Politics and the Origins of Welfare States* (New York: Routledge, 1993), 3.

16. Karen Hunt, "Journeying through Suffrage: The Politics of Dora Montefiore," in *A Suffrage Reader: Charting Directions in British Suffrage History*, ed. C. Eustace, J. Ryan, and L. Ugolini (London: Leicester University Press, 2000), 171.

17. "Workers' Children to Go to England," *Freeman's Journal*, October 21, 1913, 7: " 'I have worked amongst the workers all over the world,' Mrs. Montefiore stated. 'I have been studying economic and working-class conditions in America, South Africa, and Australia. I go down into the gold mines and do everything that is to be done, and I have written on these subjects. It is not a superficial knowledge I have of the workers. I think the condition of the children here is so deplorable. Looking from my hotel window I saw three little nippers about four or five years of age—you know how they are dressed, or undressed—turning over the garbage, putting bits of coal and stuff they found into a sack and "wolfing" any bits of bread and meat that they got mixed up in the refuse. That is an incredible state of things. It is a disgrace to any civilised country.' "

18. Sean O'Casey, *Drums under the Window*, in *Autobiographies* (1939; reprint, New York: Carroll and Graff, 1984), 602–3.

19. Interview with Paula Meehan, July 1999.

20. Montefiore, *Victorian to Modern*, 162.

21. Emmet Larkin, "Socialism and Catholicism in Ireland," *Church History* 33 (1964): 463.

22. ALS Fr. John Brophy to Archbishop Walsh, November 24, 1913, DDA, 385/2.

23. Margaret Preston, "Conversion amidst Compassion: Two Irish Charities and Their Fight for the Souls of the Poor," manuscript, courtesy of author, 1999.

24. Ibid.

25. Lyrics courtesy of Mick Moloney.

26. Dora Montefiore, *Our Fight to Save the Kiddies: Smouldering Fires of the Inquisition* (London: Utopia Press, n.d.), 2.

27. Ideas about literature, childhood, and progressive social ideas in this and the following paragraph are taken from Carolyn Steedman, *Childhood, Culture, and Class in Britain: Margaret McMillan, 1860–1931* (New Brunswick, NJ: Rutgers University Press, 1990).

28. For basic information about the Froebel Society, see ibid., 82–83; and www.members.tripod.com/~FroebelWeb/linepost.html.

29. Steedman, *Childhood, Culture, and Class*, 85.

30. Jacinta Prunty, *Lady of Charity, Sister of Faith: Margaret Aylward, 1810–1889* (Dublin: Four Courts Press, 1999), 67–68.

31. Linda Gordon, *The Great Arizona Orphan Abduction* (Cambridge: Harvard University Press, 1999), 205.

32. Ryan, "Struggle of 1913," 175.

33. "Mr. Bernard Shaw on the Strike," *Irish Times*, November 3, 1913, 3.

34. W. B. Yeats, "Dublin Fanaticism," in *Uncollected Prose*, ed. John P. Frayne and Colton Johnson (New York: Columbia University Press), 2:406.

35. W. B. Yeats to Lady Gregory, November 10, 1913, Berg Collection, NYPL. As cited in R. F. Foster, *The Apprentice Mage, 1865–1914*, vol. 1 of *W. B. Yeats: A Life* (Oxford: Oxford University Press, 1997), 621.

36. Montefiore, *Our Fight to Save the Kiddies*, 16.

37. "An Armchair for Larkin," *Irish Times*, November 7, 1913, 8.

38. Montefiore, *Our Fight to Save the Kiddies*, 6. Mrs. Rand's first name, given only at the time of her arrest, is said to be "Lucilla" in the *Freeman's Journal*, October 24, 1913, 7, and "Lucille" in the *Irish Times*, October 23, 1913, 10.

39. "Sent by Mrs. Montefiore," *Freeman's Journal*, October 24, 1913, 8.

40. "Deporting the Children. A Scheme Foiled," *Freeman's Journal*, October 23, 1913, 7.

41. "Liberty Hall Meeting," *Freeman's Journal*, October 23, 1913, 7.

42. "Deporting the Children," 7.

43. Montefiore, *Victorian to Modern*, 161.

44. Ibid., 162–63.

45. "Deporting the Children," 8.

46. Montefiore, *Our Fight to Save the Kiddies*, 10.

47. "Deported! Fifteen Victims. Priests' Protests Unheeded," *Irish Independent*, October 23, 1913, 7.

48. Montefiore, *Our Fight to Save the Kiddies*, 10–11.

49. "Rescuing the Children," *Freeman's Journal*, October 24, 1913, 7.

50. "Mrs. Montefiore at Suffrage Meeting," *Freeman's Journal*, October 22, 1913, 8.

51. *Freeman's Journal*, October 22, 1913, 7.

52. "Priests to the Rescue," *Freeman's Journal*, October 25, 1913, 7; "Mrs. Montefiore Arrested," *Freeman's Journal*, October 24, 1913, 8.

53. *Irish Independent*, October 23, 1913, 5.

54. "Another Effort to Remove Children," *Freeman's Journal*, October 25, 1913, 7.

55. "Priests to the Rescue," 7.

56. Philip O'Leary, *The Prose Literature of the Gaelic Revival, 1881–1921: Ideology and Innovation* (University Park: Pennsylvania State University Press, 1994), 26.

57. Angela Bourke, *The Burning of Bridget Cleary* (London: Pimlico, 1999), 37. My analysis in the commentary that follows is guided and inspired by the work of Angela Bourke.

58. "Tugaí Domhsa É!" ("Give It To Me!"), in *Stories of Sea and Shore*, told by John Henry, Kilgalligan, Co. Mayo; Séamas Ó Cathain, collector, trans., and annotator (Dublin: University College Dublin, 1983), 22.

59. "Girseach ar Ghoid na Síogaí í a Fuarthas arais" ("The Stolen Girl Rescued from the Fairies"), in *Fairy Legends from Donegal*, collected by Seán Ó hEochaidh, trans. Máire Mac Neill (Dublin: University College Dublin, 1977), 51.

60. "Tugaí Domhsa É!", 23.

61. "Bean a Tugadh As" ("An Abducted Woman"), in *Stories of Sea and*

Shore, 7. For the importance of the "careful observance of society's rules" in fairy legends, see Bourke, *Burning of Bridget Cleary*, 30.

62. "Gearrchaile a Tugadh As" ("An Abducted Girl"), in *Stories of Sea and Shore*, 11–12.

63. "Cath Ghleann Bholcáin" ("The Battle of Gleann Bholcain"), in *Fairy Legends from Donegal*, 71.

64. "Liberty Hall Meeting," 7.

65. ALS signed "A Catholic," to Archbishop Walsh, October 21, 1913, DDA, 385/1.

66. Canon Pinnington to Fr. Flavin, October 23, 1913, DDA, 385/2.

67. Rev. J. O'Connell to Fr. Flavin, October 23, 1913, DDA, 385/2.

68. Fr. James Leech to Fr. Flavin, October 23, 1913, DDA, 385/2.

69. Fred Bower, *Rolling Stonemason: An Autobiography* (London: Jonathan Cape, 1936), 174–75.

70. Ibid., 175.

71. "Food and Shelter. Arrival of Dublin Children in Liverpool," *Liverpool Weekly Mercury*, October 25, 1913.

72. "From Liverpool Priest," *Freeman's Journal*, October 25, 1913, 8; also printed in the *Liverpool Courier*, October 25, 1913.

73. W. P. Partridge to Fr. O'Ryan, November 21, 1913, DDA, Laity, 385/1.

74. Bower, *Stonemason*, 175–6.

75. For an analysis of the connections between *Pygmalion* and the "Maiden Tribute of Modern Babylon," the 1885 controversy provoked by W. T. Stead's purchase of a young girl for the sake of investigative journalism, see Celia Marshik, "Parodying the £ Virgin: Bernard Shaw and the Playing of Pygmalion," *Yale Journal of Criticism* 13 (2000): 321–341. On the larger issue of the relationship between middle-class humanitarian activities and sexuality, see Seth Koven, *Slumming: Sexual and Social Politics in Victorian London* (Princeton: Princeton University Press, 2004).

76. Joseph McCarroll to Archbishop Walsh, October 22, 1913, DDA, 385/1.

77. A Dubliner, letter to Archbishop Walsh, October 23, 1913, DDA, 385/1.

78. "Mr. Bernard Shaw on the Strike," 3.

79. Maud Gonne, Mary Tuohy, and Helen Laird to Archbishop Walsh, November 7, 1913, DDA, 385/1.

80. L. J. Stafford to Archbishop Walsh, December 7, 1913, DDA, 385/2.

81. Hanna Sheehy Skeffington, "Constance de Markievicz," *An Phoblacht*, April 14, 1928, 3.

82. As quoted in Margaret Ward, *Hanna Sheehy Skeffington: A Life* (Cork: Cork University Press, 1997), 63.

83. Anna MacBride White and A. Norman Jeffares, eds., *The Gonne–Yeats Letters, 1893–1938* (London: Hutchinson, 1992), 327.

84. Janis Londraville and Richard Londraville, eds., *Too Long a Sacrifice: The Letters of Maud Gonne and John Quinn* (Selinsgrove, PA: Susquehanna University Press; London: Associated University Presses, 1999), 110.

85. White and Jeffares, *Gonne–Yeats Letters*, 329. In this same letter Gonne thanks Yeats for his "generous subscription to the children's dinners." Yeats had also complained, in a public speech and a letter (see n. 33 above) about the "fa-

naticism" of the Catholics in this controversy: as in the 1937 Casement controversy, Yeats maintained numerous seemingly contradictory positions in different contexts.

86. Stephen Gwynn to Archbishop Walsh, October 29, 1913, DDA, 385/1.

87. "Charge against Mrs. Rand," *Freeman's Journal*, October 24, 1913, 8.

88. "The Priests of Dublin," *Freeman's Journal*, November 3, 1913, 7.

89. Ibid.

90. James Connolly, *The Workers' Republic: A Selection from the Writings of James Connolly* ed. Desmond Ryan (Dublin: At the Sign of the Three Candles, Fleet Street, 1951), 129–30.

91. William McMullen, "Introduction," *ibid., 23.*

92. "Mr. Bernard Shaw on the Strike," 3.

93. Sigerson and Maher letters, *Freeman's Journal*, November 6, 1913, 5; McQuilland letter, *Freeman's Journal*, November 10, 1913, 5.

94. G. K. Chesterton, "I Told You So," *New Witness*, October 30, 1913, 817: "And I say the mere surname of one of the great Jewish financial houses has probably done more harm than we can easily cure. These people will connect it, not with the unquestioned probity of one particular lady, but with a certain tribal tradition unquestionably implanted in our midst."

95. Rebecca West, "Mr. Chesterton in Hysterics," in *The Young Rebecca: Writings of Rebecca West, 1911–1917*, ed. Jane Marcus (New York: Viking in association with Virago, 1982), 222.

96. Frank Sheehy Skeffington, Letter, *Irish Times*, October 25, 1913, 8.

97. "Kidnapping Crusade," *Freeman's Journal*, October 27, 1913, 7.

98. "Mr. Sheehy Skeffington," *Freeman's Journal*, November 6, 1913, 10.

99. William Orpen, *Stories of Old Ireland and Myself* (London: Williams and Norgate, 1924), 85–86.

100. Andrée Sheehy–Skeffington, "The Hatter and the Crank," *Irish Times*, February 5, 1982, C16.

101. "Mr. Sheehy Skeffington," 10.

102. W. B. Yeats, *Collected Plays*, 2nd ed. (London: Macmillan, 1972), 120.

103. Lillian Scott Troy to Archbishop Walsh, December 29, 1913, DDA, 385/1.

104. Thomas Morrissey, S.J., *William Martin Murphy* (Dundalk: Dundalgan Press, 1997), 58.

105. See, for instance, Mike Milotte, *Banished Babies* (Dublin: New Island Books, 1997).

106. See, for instance, www.adoptionireland.com, the website of the Natural Parents Network of Ireland.

248 NOTES TO PAGES 168-169

Chapter 5. The Afterlife of Roger Casement

1. Derek Mahon, "Some Sensuous Epiphany: *The Lost Notebook* by John Montague," in *Journalism*, ed. Terence Brown (Oldcastle, County Meath: Gallery Press, 1996), 96. Originally published in the *Irish Times* in 1987.

2. References are to handwriting expert David Baxendale, chief historian of the Foreign and Commonwealth Office Gill Bennet, and gay Northern Irish writer Jeffrey Dudgeon.

3. Mary Colum, *Life and the Dream* (London: Macmillan, 1947), 176–77, 179.

4. At the RIA conference, Martin Mansergh, representing the taoiseach's office, said that there was a wish in contemporary Ireland to "co-opt [Casement] as a forerunner to Ireland's human rights tradition."

5. For information on Casement's humanitarian accomplishments, see Séamas Ó Síocháin, *Roger Casement: Imperialist, Rebel, Revolutionary* (Dublin: Lilliput, 2006); Séamas Ó Síocháin and Michael O'Sullivan, eds., *Roger Casement: The 1903–4 Congo Report and 1903 Diary* (Dublin: University College Dublin Press, 2003); B. L. Reid, *The Lives of Roger Casement* (New Haven: Yale University Press, 1976); Brian Inglis, *Roger Casement* (London: Hodder and Stoughton Ltd., 1973); Angus Mitchell, ed., *The Amazon Journal of Roger Casement* (Dublin: Lilliput, 1997); and Roger Sawyer, ed., *Roger Casement's Diaries, 1910: The Black and the White* (London: Pimlico, 1997). Although other people, such as Edouard Morel, were engaged in humanitarian work in Africa at the time Casement was, they were not familiar with the precise routes known to Casement.

6. Reid, *Lives of Roger Casement*, 418. Because my professional angle is study of the controversy, I do not take a militant position on the authenticity of the diaries. My belief in their authenticity does not derive from any expertise in handwriting identification, paper, or ink, nor have I ever inspected the diaries themselves. For the following reasons, I believe they were written by Casement: (1) In all the private memos written at the time of Casement's trial by politicians, diplomats, ministers, officials from the Home and Foreign Offices, et al., there is no reference, allusion, or hint that the diaries might not be Casement's. Every private letter and message written by people trying to get Casement hanged assumes the diaries are authentic. Gill Bennett, chief historian of the Foreign and Commonwealth Office, who spoke at the RIA symposium, asserted that no such evidence has since been found, as did a private letter from Prime Minister Tony Blair to Taoiseach Bertie Ahern (February 11, 2000), copied and made available to participants at the symposium. (2) Quite apart from the diaries, there is ample evidence of undisputed authenticity that is strongly suggestive of Casement's homosexuality: (a) the poem "The Nameless One," discussed in this chapter, takes as subject a forbidden love ("I only know 'tis Death to give / My love"); the subject is so obviously homosexuality that the Roger Casement Foundation insists, contrary to all available evidence, that the poem was written by John Addington Symonds; (b) Casement's letter of October–November 1914, written in the voice of a woman, and talking about his male lover as "that dear Norwegian girl," also discussed in this chapter; and (c) Casement's poem "The Streets of Catania," interpreted by Monk Gibbon as a poem about a

homosexual encounter, also discussed in this chapter. Certainly it contains the most erotic description of a volcano ever written. (3) Common sense dictates that no government, especially one engaged in a prolonged, terrible, and expensive overseas war, would require of a forger, or accept from one, or pay for, forgeries of such extravagant length when, as has often been observed, one or two brief letters would have done the trick; no forger would be likely to add the oddly realistic touch, in the often-quoted entry about the assignation with Millar Gordon in Warrenpoint, "Went upstairs after watching billiards," as well as many other such details. Because of the diary's precision in references to prices for sex and cruising grounds, quotations from male lovers in Northern Ireland vernacular, citations of particular places, monuments, houses, and so forth, the author is unarguably an active male homosexual who knew Northern Ireland, especially Antrim, very well. And finally, almost all of Casement's biographers—Denis Gwynn, René MacColl, Brian Inglis, B. L. Reid, Roger Sawyer, Jeffrey Dudgeon, and Séamas Ó Síocháin—have believed in the diaries' authenticity. Although Angus Mitchell (*Amazon Journal*) cites Gwynn to the contrary, see Dudgeon, *Roger Casement: The Black Diaries, with a Study of his Background, Sexuality and Irish Political Life* (Belfast: Belfast Press, 2002), 540, for Gwynn's private acknowledgment that he believed Casement to be the author of the diaries.

7. Sawyer, *Casement's Diaries*, 53.

8. Ibid., 43.

9. See Jesse Monteagudo, "Sir Roger Casement: Hero and Traitor," *Gay Today: A Global Site for Daily Gay News*, www.gaytoday.badpubby.com; and Colm Toibín, "The Casement Affair," *London Review of Books*, October 2, 1997.

10. Medbh McGuckian, interview with author, February 1994.

11. Sequences: Sean Hutton, *Seachrán Ruairí agus Dánta Eile* (Dublin: Coisceim, 1986); Philip Brady, *Forged Correspondences* (Binghamton, NY: New Myths Press, 1996); and Medbh McGuckian, typescript of unpublished sequence, courtesy of the author. Yeats's "Roger Casement" and "The Ghost of Roger Casement" are well known. Wilfrid Blunt's dreadful "Ballad of Sir Roger Casement" is fortunately available only in manuscript in the National Library of Ireland (5463 Casement/McGarrity Papers). A sample: "You are a doomed man to-day, / Hanged by the neck this morning/Before the clock strikes nine. / End here is to your treasons / Against the white man's way, / Your love for the slave peoples / Your scoff at 'rights divine.'" See also section 16 of Louis MacNeice's *Autumn Journal*, Derek Mahon's poem "Glengormleigh," Medbh McGuckian's "On Ballycastle Beach," Bernard O'Donoghue's "Casement on Banna," and Paul Muldoon's "A Clear Signal" (*New York Times*, March 17, 1992, A25), a poem about the exclusion of the Irish Lesbian and Gay Organization from the New York Saint Patrick's Day parade.

12. James Joyce, *Ulysses* (reprint, New York: Modern Library, 1961), 335.

13. Casement's cameo appearances in fiction, in addition to *Ulysses*, include Eimar O'Duffy, *The Wasted Island* (New York: Dodd, Mead, 1920); Stevie Smith, *Over the Frontier* (London: Cape, 1938); Agatha Christie, *N or M?* (1941; reprint, New York: Berkley Books, 1984); Terence de Vere White, *Lucifer Falling* (London: Cape, 1966); Neil Jordan, *The Past*, in *Collected Fiction* (New York:

Vintage, 1997; orig. pub. 1980); W. G. Sebald, *The Rings of Saturn*, trans. M. Hulse (New York: New Directions, 1998); Jamie O'Neill; *At Swim, Two Boys* (New York: Scribner, 2001); and Annabel Davis-Goff, *The Fox's Walk* (New York: Harcourt, 2003). In Emily Savin's unpublished story "A Visit from Roger Casement," Casement's ghost visits a Casement scholar who has just published an essay about him in the newspaper. See also an essayistic commentary on Casement in Rebecca Solnit, *A Book of Migrations* (London: Verso, 1997).

14. Michael Carson, *The Knight of the Flaming Heart* (New York: Doubleday, 1995). The novel *Mount Kestrel* by "An Philibin" [J. H. Pollock] (Dublin: M. H. Gill and Son, Ltd., 1945) focuses entirely on Casement's Kerry landing.

15. The plays about Casement include *Traigh Bhanna* [Banna Strand], a translation by Seamus Ó Dubhda from the English of John MacDonagh, presented at the Peacock Theatre, Dublin, as one of three plays commemorating the 1916 Rising (*Irish Times*, April 15, 1936, 8); *The Challengers* (the third of its three plays is about Casement) by Padraic Colum, produced at the Lantern Theatre, Dublin, in February 1966; *Prisoner of the Crown* by Richard F. Stockton, produced at the Abbey in 1973 (typescript in the Abbey Archives, sent to me courtesy of Teresa Kane); *Casement* by Alex Ferguson, produced at the Moving Theatre at Riverside Studios, London, May 1995; a "five-act dramatisation" of Alfred Noyes's book *The Accusing Ghost, or Justice for Roger Casement* (1957), written with "Robert" McHugh (*recte* Roger), mentioned only in the article on Noyes by Margaret B. McDowell in the *Dictionary of Literary Biography*, vol. 20, *British Poets, 1914–1915*, ed. Donald E. Sutherland (Detroit: Gale Research Co., 1983), 225; and (by far the best of the lot) David Rudkin's radio play *Cries from Casement as His Bones Are Brought to Dublin* (London: BBC, 1974), 76, commissioned by the BBC. The most recent play—evidence of Casement's international appeal—is *Terre Lointaine*, written in Brêton by Paol Keineg and performed in Brittany in 2004. Thanks to Declan Kiberd for this information. Songs about Casement include the ballad "O Lordly Roger Casement," printed in Inglis's biography (*Roger Casement*, 392); "Banna Strand" (1965), and the Christy Moore song "Delirium Tremens," which includes in its list of hallucinatory phenomena the following: "Dick Spring and Roger Casement were on board the Marita-Ann, / As she sailed into Fenit harbour they were singin' Banna Strand." Spring, TD for North Kerry, in 1984 unveiled the statue of Casement that stands in Ballyheigue.

16. Recent documentaries include a program on the diaries on BBC's radio program *Document* (September 1993) as well as two television documentaries appearing simultaneously in March 2002: "The Ghost of Roger Casement," directed by Alan Gilsenan, RTÉ, aired March 7 and 14; and "Secrets of the Black Diaries," directed by Paul Tilzey, BBC, aired March 15. In W. G. Sebald, *The Rings of Saturn*, trans. M. Hulse (New York: New Directions, 1998), the narrator falls asleep watching a BBC documentary about Casement and then dreams about Casement's meeting with Joseph Conrad in the Congo. In 1960, Peter Wyngarde starred as Casement in one segment of a television series (shown in Britain) called "On Trial." The Wyngarde program was screened most recently at the National Film Theatre, London, in 1997. The never-completed films about Casement include one mentioned in an *Irish Press* (August 6, 1956) article about Shaw's comments on a planned 1934 film about Casement that had

been "killed" by the "British Film Censorship authorities." The "Welsh film-maker" Kenneth Griffith was said to have a made a film on Casement shown at the West Belfast Festival in August 1993 (*Irish Times*, August 11, 1993). In "On the Town" (*Irish Times*, May 29, 1993, Weekend 2), Robert O'Byrne wrote of Sarah Lawson that "her interests now lie in other Irish-based projects and . . . she is actively seeking material over here, though not relating to Roger Casement. Seemingly this is one affair which has exerted an irresistible, but none too beneficial, fascination on script writers." In May 1996 Donald Taylor Black mentioned to me a Thaddeus O'Sullivan film about Casement; the *Irish Times* of May 25, 1994 (Weekend 2), quotes Mr. O'Sullivan about the film: "It's going to be a controversial project, I have no doubt. . . . It will involve intimacy, romance, and humour mixed with adventure, politics, violence and horror in the hope of constructing a modern film which will reclaim Roger Casement as a man out of his time, as an entirely modern hero." Kevin Barry has also written a film script based on episodes from Casement's life (information courtesy of author). Casement's posthumous life in English popular culture may never be explored, but a good starting point might be Agatha Christie's *N or M!* in which Sheila Perenna identifies her father this way: "His name was Patrick Maguire. He—he was a follower of Casement in the last War. He was shot as a traitor! All for nothing! For an idea—he worked himself up with those other Irishmen. Why couldn't he just stay at home quietly and mind his own business?" (59).

17. Murroe FitzGerald, letter, *Irish Times*, May 17, 1956, 7.

18. L. E. R. Peacocke, letter, *Irish Times*, June 5, 1973, 11.

19. Peter Singleton-Gates and Maurice Girodias, eds., *The Black Diaries: An Account of Roger Casement's Life and Times with a Collection of His Diaries and Public Writings* (New York: Grove Press, 1959), 121–23.

20. Ibid., 121, 123.

21. Ibid., 125.

22. Sawyer, *Casement's Diaries*, 91.

23. *The Vindication of Roger Casement*, updated ed., distributed by the Roger Casement Foundation during the Royal Irish Academy symposium, May 2000, 18.

24. Maloney Collection of Irish Historical Papers, box 2/33, NYPL.

25. James Clarence Mangan, "The Nameless One," in *The Field Day Anthology of Irish Writing*, ed. S. Deane, A. Carpenter, and J. Williams, 2:35 (Derry: Field Day, 1991).

26. Inglis, *Roger Casement*, 399.

27. Sawyer, *Casement's Diaries*, 42.

28. Ibid., 52–53.

29. Dudgeon, 215.

30. *Irish Times*, March 29, 1994, 6.

31. Holograph letter, October 28, 1914, NLI 13082-4.

32. Report from Mr. Findlay to Sir Edward Grey, Foreign Office, on information received from Adler Christensen, October 31, 1914, 3, MEPO 2/10660-1.

33. This passage is cited in virtually every biography of Casement; it may be found in Reid, *Lives of Roger Casement*, 418; Inglis, *Roger Casement*, 359–60; H. Montgomery-Hyde, *Roger Casement* (Harmondsworth, Middlesex: Penguin, 1964), 139–40.

34. In Inglis's biography of Casement, this anecdote is mentioned without any citation (381). In Reid's biography of Casement, it is cited to Roy Jenkins, *Asquith* (London: Collins, 1964), 403 (Reid 445, 513). However, the story does not appear on that page or anywhere in the Jenkins biography. The American ambassador, Walter H. Page, left the following memorandum of his dinner ("lunch" to the American) with Asquith, of which the relevant passages are quoted:

> August 1st. I lunched with Mr. Asquith. One does not usually bring away much from his conversations, and he did not say much to-day worth recording. But he showed a very eager interest in the Presidential campaign, and he confessed that he felt some anxiety about the anti-British feeling in the United States. This led him to tell me that he could not in good conscience interfere with Casement's execution, in spite of the shoals of telegrams that he was receiving from the United States. This man, said he, visited Irish prisoners in German camps and tried to seduce them to take up arms against Great Britain—their own country. When they refused, the Germans removed them to the worst places in their Empire and, as a result, some of them died. Then Casement came to Ireland in a German man-of-war (a submarine) accompanied by a ship loaded with guns. "In all good conscience to my country and to my responsibilities I cannot interfere." He hoped that thoughtful opinion in the United States would see this whole matter in a fair and just way. I asked him about anti-American feeling in Great Britain. He said: "Do not let that unduly disturb you. At bottom we understand you. At bottom the two people surely understand one another and have unbreakable bonds of sympathy. No serious breach is conceivable." He went on quite earnestly: "Mr. Page, after any policy or plan is thought out on its merits my next thought always is how it may affect our relations with the United States. That is always a fundamental consideration." I ventured to say that if he would keep our relations smooth on the surface, I'd guarantee their stability at the bottom.

Burton J. Hendrick, "Washington in the Summer of 1916," *The Life and Letters of Walter H. Page.* 1922, http://www.lib.byu.edu/~rdh/wwi/memoir/Page/Page12.htm.

35. On the day after Casement was executed, the *Times* (London) published an editorial about him, remarking, "we cannot help protesting against certain attempts which have been made to use the Press for the purpose of raising issues which are utterly damaging to Casement's character but which have no connexion whatever with the charges on which he was tried. These issues should either have been raised in a public or straightforward manner, or they should have been left severely alone" (August 4, 1916, 7). On the same day, a brief item in the *Irish Times* titled "Casement's MSS" said, in its entirety, "It is understood, says the *Daily Mail*, that the documents, on the writing of which Casement was engaged before his execution, are intended for his friends" (August 4, 1916, 5). This odd bit of information on "manuscripts" may have been intended to suggest that there were no diaries at all or simply to confuse the issue.

36. As quoted in Sinéad McCoole, *Hazel: A Life of Lady Lavery, 1880–1935* (Dublin: Lilliput, 1996), 65–66.

37. As quoted in Reid, *Lives of Roger Casement*, 418.

38. René MacColl, *Roger Casement* (London: Hamish Hamilton, 1956), 268.

39. Lady Gregory's play *Spreading the News* does in fact reconstruct the channels through which information moves, showing successive misquotations and distortions of content.

40. Janet Dunbar, *Mrs. GBS: A Portrait* (New York: Harper and Row, 1963), 256–57.

41. Dudgeon, *Roger Casement*, 398, 497.

42. Dunbar, *Mrs. GBS*, 256, 257.

43. Reid, *Lives of Roger Casement*, 386.

44. Dudgeon, *Roger Casement*, 494.

45. Dunbar, *Mrs. GBS*, 256.

46. As quoted in Dudgeon, *Roger Casement*, 540.

47. Lady Gregory, *The Journals*, Vol. 2, Books 30–44, ed. Daniel J. Murphy (New York: Oxford University Press, 1987), 571.

48. Reid, *Lives of Roger Casement*, 434.

49. Eva Gore-Booth, "Heroic Death, 1916," in *Selected Poems of Eva Gore-Booth* (London: Longmans, Green, 1933), 77.

50. Gregory, *Journals*, 2:572.

51. "Roger Casement's Remains. Irish Demonstration in Hyde Park," *Irish Times*, April 13, 1936, 8.

52. P. J. Little's remark may be found in "Vindication of Casement," *Irish Press*, February 3, 1937, 9.

53. Baldwin to de Valera, February 24, 1936, as quoted in Deirdre McMahon, "Roger Casement: An Account from the Archives of His Reinterment in Ireland," *Journal of the Irish Society for Archives*, n.s., 3, 1 (Spring 1996): 5.

54. Churchill to de Valera, October 14, 1953, as quoted ibid., 7.

55. Mary Douglas, *Purity and Danger*, rev. ed. (New York: Routledge, 1991), 113.

56. Reid, *Lives of Roger Casement*, 460–61.

57. Alfred Noyes, *Two Worlds for Memory* (Philadelphia: J. B. Lippincott, 1953), 124–25.

58. Douglas, *Purity and Danger*, 135.

59. Reid, *Lives of Roger Casement*, 417.

60. W. B. Yeats, *The Variorum Edition of the Poems*, ed. Peter Allt and Russell K. Alspach (New York: Macmillan, 1975), 460.

61. W. B. Yeats, *Letters on Poetry from W. B. Yeats to Dorothy Wellesley* (1940; reprint, Oxford: Oxford University Press, 1964), 93.

62. William J. Maloney, *The Forged Casement Diaries* (Dublin and Cork: Talbot Press, 1936).

63. W. B. Yeats, "Roger Casement," *Irish Press*, February 2, 1937, 6.

64. Yeats, *Letters on Poetry*, 126.

65. Yeats, *Letters*, 867.

66. Yeats, *Letters on Poetry*, 128.

67. *Irish Press*, February 18, 1937, 9. For additional commentary on de Valera's attitude to the diaries, see McMahon, "Account from the Archives," 4.

68. Tom Casement to Michael Collins, May 25, 1922, as quoted in McMahon, "Account from the Archives," 4.

69. *Irish Press*, February 2, 1937, 6.

70. *Irish Press*, February 12, 1937, 8–9.

71. John Unterecker, ed., *Yeats and Patrick McCartan, a Fenian Friendship: Letters with a Commentary* (Dublin: Dolmen Press, 1967), 393.

72. Yeats, *Letters on Poetry*, 128.

73. Yeats, *Letters*, 881–82.

74. Noyes, *Two Worlds*, 133.

75. Alfred Noyes, *The Accusing Ghost, or, Justice for Roger Casement* (London: Victor Gollancz, 1957), 180.

76. *Irish Press*, February 12, 1937, 9.

77. Noyes, *Accusing Ghost*, 152, 38–39.

78. *Irish Press*, February 11, 1937, 9.

79. Yeats, *Letters on Poetry*, 128.

80. *Irish Press*, February 13, 1937, 8.

81. *Irish Press*, February 16, 1937, 14.

82. *Irish Press*, February 22, 1937, 2.

83. Ibid.

84. *Irish Times*, April 7, 1956, 9, 12.

85. *Irish Times*, April 14, 1956, 9; April 16, 1956, 5; April 18, 1956, 5; April 19, 1956, 7.

86. *Irish Times*, April 17, 1956, 7; April 25, 1956, 5; April 30, 1956, 5.

87. *Irish Times*, April 21, 1956, 9.

88. As Luke Gibbons has written, "It was the formats, generic conventions and production contexts of key programmes such as the television serial *The Riordans* and the talk show *The Late Late Show* which allowed them to ventilate certain controversial topics, thus helping substantially to mould public opinion on these issues. Had the programmes' styles and modes of representation been different, it would have proved much more difficult to challenge prevailing attitudes and lift the taboo off sensitive issues regarding the family, sexuality, property, and the traditional pieties of faith and fatherland" (*Transformations in Irish Culture* [Cork: Cork University Press, 1996], 11).

89. Author interview with Eilis Pearce, July 9, 1995.

90. *Irish Times*, February 25, 1965, 9.

91. *Irish Times*, February 27, 1965, 11. Once Deirdre McMahon published "Roger Casement: An Account from the Archives of His Reinterment in Ireland," the official list of the actual bones that were returned to Ireland in the coffin became available to all. Those interested in Casement's remains may want to know of another remains-related ritual, one that took place on August 2, 1953, when de Valera addressed a meeting called by the Casement Commemoration Committee at Murlough Bay (see the *Irish News and Belfast Morning News* and the *Belfast Telegraph* for predictably different accounts of the occasion). At this event, a grave site was chosen, in anticipation of the return of the remains to Casement's own chosen site. In the Rudkin play, Casement complains when he realizes he is being buried in Glasnevin, not Murlough Bay.

92. Rudkin, *Cries from Casement*, 10.

93. *Belfast Newsletter*, March 3, 1965, 1.

94. Ibid.

95. Author interview with Eilis Pearce, July 9, 1995.

96. Ibid. For recent commentary on the reinterment, see Kevin Grant, "Bones of Contention: The Repatriation of the Remains of Roger Casement," *Journal of British Studies* 41, no. 3 (July 2002), 329–353.

97. *Irish Times*, March 2, 1965, 1.

98. Ibid., 6.

99. Rudkin, *Cries from Casement*, 74–75.

100. Richard Murphy, *Collected Poems* (Winston-Salem, NC: Wake Forest University Press, 2001), 47.

101. *Kerryman*, April 9, 1966, 1, 5.

102. For an analysis of Casement's continuing presence in the stories and relics of North Kerry, see Lucy McDiarmid, "Secular Relics: Casement's Boat, Casement's Dish," *Textual Practice* (Summer 2002): 277–302. The Oisín Kelly statue of Casement now situated in Ballyheigue was "specifically commissioned for the Borough of Dun Laoghaire" (www.oireachtas-debates.gov .ie/D.0346.198312060002.html).

103. Mrs. Irving's letter, *Irish Times*, June 19, 1973, 11; Mrs. Kelly's letter, *Irish Times*, June 22, 1973, 13.

104. *Irish Times*, June 5, 1973, 11.

105. Kieran Rose, *Diverse Communities* (Cork: Cork University Press, 1994), 9.

106. Anecdote told to me by Brian Walker, October 1, 1994.

107. Author interview with Medbh McGuckian, February 1994.

108. Anecdote told to me by students at the Yeats International Summer School, Sligo, August 1993.

109. The book in question is Anthony Bradley and Maryanne Valiulis, eds., *Gender and Sexuality in Modern Ireland* (Amherst: University of Massachusetts Press, 1997).

110. *Swoon*, directed by Tom Kalin, produced by Christine Vachon, and screenplay by Tom Kalin and Hilton Als (1992).

111. Rose, *Diverse Communities*; Eibhear Walshe, "Oscar's Mirror," in *Lesbian and Gay Visions of Ireland*, ed. Ide O'Carroll and Eoin Collins (New York: Cassell, 1995), 150.

112. Paul Muldoon, "A Clear Signal," *New York Times*, March 17, 1992, A25.

113. Dudgeon, *Roger Casement*.

114. Conversation with Nigel Acheson, September 1996.

115. *Irish Times*, March 29, 1994, 6.

116. Ibid.

117. *Sunday Independent*, April 3, 1994.

118. Mansergh's essay "Roger Casement and the Idea of a Broader Nationalist Tradition: His Impact on Anglo-Irish Relations" will be published along with the other papers from the RIA symposium in a forthcoming volume edited by Mary E. Daly.

119. Eunan O'Halpin coined the term *Casementistas*; the term *Casementalists* is Jeff Dudgeon's.

120. As Liam Fay noted in a review of the Gilsenan documentary, "it became apparent that what we were watching was in fact a slow-burn comedy, a subtle

satire on the tomfoolery of men who call themselves academics" (*Sunday Times*, March 17, 2002, 34). For the record, the Casementistas include among others Frank Callanan, Mary E. Daly, Reinhard Doerries, Jeffrey Dudgeon, Owen Dudley Edwards, Siobhán Kilfeather, William McCormack, Deirdre McMahon, Angus Mitchell, Jack Moylett, Margaret O'Callaghan, Eunan O'Halpin, Séamas Ó Síocháin, Roger Sawyer, and the present author. I don't know if it's an insult or a compliment to be omitted from this list, but apologies to any writers who feel they should have been included. Others who have published on Casement recently include Robert L. Caserio, Katie Conrad, Ruth Dudley Edwards, Kevin Grant, Richard Kirkland, Kieran F. Kennedy, Patrick Mullen, Michael Taussig, and Colm Tóibín. Handwriting experts who have made public comments on the diaries include David Baxendale (who inspected the diaries for the 1993 BBC radio program *Document*), John Horan (who commented on techniques of handwriting analysis for the RIA symposium), and Audrey Giles, whose 2002 report declared the diaries to be authentic (*Report of Dr. Audrey Giles* [Amersham, Buckinghamshire: Giles Document Laboratory, February 8, 2002]). Forgery theorists were not convinced by the report, and believers in the diaries' authenticity did not require it in the first place. For a set-to between two Casementalists, see Angus Mitchell's review of recent books by William McCormack and Jeffrey Dudgeon in *Irish Economic and Social History* 30 (2003): 191–92; and McCormack's reply in the *IESH Newsletter* 15 (Spring/Summer 2004): 1–4. At the end of the reply, the editor has wisely written, "no further correspondence will be entered into on this or related matters."

Epilogue

1. For comments on the *Contention* as controversy, see the introduction, n. 2.

2. The McKenna translation has been the standard edition since it was published in 1918. The website http://ucc.ie/celt/published/G405990/mentions John Minahan, *The Contention of the Poets: An Essay in Irish Intellectual History, with a Parallel Translation of the Irish Text in English* (Sansa, 2000), but it appears nowhere else on the web. See also comments on Leerssen, in chap. 1, n. 2.

3. Description of Joe Steve Ó Neachtain, "Fead Ghlaice," in *Cúpla Focal, Siopa Leabhar*, www.eofeasa.ie/cuplafocal.catalog/product_info.php. See also the introduction, n. 2., for Moore Quinn's analysis.

4. Ursula Barry and Clair Wills, eds., "The Republic of Ireland: The Politics of Sexuality, 1965–2000," in Angela Bourke et al., *The Field Day Anthology of Irish Writing*, vol. 5, *Irish Women's Writings and Traditions* (Cork: Cork University Press in association with Field Day; New York: New York University Press, 2002).

5. Veronica Guerin, "From 'Interview with Eamonn Casey' (1993)," ibid.

6. Text is translated into English by Eileen Moore Quinn. See the introduction, n. 2.

7. See the introduction, n. 1.

8. Seamus Heaney, *The Midnight Verdict* (Loughcrew, Oldcastle, County Meath: Gallery Press, 1993), 33.

9. Ibid., 39.

10. Ibid., 11.

11. *Aqua*, unpublished film script by Nina FitzPatrick, directed by Edel O'Brien, 1998, and screened at the Cork Film Festival and on Telefís na Gaeilge.

12. For an analysis of conflicts over heritage and "interpretive centres," see Ruth McManus, "Heritage and Tourism in Ireland—An Unholy Alliance?" www.ucd.ie/gsi/pdf/30-2heritage.pdf, p. 1; for commentary on the larger issues, see Fintan O'Toole, "Tourists in Our Own Land," in *Black Hole, Green Card: The Disappearance of Ireland* (Dublin: New Island Books, 1994).

13. Rev. L. McKenna, S.J., trans. and ed., *Iomarbhágh na bhFileadh: The Contention of the Bards* (London: Irish Texts Society, 1918), viii.

14. Controversies were plentiful in Ireland between the mid-1980s and the end of the 1990s, but they were not functionally identical to the pre-Rising controversies. See introduction for discussion. In the United States, a series of dramatic cultural controversies followed immediately upon the end of the Cold War: just after the fall of the Berlin Wall in 1989 came the controversy about the "NEA Four," the artists recommended for, and then denied, fellowships by the National Endowment for the Arts. The Irish Lesbian and Gay Organisation made its first, contested march up Fifth Avenue in the spring of 1991, as Mikhail Gorbachev began the work of dismantling the Soviet Union.

▣ Sources

Archives

Abbey Theatre Archives, Dublin
Henry W. and Albert A. Berg Collection, New York Public Library
Bodkin Papers, Trinity College, Dublin
Department of Early Printed Books, Trinity College, Dublin
Diocesan Archives, Armagh
Diocesan Archives, Dublin
Dublin City Archives
Gilbert Library, Dublin
Hugh Lane Municipal Gallery of Modern Art Archives, Dublin
Maloney Collection of Irish Historical Papers, New York Public Library
National Archives of Ireland, Dublin
National Library of Ireland, Dublin
O'Hickey File, Russell Library, St. Patrick's College, Maynooth
Radio Archives, Radio Telefís Éireann, Dublin

Newspapers

An Claidheamh Soluis
An Phoblacht
Belfast Newsletter
Daily Mail
Dublin Evening Mail
Dublin Opinion
Freeman's Journal
Irish Catholic
Irish Citizen
Irish Independent
Irish Nation and Peasant

Irish News and Belfast Morning News
Irish Press
Irish Times
Kerryman
Liverpool Weekly Mercury
Nationalist and Munster Advertiser
New Witness
New York Times
Sinn Féin
Times (London)
Waterford News

Interviews

Nigel Acheson, September 1993, September 1996
Mícheál Briody, May 1996, March 1997, July 2001
Nora Briody (née Hickey), June 1995
Michael Coady, March 1996, February 1997, July 2001
Maura Cronin, December 1998
Barbara Dawson, August 1993, June 1998
Medbh McGuckian, February 1994
Paula Meehan, July 1999
Mary Murphy (née Hickey), June 2000
Helen O'Carroll, July 1995
Eilis Pearce, July 1995
Brian Walker, October 1994

Published and Recorded Works

Aberdeen and Temair, Marquess of, K. T. *Tell Me Another.* London: Edward
    Arnold and Co., 1926.
Acheson, Nigel, and Roisín McAuley, producers. *Document.* BBC: September
    24, 1993.
Arnold, Bruce. *Orpen: Mirror to an Age.* London: Cape, 1981.
Bodkin, Thomas. *Hugh Lane and His Pictures.* Dublin: Browne and Nolan,
    1934.
Bourke, Angela. *The Burning of Bridget Cleary.* London: Pimlico, 1999.
Bourke, Angela, Siobhán Kilfeather, Maria Luddy, Margaret MacCurtain,
    Gerardine Meaney, Máirin Ní Dhonnchadha, Mary O'Dowd, and Clair
    Wills, eds. *The Field Day Anthology of Irish Writing.* Vols. 4 and 5, *Irish
    Women's Writing and Traditions.* Cork: Cork University Press in associa-
    tion with Field Day; New York: New York University Press, 2002.
Bowe, Nicola Gordon. "The Friends of the National Collections of Ireland."
    In *Art Is My Life: A Tribute to James White,* ed. Brian P. Kennedy, 15–30.
    Dublin: National Gallery, 1991.

Bower, Fred. *Rolling Stonemason: An Autobiography.* London: Jonathan Cape, 1936.

Bradley, Anthony. "Yeats's *Poems Written in Discouragement, 1912–1913:* The Politics of Culture." *Éire–Ireland: A Journal of Irish Studies* 30, 3 (1995): 103–32.

Bradley, Anthony, and Maryanne Valiulis, eds. *Gender and Sexuality in Modern Ireland.* Amherst: University of Massachusetts Press, 1997.

Brady, Philip. *Forged Correspondences.* Binghamton, NY: New Myths Press, 1996.

Breathnach, Diarmuid, and Máire Ní Mhurchú. "Additions and Corrections to Volumes I and II." In *1882–1982 Beathaisnéis a Trí.* Leabhair Thaighde 72. Dublin: Clóchomar, 1992.

Briody, Mícheál. "From Carrickbeg to Rome—The Story of Fr Michael O'Hickey." *Decies: Journal of the Waterford Archaeological and Historical Society* 57 (2001): 143–66.

Brown, Terence. *Ireland: A Social and Cultural History, 1922 to the Present.* Ithaca: Cornell University Press, 1985.

Buckley, Fr. Pat. *Faith and Fatherland.* Belfast: Belfast Historical and Educational Society, 1991.

Carroll, Denis. *Unusual Suspects: Twelve Radical Clergy.* Dublin: Columba Press, 1998.

Carson, Michael. *The Knight of the Flaming Heart.* New York: Doubleday, 1995.

Caserio, Robert L. "Casement, Joyce, and Pound: Some New Meanings of Treason." In *Quare Joyce,* ed. Joseph Valente, 139–55. Ann Arbor: University of Michigan Press, 1998.

——. "Shades of Casement." Manuscript courtesy of author, 2000.

Christie, Agatha. *N or M?* Rev. ed. New York: Berkley Books, 1984.

Coady, Michael. "The Rehabilitation of Michael O'Hickey." *Nationalist and Munster Advertiser* (centenary supplement), December 1990, 97.

Colum, Mary. *Life and the Dream.* London: Macmillan, 1947.

Connolly, James. *The Workers' Republic: A Selection from the Writings of James Connolly.* Ed. Desmond Ryan. Dublin: At the Sign of the Three Candles, Fleet Street, 1951.

Conrad, Kathryn. "Queer Treasons: Homosexuality and Irish National Identity." *Cultural Studies* 15, 1 (January 2001): 124–37.

Corish, Mgsr. Patrick J. *Maynooth College, 1795–1995.* Dublin: Gill and Macmillan, 1995.

Coulter, Carol. *The Hidden Tradition: Feminism, Women, and Nationalism in Ireland.* Cork: Cork University Press, 1993.

——. "Archbishop Criticises Child-as-Product View." *Irish Times,* March 3, 1999.

Coxhead, Elizabeth. *Lady Gregory: A Literary Portrait.* London: Secker and Warburg, 1961.

Curriculum Development Unit. *Dublin 1913: A Divided City.* 1978. Reprint, Dublin: O' Brien Press, 1982.

Daly, Mary E. *Dublin: The Deposed Capital. A Social and Economic History, 1860–1914*. Cork: Cork University Press, 1984.

Davin, Anna. "Imperialism and Motherhood." *History Workshop Journal* 5 (Spring 1978): 9–65.

Dawson, Barbara. "Hugh Lane and the Origins of the Collection." In *Images and Insights*, 13–31. Dublin: Hugh Lane Municipal Gallery of Modern Art, 1993.

Deane, Seamus. "What Is Field Day." Insert in the program for the production of Brian Friel's translation of Chekhov's *Three Sisters*. Derry: Field Day Theatre Company, 1981.

Deane, Seamus, Andrew Carpenter, and Jonathan Williams. *The Field Day Anthology of Irish Writing*. Vol. 2. Derry: Field Day Publications, 1991.

Denvir, Gearóid. *An Ghaeilge, an Ghaeltacht agus 1992*. Baile Átha Cliath: Glór na nGael, 1991.

Douglas, Mary. *Purity and Danger*. Rev. ed. New York: Routledge, 1991, 113.

Dudgeon, Jeffrey. *Roger Casement: The Black Diaries, with a Study of His Background, Sexuality and Irish Political Life*. Belfast: Belfast Press, 2002.

Dunbar, Janet. *Mrs. GBS: A Portrait*. New York: Harper and Row, 1963.

Duncan, Carol. *Civilizing Rituals: Inside Public Art Museums*. London: Routledge, 1995.

Eliot, T. S. "Tradition and the Individual Talent." In *Selected Essays*. 1932. Reprint, London: Faber and Faber, 1953, 13–22.

Ellmann, Richard. *Oscar Wilde*. London: Penguin Books, 1988.

Fingall, Countess of, Elizabeth, as told to Pamela Hinkson. *Seventy Years Young*. Dublin: Lilliput, 1991.

Fogarty, William P. "Coup de Tate." *Pegasus: Magazine of the Veterinary Students' Union* (1956): 13–18.

——. "Theft of Lane Collection Picture 1956" (interview). RTÉ Radio Archives IDLPROC, L127/77. Produced August 18, 1976 (never aired).

Foster, R. F. *W. B. Yeats: A Life. Vol. 1, The Apprentice Mage: 1865–1914*. Oxford: Oxford University Press, 1997.

Frazier, Adrian. *Behind the Scenes: Yeats, Horniman, and the Struggle for the Abbey Theatre*. Berkeley: University of California Press, 1990.

——. *George Moore, 1852–1933*. New Haven: Yale University Press, 2000.

Gibbons, Luke. *Transformations in Irish Culture*. Cork: Cork University Press, 1996.

Giles, Audrey. *Report of Dr. Audrey Giles*. Amersham, Buckinghamshire: Giles Document Laboratory, February 8, 2002.

Gilsenan, Alan, director. "The Ghost of Roger Casement." RTÉ. March 14 and 21, 2002.

Gordon, Linda. *The Great Arizona Orphan Abduction*. Cambridge: Harvard University Press, 1999.

Gore-Booth, Eva. Selected Poems of Eva Gore-Booth. London: Longmans, Green, 1933.

Grant, Kevin. "Bones of Contention: The Repatriation of the Remains of Roger Casement." *Journal of British Studies* 41 (2002), 329–353.

Great Britain. Parliament. Commons. Select Committee on Theatres and Places of Entertainment. *Report from the Select Committee on Theatres and Places of Entertainment Together with the Proceedings. . . .* London: HMSO, 1892.

——. Lords and Commons. Joint Select Committee of the House of Lords and the House of Commons on the Stage Plays (Censorship). *Report from the Joint Select Committee of the House of Lords and the House of Commons on the Stage Plays (Censorship) Together with the Proceedings. . . .* London: HMSO, 1909.

Greaves, C. Desmond. *The Irish Transport and General Workers' Union: The Formative Years, 1909–1923.* Dublin: Gill and Macmillan, 1982.

Greenblatt, Stephen. "Culture." In *Critical Terms for Literary Study,* ed. Frank Lentricchia and Thomas McLaughlin, 225–232. Chicago: University of Chicago Press, 1990.

Gregory, Augusta. *Hugh Lane's Life and Achievement.* London: John Murray, 1921.

——. *Lady Gregory: Selected Writings.* Ed. Lucy McDiarmid and Maureen Waters. London: Penguin, 1995.

——. *Lady Gregory's Diaries, 1892–1902.* Ed. James Pethica. Gerrards Cross: Colin Smythe, 1996.

——. *Our Irish Theatre.* 1913. Reprint, New York: Oxford University Press, 1972.

——. *Seventy Years: 1852–1922.* New York: Macmillan, 1976.

Gregory, Lady. *The Journals.* Vol. 2. Books 30–44. Ed. Daniel J. Murphy. New York: Oxford University Press, 1987.

Grene, Nicholas. *The Politics of Irish Drama.* Cambridge: Cambridge University Press, 1999.

Gwynn, Denis. *The Life and Death of Roger Casement.* London: Cape, 1930.

Hart-Davis, Rupert, ed. *A Catalogue of the Caricatures of Max Beerbohm.* London: Macmillan, 1972.

Haverty, Anne. *Constance Markiewicz: An Independent Life.* London: Pandora, 1988.

Heaney, Seamus. *The Midnight Verdict.* Loughcrew, Oldcastle, County Meath: Gallery Press, 1993.

Hogan, Robert, and James Kilroy, eds. *The Abbey Theatre: The Years of Synge, 1905–1909* (Atlantic Highlands, NJ: Humanities Press, 1978).

Hunt, Karen. "Journeying through Suffrage: The Politics of Dora Montefiore." In *A Suffrage Reader: Charting Directions in British Suffrage History,* ed. C. Eustace, J. Ryan, and L. Ugolini, 162–176. London: Leicester University Press, 2000.

Hutton, Seán. *Seachrán Ruairí agus Dánta Eile.* Dublin: Coisceim, 1986.

Hynes, Samuel. *The Edwardian Turn of Mind.* Princeton: Princeton University Press, 1968.

Inglis, Brian. *Roger Casement.* London: Hodder and Stoughton Ltd., 1973.

Jenkins, Roy. *Asquith.* London: Collins, 1964.

Johnston, John. *The Lord Chamberlain's Blue Pencil.* London: Hodder, 1990.

Jordan, Neil. *The Past.* In *Collected Fiction.* New York: Vintage, 1997.

Joyce, James. *A Portrait of the Artist as a Young Man.* Reprint, New York: Viking Press, 1966.

——. Review of *The Shewing-up of Blanco Posnet* (as published in *Piccolo della Sera*). In *Shaw: The Critical Heritage,* ed. T. F. Evans, 197–199. London: Routledge, 1976.

——. *Ulysses.* Reprint, New York: Modern Library, 1961.

Kalin, Tom, director. *Swoon.* Produced by Christine Vachon; screenplay, Tom Kalin and Hilton Als. 1992.

Kelly, James, and Daire Keogh, eds. *History of the Catholic Diocese of Dublin.* Dublin: Four Courts Press, 2000.

Kelly, John. " 'Friendship is the only house I have.' " In *Lady Gregory, Fifty Years After,* ed. Ann Saddlemyer and Colin Smythe, 179–257. Gerrards Cross, Bucks.: Colin Smythe, 1987.

Kennedy, Kieran. "Official Secrets, Unauthorized Acts." *Irish Literary Supplement* 17, 1 (Spring 1998): 27.

Kiberd, Declan. *Inventing Ireland: The Literature of the Modern Nation.* Cambridge: Harvard University Press, 1995.

Kiernan, Colm. *Daniel Mannix and Ireland.* Dublin: Gill and Macmillan, 1984; Morwell, Victoria: Alella Books, 1984.

Kirkland, Richard. "Rhetoric and (Mis)recognitions: Reading Casement." In special issue *Post–Colonial Theory and Ireland,* ed. Colin Graham and Willy Maley. *Irish Studies Review* 7 (1999): 163–72.

Kopytoff, Igor. "The Cultural Biography of Things: Commodity as Process." In *The Social Life of Things: Commodities in Cultural Perspective,* ed. Arjun Appadurai, 64–91. Cambridge: Cambridge University Press, 1986.

Koven, Seth, and Sonya Michel, eds. *Mothers of a New World: Maternalist Politics and the Origins of Welfare States.* New York: Routledge, 1993.

Larkin, Emmet. "Socialism and Catholicism in Ireland." *Church History* 33 (1964): 462–83.

Laurence, Dan H., and Nicholas Grene, eds. *Shaw, Lady Gregory, and the Abbey: A Correspondence and a Record.* Gerrards Cross, Bucks: Colin Smythe, 1993.

Lee, J. J. *The Modernisation of Irish Society.* Dublin: Gill and Macmillan Ltd., 1973.

Leerssen, Joep. *The Contention of the Bards (Iomarbhágh na bhFileadh) and Its Place in Irish Political and Literary History.* London: Irish Texts Society, 1994.

——. *Remembrance and Imagination: Patterns in the Historical and Literary Representation of Ireland in the Nineteenth Century.* South Bend, IN: Notre Dame University Press; Cork: Cork University Press, 1997.

Levenson, Leah. *With Wooden Sword: A Portrait of Francis Sheehy Skeffington, Militant Pacifist*. Boston: Northeastern University Press, 1983.

Levitas, Ben. *The Theatre of Nation: Irish Drama and Cultural Nationalism, 1890–1916*. Oxford: Clarendon Press, 2002.

Londraville, Janis, and Richard Londraville, eds. *Too Long a Sacrifice: The Letters of Maud Gonne and John Quinn*. Selinsgrove, PA: Susquehanna University Press; London: Associated University Presses, 1999.

Longley, Michael. *Tuppeny Stung: Autobiographical Chapters*. Belfast: Lagan Press, 1994.

Lyons, F. S. L. *Ireland since the Famine*. Bungay: Collins, 1973.

MacColl, René. *Roger Casement*. London: Hamish Hamilton, 1956.

Mac Fhinn, Msgr. Padraig. *An tAthair Mícheál Ó hIceadha*. Baile Átha Cliath: Sairseal agus Dill, 1974.

Mackey, Herbert O. *The Life and Times of Roger Casement*. Dublin: C. J. Fallon, 1954.

MacNeice, Louis. *Collected Poems of Louis MacNeice*. Boston: Faber and Faber, 1966.

Magray, Mary Peckham. "The Queen vs. Margaret Aylward: Religion, Gender, Politics, and the Construction of Irish Catholic Identity." Manuscript, courtesy of author, 1997.

Mahon, Derek. *Collected Poems*. Loughcrew, Oldcastle, County Meath: Gallery Press, 1999.

———. "Some Sensuous Epiphany: *The Lost Notebook* by John Montague." In *Journalism*, ed. Terence Brown, 95–97. Oldcastle, County Meath: Gallery Press, 1996.

Maloney, William J. *The Forged Casement Diaries*. Dublin and Cork: Talbot Press, 1936.

Marcus, Jane. *The Young Rebecca: Writings of Rebecca West, 1911–1917*. New York: Macmillan in association with Virago Press, 1982.

Martin, Alec. "Talk on Hugh Lane by Sir Alec Martin." RTÉ Radio Archives IDLPROC, 00004. Produced July 12, 1955; transmitted July 30, 1955. No producer listed.

McCoole, Sinéad. *Hazel: A Life of Lady Lavery, 1880–1935*. Dublin: Lilliput, 1996.

McDiarmid, Lucy. "Secular Relics: Casement's Boat, Casement's Dish." *Textual Practice* (Summer 2002): 277–302.

McDonald, Walter. *Reminiscences of a Maynooth Professor*. London: Cape, 1925.

McDowell, John. "Verbal Dueling." In *Discourse and Dialogue*, vol. 3 of *Handbook of Discourse Analysis*, ed. Teun A. Van Dijk, 203–12. Orlando, FL: Harcourt, 1985.

McDowell, Margaret B. "Alfred Noyes." In *Dictionary of Literary Biography*, vol. 20, *British Poets, 1914–1915*, ed. Donald E. Sutherland. Detroit: Gale Research Co., 1983.

McGuckian, Medbh. *On Ballycastle Beach.* Oxford: Oxford University Press, 1988.

McKenna, Rev. L., S.J., trans. and ed. *Iomarbhágh na bhFileadh: The Contention of the Bards.* London: Irish Texts Society, 1918.

McMahon, Deirdre, ed. *The Moynihan Brothers in Peace and War, 1908–1918: Their New Ireland,* with an introduction by D. McMahon. Dublin: Irish Academic Press, 2004.

——. "Roger Casement: An Account from the Archives of His Reinterment in Ireland." *Journal of the Irish Society for Archives,* n.s., 3, 1 (Spring 1996).

McManus, Ruth. "Heritage and Tourism in Ireland–An Unholy Alliance?" www.ucd.ie/gsi/pdf/30-2/heritage.pdf.

Milotte, Mike. *Banished Babies.* Dublin: New Island Books, 1997.

Mitchell, Angus, ed. *The Amazon Journal of Roger Casement.* Dublin: Lilliput, 1997.

Montefiore, Dora. *From a Victorian to a Modern.* London: E. Archer, 1927.

——. *Our Fight to Save the Kiddies: Smouldering Fires of the Inquisition.* London: Utopia Press, n.d.

Montgomery-Hyde, H. *Roger Casement.* Harmondsworth, Middlesex: Penguin, 1964.

Morash, Christopher. *A History of Irish Theatre, 1601–2000.* Cambridge: Cambridge University Press, 2002.

Moriarty, Theresa. "Larkin and the Women's Movement." In *James Larkin: Lion of the Fold,* ed. D. Nevin, 93–101. Dublin: Gill and Macmillan, in association with RTÉ and SIPTU, 1998.

Morrissey, Thomas J., S.J. *Towards a National University: William Delany S.J. (1835–1924).* Dublin: Wolfhound Press, 1983.

——. *William J. Walsh, Archbishop of Dublin, 1841–1921: No Uncertain Voice.* Dublin: Four Courts Press, 2000.

——. *William Martin Murphy.* Dundalk: Dundalgan Press, 1997.

Muldoon, Paul. "A Clear Signal." *New York Times,* March 17, 1992, A25.

Mulhern, Francis. *The Present Lasts a Long Time: Essays in Cultural Politics.* Cork: Cork University Press; South Bend, IN: University of Notre Dame Press, 1998.

Mullen, Patrick. "Roger Casement's Global English: From Human Rights to the Homoerotic." *Public Culture* 15, 3 (Fall 2003): 559–78.

Murphy, Richard. *Collected Poems.* Winston-Salem, NC: Wake Forest University Press, 2001.

Murray, Christopher. "The Last Battle: *The Drums of Father Ned* and O'Casey's Final Myth." Manuscript, courtesy of the author, 1999.

——. "O'Casey's *The Drums of Father Ned* in Context." In *A Century of Irish Drama: Widening the Stage,* ed. Stephen Watt, Eileen Morgan, and Shakir Mustafa, 117–29. Bloomington: Indiana University Press, 2000.

Nevin, Donal. "AE and the Dublin Lock-out." In *James Larkin: Lion of the Fold,* ed. D. Nevin, 211–22. Dublin: Gill and Macmillan, in association with RTÉ and SIPTU, 1998.

Newman, Jeremiah. *St. Patrick's College Maynooth.* Irish Heritage Series, no. 47 (no pagination).

Newton, Lord. *Retrospection.* London: Murray, 1941.

Ní Dhomhnaill, Nuala. *Pharoah's Daughter.* Oldcastle, County Meath: Gallery Press, 1990.

Noyes, Alfred. *The Accusing Ghost, or, Justice for Roger Casement.* London: Victor Gollancz, 1957.

———. *Two Worlds for Memory.* Philadelphia: J. B. Lippincott, 1953.

O'Brien, Joseph. *"Dear, Dirty Dublin": A City in Distress, 1899–1916.* Berkeley: University of California Press, 1982.

Ó Broin, Leon. "The Gaelic League and the Chair of Irish at Maynooth." *Studies* 52 (1963): 348–62.

O'Byrne, Robert. *Hugh Lane, 1875–1915.* Dublin: Lilliput, 2000.

O'Casey, Sean. *The Drums of Father Ned.* New York: St. Martin's Press, 1960.

———. *Drums under the Window.* In *Autobiographies,* vol. 1. 1939. Reprint, New York: Carroll and Graff, 1984.

Ó Cathain, Séamas, ed. *Stories of Sea and Shore,* told by John Henry, Kilgalligan, Co Mayo. Dublin: UCD, 1983.

O'Connor, Frank. "The Future of Irish Literature." *Horizon* 5, 25 (January 1942), 55–63.

O'Donoghue, Bernard. *The Weakness.* London: Chatto and Windus, 1991.

O'Donovan, Gerald. *Father Ralph.* 1913. Reprint, Dingle, County Kerry: Brandon, 1993.

O'Driscoll, Padraig, producer. "Coup de Tate." RTÉ television. December 19, 2002.

O'Duffy, Eimar. *The Wasted Island.* New York: Dodd, Mead, 1920.

Ó hEochaidh, Seán, collector; trans. Maire MacNeill. *Fairy Legends from Donegal.* Dublin: UCD, 1977.

O'Faolain, Sean. *The Irish: A Character Study.* London: Penguin, 1947.

O'Farrell, Padraic. *Tales for the Telling: True Life Stories of Irish Scandals.* Cork: Collins Press, n.d.

Ó Fiaich, Tomás. "The Great Controversy." In *The Gaelic League Idea,* ed. Seán Ó Tuama, 63–75. Cork: Mercier Press, 1972.

Ó Fiannachta, Pádraig. "An tAthair Mícheál Ó hIci." In *Léachtai Cholm Cille,* 16:140–74. Maigh Nuad: An Sagart, 1986.

O'Hickey, Michael. *The Irish Bishops and an Irish University.* Dublin: Sealy, Bryers, and Walker, 1909. (Published anonymously "By an Irish Priest.")

———. *The Irish Language Movement: Its Genesis, Growth, and Progress.* Gaelic League Pamphlets, no. 29. N.d.

———. *An Irish University, or Else.* Dublin and Waterford: M. H. Gill and Sons, Ltd., 1909.

———. *The True National Idea.* Dublin: Gaelic League, 1898.

———. *Wanted—An Irish University.* Dublin: Sealy, Bryers, and Walker, 1909. (Published anonymously "By an Irish Priest.")

O'Leary, Philip. *The Prose Literature of the Gaelic Revival, 1881–1921: Ide-*

ology and Innovation. University Park: Pennsylvania State University Press, 1994.

Ó Maoleóin, Séamus. *B'fhiú an Braon Fola.* 2nd ed. Dublin: Sairseal and Dill, 1972. (Originally published 1958.)

O'Rourke, Joseph. "John Philpot Curran: The Development of a Speaker." Doctoral dissertation, University of Missouri, 1967.

Ó Síocháin, Séamas. *Roger Casement: Imperialist, Rebel, Revolutionary.* Dublin: Lilliput, 2006.

Ó Síocháin, Séamas, and Michael O'Sullivan, eds. *Roger Casement: The 1903–4 Congo Report and 1903 Diary.* Dublin: University College Dublin Press, 2003.

O'Toole, Fintan. *Black Hole, Green Card: The Disappearance of Ireland.* Dublin: New Island Books, 1994.

Orpen, William. *Stories of Old Ireland and Myself.* London: Williams and Norgate, 1924.

Owens, Gary. "Popular Mobilisation and the Rising of 1848: The Clubs of the Irish Confederation." In *Rebellion and Remembrance in Modern Ireland,* ed. Laurence Geary, 51–63. Dublin: Four Courts, 2001.

Parks, Ward. *Verbal Dueling in Heroic Narrative: The Homeric and Old English Traditions.* Princeton: Princeton University Press, 1990.

Patterson, Nerys Thomas. *Cattle Lords and Clansmen: The Social Structure of Early Ireland.* South Bend, IN: Notre Dame University Press, 1994.

Pearse, Patrick H. *A Significant Irish Educationalist: The Educational Writings of P. H. Pearse.* Ed. Séamus Ó Buachalla. Dublin and Cork: Mercier Press, 1980.

"An Philibín" [J. H. Pollock]. *Mount Kestrel.* Dublin: M. H. Gill and Son, Ltd., 1945.

Pilkington, Lionel. *Theatre and the State in Twentieth-Century Ireland.* New York: Routledge, 2001.

Preston, Margaret. "Conversion amidst Compassion: Two Irish Charities and Their Fight for the Souls of the Poor." Manuscript, courtesy of author, 1999.

Prunty, Jacinta. *Lady of Charity, Sister of Faith: Margaret Aylward, 1810–1889.* Dublin: Four Courts Press, 1999.

Quinn, Eileen Moore. "Anthropological Poetics and Ireland: *An t'Oireachtas,* 1994." Paper delivered at the meeting of the American Conference for Irish Studies at Queen's University, Belfast, June 1994.

Reid, B. L. *The Lives of Roger Casement.* New Haven: Yale University Press, 1976.

Report of the Committee of Inquiry into the Work Carried on by the Royal Hibernian Academy and the Metropolitan School of Art, Dublin. Parliamentary Papers 31. Cd 3256 (1906).

Reynolds, John J. *Statement of the Claim for the Return to Dublin of the 39 Lane Bequest Pictures Now at the Tate Gallery.* Dublin: Educational Company of Ireland Ltd., 1932.

Richards, Grant. *Caviare.* New York: Houghton Mifflin, 1912.

Robertson, Nora. *Crowned Harp: Memories of the Last Years of the Crown in Ireland.* Dublin: Figgis, 1960.

Roche, Anthony. *Contemporary Irish Drama: From Beckett to McGuinness.* London: Palgrave-Macmillan, 1995.

Roger Casement Foundation, distributor. *The Vindication of Roger Casement.* "Updated Edition 11th April 2000."

Rose, Kieran. *Diverse Communities.* Cork: Cork University Press, 1994.

Rothery, Sean. *Ireland and the New Architecture, 1900–1940.* Dublin: Lilliput, 1991.

Rudkin, David. *Cries from Casement as His Bones Are Brought to Dublin.* London: BBC, 1974.

Ryan, John. "Gerald O'Donovan: Priest, Novelist, and Irish Revivalist." *Journal of the Galway Archaeological and Historical Society* 48 (1996): 1–47.

Ryan, W. P. *The Pope's Green Island.* Boston: Small, Maynard, 1912.

Ryan, W. P. "The Struggle of 1913: An Overview." In *James Larkin: Lion of the Fold,* ed. D. Nevin. Dublin: Gill and Macmillan, in association with RTÉ and SIPTU, 1998.

Sawyer, Roger, ed. *Roger Casement's Diaries, 1910: The Black and the White.* London: Pimlico, 1997.

Sebald, W. G. *The Rings of Saturn.* Trans. M. Hulse. New York: New Directions, 1998.

Shaw, Bernard. *Collected Letters, 1874–1897.* Ed. Dan H. Laurence. New York: Dodd, Mead, 1965.

——. *Collected Letters, 1898–1910.* Ed. Dan H. Laurence. New York: Viking, 1985.

——. *John Bull's Other Island.* In *Complete Plays with Prefaces,* vol. 2. New York: Dodd, Mead, 1963.

——. *The Shewing-up of Blanco Posnet.* In *Complete Plays with Prefaces,* vol. 5. New York: Dodd, Mead, 1962.

Sheehy Skeffington, Andrée. *Skeff: A Life of Owen Sheehy Skeffington, 1909–1970.* Dublin: Lilliput, 1991.

Singleton-Gates, Peter, and Maurice Girodias, eds. *The Black Diaries: An Account of Roger Casement's Life and Times with a Collection of His Diaries and Public Writings.* New York: Grove Press, 1959.

Smith, Stevie. *Over the Frontier.* London: Cape, 1938.

Solnit, Rebecca. *A Book of Migrations.* London: Verso, 1997.

Steedman, Carolyn. *Childhood, Culture, and Class in Britain: Margaret McMillan, 1860–1931.* New Brunswick, NJ: Rutgers University Press, 1990.

Steinman, Michael. *Yeats's Heroic Figures: Wilde, Parnell, Swift, Casement.* Albany: State University of New York at Albany Press, 1984.

Synge, J. M. *Collected Works.* Vol. 2. Ed. Robin Skelton. London: Oxford University Press, 1962–68.

Taussig, Michael. *Shamanism, Colonialism, and the Wild Man: A Study in Terror and Healing.* Chicago: University of Chicago Press, 1987.

Taylor, Lawrence. *Occasions of Faith: An Anthropology of Irish Catholicism.* Philadelphia: University of Pennsylvania Press, 1995.

Thuente, Mary Helen. *The Harp Restrung: The United Irishmen and the Rise of Irish Literary Nationalism.* Syracuse, NY: Syracuse University Press, 1994.

Tilzey, Paul, director. "Secrets of the Black Diaries." BBC. Screened March 15, 2003.

Tóibín, Colm. "A Whale of a Time." *London Review of Books 19,* 19 (October 2, 1997): 25–28.

——. *Love in a Dark Time: Gay Lives from Wilde to Almodovar.* London: Picador, 2002.

Tribute to Sir Hugh Lane. Cork: Cork University Press, 1961.

Unterecker, John, ed. *Yeats and Patrick McCartan, a Fenian Friendship: Letters with a Commentary.* Dublin: Dolmen Press, 1967.

Walsh, Archbishop William. *The Dublin Children's Distress Fund, The Society of St. Vincent de Paul: The Archbishop's Statement.* Pamphlet. October 27, 1913. N.p.

Walshe, Eibhear. "Oscar's Mirror." In *Lesbian and Gay Visions of Ireland,* ed. Ide O'Carroll and Eoin Collins. New York: Cassell, 1995.

Ward, Margaret. *Hanna Sheehy Skeffington: A Life.* Cork: Cork University Press, 1997.

Watt, Stephen, Eileen Marie Morgan, and Shakir M. Mustafa. *A Century of Irish Drama: Widening the Stage.* Bloomington: Indiana University Press, 2000.

West, Rebecca. *The Young Rebecca: Writings of Rebecca West, 1911–1917.* Ed. Jane Marcus. New York: Viking, in association with Virago, 1982.

Whelan, Gerard, with Carolyn Swift. *Spiked: Church–State Intrigue and the Rose Tattoo.* Dublin: New Island, 2002.

White, Anna MacBride, and A. Norman Jeffares, eds. *The Gonne–Yeats Letters, 1893–1938.* London: Hutchinson, 1992.

White, Terence de Vere. *Lucifer Falling.* London: Cape, 1966.

Winslow, Barbara. *Sylvia Pankhurst: Sexual Politics and Political Activism.* London: UCL Press, 1996.

Yeates, Pádraig. *Lockout: Dublin 1913.* Dublin: Gill and Macmillan, 2000.

Yeats, W. B. *Collected Plays.* 2nd ed. London: Macmillan, 1972. (Originally published 1934.)

——. *Letters.* Ed. Allan Wade. London: Rupert Hart-Davis, 1954.

——. *Letters on Poetry from W. B. Yeats to Dorothy Wellesley.* 1940. Reprint, Oxford: Oxford University Press, 1964.

——. *Uncollected Prose.* Vol. 2. Ed. John P. Frayne and Colton Johnson. New York: Columbia University Press, 1976.

——. *The Variorum Edition of the Poems.* Ed. Peter Allt and Russell K. Alspach. New York: Macmillan, 1975.

❖ Index